Ten Years of Protests in the Middle East and North Africa

GLOBAL POLITICS AND SECURITY

Volume 8

Edited by

Prof. Lorenzo Kamel,
University of Turin's History Department,
and Istituto Affari Internazionali (IAI)

PETER LANG

Bern · Berlin · Bruxelles · New York · Oxford

Silvia Colombo and Daniela Huber (eds)

Ten Years of Protests in the Middle East and North Africa

Dynamics of Mobilisation in a Complex (Geo)Political Environment

PETER LANG

Bern · Berlin · Bruxelles · New York · Oxford

Bibliographic Information published by the Deutsche Nationalbibliothek
The Deutsche Nationalbibliothek lists this publication in the Deutsche
Nationalbibliografie; detailed bibliographic data is available in the internet
at http://dnb.d-nb.de.

Library of Congress Cataloging-in-Publication Data
A CIP catalog record for this book has been applied for
at the Library of Congress.

Volume prepared in the framework of the IAI-ECFR-CeSPI project 'Ten Years into the
Protests in the Middle East and North Africa. Dynamics of Mobilisation in a Complex
(Geo)Political Environment and the Role of the European Union'. This publication has
benefited from the financial support of the Policy Planning Unit of the Italian Ministry
of Foreign Affairs and International Cooperation pursuant to art. 23-bis of Presidential
Decree 18/1967 and of the Compagnia di San Paolo Foundation. The views expressed
in this report are solely those of the author and do not necessarily reflect the
views of the Italian Ministry of Foreign Affairs and International
Cooperation and of the Compagnia di San Paolo Foundation.

ISSN 2624-8905 • ISBN 978-3-0343-2894-4 (Print)
E-ISBN 978-3-0343-4478-4 (E-PDF) • E-ISBN 978-3-0343-4479-1 (EPUB)
• DOI 10.3726/b19347

This publication has been peer reviewed.

© Peter Lang Group AG, International Academic Publishers, Bern 2022
bern@peterlang.com, www.peterlang.com

Contents

6 Contents

Andrea Dessì

Chapter 10: Popular Mobilisation and Authoritarian Reconstitution in
the Middle East and North Africa: Ten Years of Arab Uprisings 191

Contributors 207

Abbreviations 211

Lorenzo Kamel

Foreword – Preserving Tyrannies

'The Arab uprisings failed'. This claim, repeated as a mantra by countless analysts and observers (mainly non 'Middle Easterners'), is both largely misleading and arrogant. It is misleading because it tends to cherry-pick the parameters through which it is allegedly possible to assess the failures and successes of movements and efforts that have involved millions of human beings. It is arrogant inasmuch as it implicitly fosters the idea that 'we [Westerners] are better than them' (or, quoting Steven A. Cook on *Foreign Policy*,[1] 'Maybe Tunisians never wanted democracy') and denies or downplays the role played by external actors in the alleged failure of those very same movements and trajectories.

From *Tul'it rihetkun* – the 'You Stink!' movement born out of spontaneous protests that took place in Lebanon in 2015 and 2016 – to the Hirak protests in Algeria in 2019, and to dozens of other recent movements mentioned in this volume, the spirit of the revolts is indeed far from extinguished. More than focusing on a simplistic dichotomy (failure/success), *Ten Years of Protests in the Middle East and North Africa* sheds light on a number of little known bottom-up dynamics and perspectives. These appear even more meaningful and 'revolutionary' in light of the two main competing regional and international agendas for the region in the last decade, both of them underpinned by uncompromising and autocratic ideologies, and by an interest in fostering proxy wars.

The first of these agendas aims at maintaining and strengthening an intra-regional geopolitical line across Tehran, Baghdad, Damascus and Beirut: while searching for a less externally-dependent order, the regimes and most of the leaders in power in these cities/countries perceive their citizens as passive 'subjects' in need of guidance. The second aims at imposing a new, largely Western-led order in the region. At the moment, this second agenda – which also involves Israel and three local 'tyrannies' considered useful by many Western countries (Saudi Arabia, the United Arab Emirates and Egypt) – would seem to have higher chances of success. This was also confirmed by the 2018 US sanctions on Iran (despite the appearances, a despotic and uncompromising Iran appears far more useful to Washington and its allies), which followed the

---

[1] Steven A. Cook, 'How the West Misunderstood Tunisia', in *Foreign Policy*, 27 July 2021, https://bit.ly/3l11M50.

unilateral breach of the Iran nuclear deal by the Trump administration, as well as by numerous other strategic dynamics. The latter include, for instance, the decision whereby Mohammed Bin Salman (2017) was made first in line to the throne at the expense of his cousin Mohammed Bin Nayef: a strategy that was first accepted and then employed by Washington on the condition of compliance with US and Israeli goals in the region.

A hundred years ago the Sykes-Picot mentality (the Sykes-Picot Agreement, on the other hand, was never implemented) hindered or postponed the rise of a new order shaped from within the region. In some respects, what many areas in the Middle East have witnessed in recent years is the final point of an historical impasse that lasted for a century. The final result, however, will most likely be not the one hoped for by most of the region's inhabitants. Particularly under the Trump administration (and with no change in sight under the current US President Joe Biden), oppressive regimes are once again considered part of the solution, rather than the problem. As one Israeli ex-general said in 2015 to Michael Oren, his country's former ambassador to Washington: 'Why won't Americans face the truth? To defend Western freedom, they must preserve Middle Eastern tyranny'.[2]

Local 'tyrannies', for their part, are ready to pay a high price to guarantee their survival. This explains, for instance, the reason why over the last decade Riyadh has invested an enormous amount of resources in opposing the rise of any government or party that, in the Arab world, could have represented a credible alternative to the 'Saudi model'. It also sheds light on the deeper reasons connected to Riyadh's decision to support the Egyptian army in its coup against former Islamist president Mohamed Morsi (1951–2019), as well as the attempt made by the UAE leadership to interfere in the internal affairs of a number of countries, including Tunisia, where the Ennahda party was (and is still) seen by many as an example of how Islamists can participate in democratic transitions to power (winning the elections in 2011 and stepping down in 2013).

In the short term, ruling families and regimes will gain much from these strategies and the new order in the making. The long-term scenario, however, is far less promising for them. The region has changed substantially from the previous decades and particularly since 2011: grab-and-go 'solutions' and ideologies used in the past to divert the attention of the region's people (including sectarian strategies conceived by autocratic and cleptocratic elites) will have much less appeal

---

[2]   Michael B. Oren, *Ally. My Journey Across the American-Israeli Divide*, New York, Random House, 2015, p. 302.

in the near future. This further confirms that the new Western-supported order fostered by Riyadh and its allies has high chances of backfiring. It will in fact lead to an even more externally dependent Middle East, but also to the further weakening of the Saudi Kingdom itself and, more in general, of a large part of the region.

Daniela Huber

Chapter 1: Ten Years of Arab Uprisings: A Conceptual Appraisal

Almost ten years since the onset of the Arab uprisings, protest, mobilisation, and contestation in the Middle East and North Africa are continuing. While research has grown substantially,[1] it has typically focused either on internal factors (comparative politics)[2] or the regional dimension (international relations),[3] while neglecting dynamics between these levels. Therefore, a more comparative and comprehensive approach is crucial, particularly also from a policy perspective which necessarily needs to take all factors into account.[4] On top of this, covid-19 has also substantially impacted the uprisings and the EU's response.

In light of these observations, three research institutions based in Italy – the Istituto Affari Internazionali (IAI), the European Council of Foreign Relations (ECFR) Rome office and the Centro Studi di Politica Internazionale (CeSPI) – have joined forces in this research project which has been financially supported by the Italian Ministry of Foreign Affairs and International Cooperation, as well as the Fondazione Compagnia di San Paolo. It has been guided by two research questions:

---

[1] Marc Lynch (ed.), *The Arab Uprisings Explained. New Contentious Politics in the Middle East*, New York, Columbia University Press, 2014; Raymond Hinnebusch, *After the Arab Uprisings. Between Democratization, Counter-revolution and State Failure*, London/ New York, Routledge, 2016; Andrea Teti, Pamela Abbott and Francesco Cavatorta, *The Arab Uprisings in Egypt, Jordan and Tunisia. Social, Political and Economic Transformations*, Cham, Palgrave Macmillan, 2018; MERIP, 'Return to Revolution', in *Middle East Report*, No. 292/293 (Fall/Winter 2019), https://merip.org/magazine/ 292-3.

[2] Steven Heydemann, 'Explaining the Arab Uprisings: Transformations in Comparative Perspective', in *Mediterranean Politics*, Vol. 21, No. 1 (2016), p. 192–204, https://doi. org/10.1080/13629395.2015.1081450.

[3] Federica Bicchi, Benoit Challand and Steven Heydermann (eds), *The Struggle for Influence in the Middle East. The Arab Uprisings and Foreign Assistance*, London/ New York, Routledge, 2016.

[4] On this, see also the publications of the MENARA project: https://www.iai.it/en/pubbli cazioni/lista/all/MENARA-Papers.

1. How has contestation evolved over time regarding the protest movements themselves and the (geo)political context in which they occurred? How has the covid-19 crisis impacted the trajectory of the protests?
2. How has the EU reacted to the uprisings over time and what feasible paths for EU engagement exist, particularly in light of the covid-19 crisis?

Observing these questions for seven cases – Algeria, Egypt, Iraq, Lebanon, Morocco, Sudan and Tunisia – the project has aimed to foster a better understanding of both local agency (the protest movements), as well as the dynamics at the national level (authoritarian resilience / relation to organised opposition) and the regional level (involvement of regional powers). This allowed us to assess how *the political space has evolved over time*, and what major political fault lines this may imply for the near and medium futures, whilst also taking account of the impact of covid-19.

In addition to this, observing the EU response in terms of rhetoric (perceptions of uprisings and stated goals) and practice (towards the movements, as well as the government/opposition, and regional powers) over time served to assess how the EU has imagined its own place in the region over time, also in light of the covid-19 crisis, and how (dis)connected this is from the regional political space assessed in the seven case studies. Indeed, one of the core objectives of this research project has been to identify paths towards a more attune EU engagement on the local, national and regional levels.

1. Rationale and analytical framework for the seven country case studies

The chapters of this book cover seven case studies, a comparative analysis, as well as a study of EU policies. The in-depth case studies include countries where protests have been substantially proliferating since 2005 (Lebanon), since 2010/11 (Egypt, Morocco and Tunisia), since 2015 (Iraq) and since 2019 (Algeria, Sudan). This wide range of case studies ensures variance over diverse histories of protests, political systems and their reactions/changes, and different geopolitical configurations. Such a cross-temporal comparative analysis helped us not only to identify continuity, change and processes of sequencing across time, but also to inductively reveal potential categories by which these protests can be compared.

The evolution of contestation over time in each case study is analysed across three levels of analysis, which are: 1) the local level (the protest movements); 2) the national level (government response and relationship to major political forces); and 3) the regional level (support for or opposition to protests by regional/global powers). Whilst these levels of analysis are useful for the comparative purpose of this project, as well as for devising comprehensive policy recommendations, the authors of each case study have addressed the interlinkage and interaction between these levels differently, while also keeping in mind a gender perspective.

2. First level of analysis: The protest movements

Regarding the protest movements themselves, their composition, strategies and demands of mobilisation converge rather than differ across the cases, but there are processes of learning from each other over time, as well as particularities in light of different histories of each country.

The *composition of the mobilisation* has typically been broad, cross-sectarian and diverse, spanning all classes, sectors, ethnicities, gender and age groups of societies with whole families participating, including the youngest and the oldest. As Asef Bayat has framed it, this has in many respects been a revolution without revolutionaries.[5] They have mobilised not only in the centres and capitals, but across the countries, including in 'peripheries'.[6] Women have played a prominent role in political resistance since the uprisings began.[7] Whilst research in the past ten years has put much focus on the interclass, age-group and male/female participation features of the protests, a lacuna exists in shedding more light on the ideational side of the movements. This is, however, necessary to explain why demands from the 'square' and policies of governments have never met, not even in Tunisia. This point directly links to the dimension of strategy, as the (lack of) political organisation within the 'squares' shaped the 'revolution without revolutionaries' or 'mobilisation without change'.

The rather loose *strategy of mobilisation* of the protest movements[8] has meant that they have been difficult to control; at the same time such loose strategies lead to difficulties in representing coherent alternatives to existing policies and

---

5   Asef Bayat, *Revolution without Revolutionaries. Making Sense of the Arab Spring*, Stanford, Stanford University Press, 2017.

6   Daniela Huber and Lorenzo Kamel (eds), *Arab Spring and Peripheries. A Decentring Research Agenda*, London/New York, Routledge, 2016.

7   Rita Stephan and Mounira M. Charrad (eds), *Women Rising. In and Beyond the Arab Spring*, New York, New York University Press, 2020.

8   The movements have been largely non-hierarchical, including from a gender perspective; see Diane Singerman, 'Youth, Gender, and Dignity in the Egyptian Uprising', in *Journal of Middle East Women's Studies*, Vol. 9, No. 3 (Fall 2013), p. 1–27, https://doi.org/10.2979/jmiddeastwomstud.9.3.1.

political systems. Whilst this is a similarity across countries, protest movements have learnt from each other over time. Firstly, in light of the experiences of Egyptian counterparts, protesters in both Sudan and Algeria have, for example, been very wary of deals with the respective armies. At the same time, they continue – for now – to mobilise the square as 'guardians of the transitions' to promote an alternative in terms of political organisation as protagonists. Secondly, the strategies have been influenced by the memory of protests in the past which is particularly important for countries such as Lebanon, Iraq or Algeria which have been shaken by civil wars. How are protesters dealing with this memory? In both Iraq and Lebanon, for example, protesters argued for cross-sectarian solidarity and against *any* form of foreign intervention. Thirdly, more recently protesters have needed to deal with the covid-19 crisis. As the latter evolved many of the protest movements also needed to decide how to deal with lockdowns as governments imposing the standard global containment measures. How have activists dealt with this crisis in terms of strategy?

Like all uprisings, the Arab uprisings have developed their own 'language'. What are the *demands and dreams of these uprisings*? As Sune Haugbolle and Andreas Bandak have pointed out, '[t]aking the practice of politics seriously means that we pay attention to what revolutionaries do – their repertoires of contention – as much as we pay attention to what they say and write as they seek to create a new political world'.[9] Protestors have asked for social and ecological justice, and for provision of education and health services. In many of the protest countries, #metoo movements have also been growing.[10] The movements have also criticised austerity measures which have been imposed by international financial institutions but also by the EU, as for example in Lebanon or Tunisia. This critique has intensified with the covid-19 crisis particularly, because basic health services are generally underfunded and ill-prepared for a pandemic. Sudan, for example, has practically no intensive care units for a population of almost 42 million people. In Lebanon, health services are often private, which reduces access to healthcare or makes it conditional on identity criteria. Leeway for expanding access to healthcare is limited, as the country is undergoing an existential economic crisis. After the blast in Beirut's harbour, it has been the

---

[9]   Sune Haugbolle and Andreas Bandak, 'The Ends of Revolution: Rethinking Ideology and Time in the Arab Uprisings', in *Middle East Critique*, Vol. 26, No. 3 (3 July 2017), p. 191–204 at p. 193.

[10]   Tom Allinson, 'Setback to Egypt's #MeToo Movement as Rape Witnesses Reportedly Charged', in *Deutsche Welle*, 17 September 2020, https://p.dw.com/p/3ibKm.

Lebanese Red Cross/Red Crescent and local groups and volunteers that have provided the services the government has failed to deliver.

Thus, at a first level of analysis, all chapters investigate the composition, strategies and demands of the protest movements, including from a gender perspective and also in light of the covid-19 crisis, vis-à-vis their respective governments, but also regional powers and international actors such as the European Union. This sets the stage to explain why these movements have experienced a rather huge mobilisation, but have had relatively little impact on alternative policies and change (like similar movements in other world regions such as the Occupy movements, the Indignados in Spain or Orange Revolutions in Ukraine). It exposes potential weaknesses inherent in these movements which make it difficult for them to create a new political community, particularly when they interact with power structures, as addressed next at the second level of analysis.

3. Second level of analysis: National political dynamics

At a second level, the dynamics between these movements and the respective governments and major political forces in each country are investigated. Governments have reacted with diverse strategies to the protest movements. The first strategy has been violence, including particularly gendered violence,[11] and it is indeed important to also observe the role of the military and the security apparatus here, as evident in the case of Egypt.[12] Such responses are typically justified with the claim of preventing the emergence of a 'Syria situation' (in denial of the fact that violence in Syria also escalated due to the violent response of the regime to the protests). In Iraq which has more hybrid governance structures than Egypt, also non-state actors have exercised violence against protestors. Furthermore, authoritarian regimes have learnt from each other how to respond to protests.[13] As Steven Heydemann has pointed out, the reassertion of authoritarianism in Arab states after 2011 does not 'represent a 'back-to-the-future'

---

[11] Elisabeth Johansson-Nogués, 'Gendering the Arab Spring? Rights and (In)security of Tunisian, Egyptian and Libyan Women', in *Security Dialogue*, Vol. 44, No. 5/6 (October-December 2013), p. 393–409.

[12] Yezid Sayigh, *Owners of the Republic. An Anatomy of Egypt's Military Economy*, Washington, Carnegie Endowment for International Peace, 2019, https://carnegieen dowment.org/publications/80325.

[13] Steven Heydemann and Reinoud Leenders, 'Authoritarian Learning and Authoritarian Resilience: Regime Responses to the 'Arab Awakening'', in *Globalizations*, Vol. 8, No. 5 (2011), p. 647–653.

process'. Rather, Arab regimes have responded to the uprisings 'through the imposition of repressive-exclusionary social pacts in which previously universal economic and social rights of citizens are being redefined as selective benefits'.[14] A second strategy has been some minor reforms, reshuffling of government or the co-optation of protest movements, as happened in different forms in Morocco, Algeria, Iraq or Lebanon. A third path has been a genuine change of the political system as in Tunisia.

Secondly, the relationship of the protest movements to the major political forces in their countries is also crucial. In some of the case studies, the Muslim Brotherhood or related parties of political Islam constituted major organised oppositional forces and thus a serious threat to autocratic regimes, particularly in Tunisia or Egypt. In other countries such as Morocco, political Islam has been more directly co-opted into the political system. In each of these countries, political Islam has acted in diverse ways within the uprisings and their aftermath. Ennahda in Tunisia, for example, made sure to highlight its different approach from the Muslim Brotherhood in Egypt.[15] In general, Islamist politics have changed decisively in light of the experiences with the Arab uprisings.[16] In other countries such as Iraq, Lebanon or Algeria political Islam is not a major political force, but there are other important political forces with which the protest movements interact in particular ways. In Iraq, protests are taking place in Shia-dominated areas of the country to which parts of the Popular Mobilization Units have reacted violently, while members of other parts of it actually participated in the protests. In Lebanon, Hezbollah has on one hand shown sympathy with demands of the protesters, while at the same time also showing potential force. These interactions are important as they also structure the political space in which protests movements act, whilst impacting on the political imagination of all sides.

Thus, at a second level of analysis, all chapters investigate how the government, as well as major political forces in each country have framed the mobilisations

---

[14] Steven Heydemann, 'Rethinking Social Contracts in the MENA Region: Economic Governance, Contingent Citizenship, and State-Society Relations after the Arab Uprisings', in *World Development*, Vol. 135 (November 2020, Article 105019.

[15] Georges Fahmi at the workshop 'At the Crossroads: Understanding the Different Trajectories of Political Islam in Egypt and Tunisia', organised by the European University Institute in Fiesole on 17 March 2017.

[16] Marc Lynch and Jillian Schwedler, 'Introduction to the Special Issue on 'Islamist Politics After the Arab Uprisings'', in *Middle East Law and Governance*, Vol. 12, No. 1 (April 2020), p. 3–13.

and justified their reactions to or interactions with them, including from a gender perspective.

4. Third level of analysis: The regional geopolitical context

Finally, also the geopolitical context in which the protests occurred has evolved substantially. The US-led invasion and Iraq's societal disintegration raised fears of an increasing power projection of Iran into the region, particularly on the side of Saudi Arabia, the UAE, Egypt, Jordan and Israel. This fear had already emerged in the wake of the US-led invasion when the Jordanian king first spoke of a developing 'Shia crescent'. It intensified with the US 'retrenchment' from Iraq and its pivot to Asia, as well as the Arab uprisings. Wars emerged in both Syria and Yemen, and also influenced Lebanon and Iraq decisively.

Secondly, with the rise of political Islam coupled with what seemed a loss of US determination, Arab autocrats who have traditionally been more dependent on the West than their own people perceived this evolution as an essential threat to their regime security. This fear opened a second geopolitical rupture of the counter-revolutionary Arab regimes (UAE, KSA, post-coup Egypt) vis-à-vis Turkey and Qatar. This rupture has been particularly evident in Libya but also in Egypt, Morocco, Tunisia or Algeria (to varying degrees).

In this complex geopolitical picture, the norms of sovereignty and non-interference – violated already for decades by global powers such as the US in what Raymond Hinnebusch has called a 'penetrated region'[17] – have been further trumped by all global and regional powers active in the region. Foreign meddling became increasingly pronounced as the uprisings evolved, by regional but also global powers such as the US, Russia or EU member states which provided support to the protest movements or supported militias/governments in violently seeking to suppress them. What is notable in many protest movements is the outright rejection of foreign intervention. One of the protest leaders in Algeria has, for example, asserted: 'Count only on your unity and determination to carry on with this peaceful revolution. Do not expect foreign help. A revolution succeeds only with the solidarity and unity of the people. No revolution has won when foreigners intervened in it'.[18]

---

[17]   Raymond Hinnebusch, *The International Politics of the Middle East*, Manchester/ New York, Manchester University Press, 2003, http://library.oapen.org/handle/ 20.500.12657/35008.

[18]   Lamine Ghanmi, 'European Support for Algeria's Protests Finds No Takers', in *The Arab Weekly*, 2019, https://thearabweekly.com/node/46733. This, it should be noted,

Thus, the political space is also directly structured by the geopolitical context in which these protest movements emerged.

5. EU policies

While the EU reacted rather quickly to the protests in 2011 with a revised European Neighbourhood Policy (ENP), the new European Endowment for Democracy as well as ad-hoc instruments such as the trilateral dialogue in Tunisia, from 2013 onwards, its reaction to protests has been extremely cautious and limited. Whilst it has voiced support for the protesters in rhetoric, no concrete instruments have been adopted – as opposed for example to migration and security where an array of new and often informal instruments have been developed.

On the *local dimension*, the EU has boosted its capacities to support civil society in the region, particularly in the initial phase of the uprisings. Nonetheless, EU policies often do not respond to local needs,[19] also from a gender perspective as it treats 'gender' in a technocratic, box-ticking approach.[20] Resentment towards the EU has increased with the first uprisings, particularly in light of its cooperation with autocrats and its (arms) trade and migration policies,[21] as well as – more recently – its reaction to the covid-19 crisis which has been limited to a re-shuffling of funds instead of a major new initiative to support these countries including with sufficient vaccines. Nonetheless, before the covid-19 crisis, the EU has still been perceived more positively than the Gulf states, Russia or the US.[22]

On the *national dimension*, the EU continues to mainly interact with mostly autocratic governments through its ENP which has not gone through a revision

---

aims not only at regional powers and the US, but also Europe. After a resolution of the European Parliament on the protests in Algeria, one protest leader tweeted that 'If Europe wants to help Algeria, it must help it recover the stolen money'. Protesters in Lebanon pointed out how the tear gas the security forces threw at them had been produced in France.

[19] Andrea Teti et al., *Democratisation against Democracy. How EU Foreign Policy Fails the Middle East*, Cham, Palgrave Macmillan, 2020.

[20] Hala Ghosheh, 'EU Approach to Gender Equality in the Southern and Eastern Mediterranean Region', in *MEDRESET Policy Papers*, No. 9 (April 2019), https://www.iai.it/en/node/10234.

[21] Daniela Huber and Maria Cristina Paciello (eds), '10 Years of Arab Uprisings and the EU's Pragmatist Turn: Grassroots Perceptions from the Mediterranean Space', in *European Foreign Affairs Review*, Vol. 25, Special issue (May 2020).

[22] European Institute of the Mediterranean (IEMed), 'Changing Euro-Mediterranean Lenses', in *Euromed Surveys*, No. 9 (2018), https://www.iemed.org/?p=6358.

despite the EU's turn towards a policy of building societal 'resilience'.[23] The EU's relationship with political Islam is evolving,[24] whilst it is divided on how to interact with political forces such as Hezbollah. Some of the countries in the region – Sudan and Iraq – are not even included in the ENP and the EU is not particularly interested in them. Furthermore, as the EU seems to have lost momentum, its member states are becoming more active, most notably France. The increasing activity of single EU member states, however, impacts decisively on EU cohesiveness and credibility.

On the *regional dimension*, despite the 25th anniversary of the Barcelona Process, there is no new EU initiative to support the building of a security architecture in the region. As pointed out by Waleed Hazbun, the international community needs to 'work with regional states to manage ongoing conflicts, define norms for regional power projection and establish inclusive regional negotiations'.[25] Whilst the EU's (and EU UNSC members) commitment to the JCPOA might be stepping stones, no major initiative by the EU to protect international law (including international humanitarian and human rights law) in the region has been forthcoming.

Conclusions

Ten years ago, a major historical transformation commenced in the Arab world with the uprisings that are continuing until this day, even though they are being challenged by authoritarian counter-revolutionary responses, a complex (geo) political context, as well as the covid-19 pandemic. Also in these past ten years, the EU has changed decisively, internally with the rise of nationalist right-wing populism and Brexit; and externally as its foreign policy in the Middle East and North Africa has focused on security and migration rather than democracy or international law. Through a multilevel and comparative approach, this book draws a comprehensive picture of this transformation which can set the stage for the EU to reimagine its own policies vis-à-vis the region in a way that is more connected to the regional political space.

---

23 Silvia Colombo, Andrea Dessi and Vassilis Ntousas (eds), *The EU, Resilience and the MENA Region*, Brussels/Rome, Foundation for European Progressive Studies/Istituto Affari Internazionali, 2017, https://www.iai.it/en/node/8767.

24 Sarah Wolff, *Secular Power Europe and Islam. Identity and Foreign Policy*, Ann Arbor, University of Michigan Press, 2021.

25 Waleed Hazbun, 'Regional Powers and the Projection of Insecurity in the Middle East', in *MENARA Working Papers*, No. 11 (September 2018), p. 2, https://www.iai.it/en/node/9518.

References

Tom Allinson, 'Setback to Egypt's #MeToo Movement as Rape Witnesses Reportedly Charged', in *Deutsche Welle*, 17 September 2020, https://p.dw.com/p/3ibKm

Asef Bayat, *Revolution without Revolutionaries. Making Sense of the Arab Spring*, Stanford, Stanford University Press, 2017

Federica Bicchi, Benoit Challand and Steven Heydermann (eds), *The Struggle for Influence in the Middle East. The Arab Uprisings and Foreign Assistance*, London/New York, Routledge, 2016

Silvia Colombo, Andrea Dessi and Vassilis Ntousas (eds), *The EU, Resilience and the MENA Region*, Brussels/Rome, Foundation for European Progressive Studies/Istituto Affari Internazionali, 2017, 2017, https://www.iai.it/en/node/8767

European Institute of the Mediterranean (IEMed), 'Changing Euro-Mediterranean Lenses', in *Euromed Surveys*, No. 9 (2018), https://www.iemed.org/?p=6358

Lamine Ghanmi, 'European Support for Algeria's Protests Finds No Takers', in *The Arab Weekly*, 2019, https://thearabweekly.com/node/46733

Hala Ghosheh, 'EU Approach to Gender Equality in the Southern and Eastern Mediterranean Region', in *MEDRESET Policy Papers*, No. 9 (April 2019), https://www.iai.it/en/node/10234

Sune Haugbolle and Andreas Bandak, 'The Ends of Revolution: Rethinking Ideology and Time in the Arab Uprisings', in *Middle East Critique*, Vol. 26, No. 3 (3 July 2017), p. 191–204

Waleed Hazbun, 'Regional Powers and the Projection of Insecurity in the Middle East', in *MENARA Working Papers*, No. 11 (September 2018), p. 2, https://www.iai.it/en/node/9518

Steven Heydemann, 'Explaining the Arab Uprisings: Transformations in Comparative Perspective', in *Mediterranean Politics*, Vol. 21, No. 1 (2016), p. 192–204, https://doi.org/10.1080/13629395.2015.1081450

Steven Heydemann, 'Rethinking Social Contracts in the MENA Region: Economic Governance, Contingent Citizenship, and State-Society Relations after the Arab Uprisings', in *World Development*, Vol. 135 (November 2020, Article 105019

Steven Heydemann and Reinoud Leenders, 'Authoritarian Learning and Authoritarian Resilience: Regime Responses to the 'Arab Awakening'', in *Globalizations*, Vol. 8, No. 5 (2011), p. 647–653

Raymond Hinnebusch, *After the Arab Uprisings. Between Democratization, Counter-revolution and State Failure*, London/New York, Routledge, 2016

Raymond Hinnebusch, *The International Politics of the Middle East*, Manchester/New York, Manchester University Press, 2003, http://library.oapen.org/handle/20.500.12657/35008

Daniela Huber and Lorenzo Kamel (eds), *Arab Spring and Peripheries. A Decentring Research Agenda*, London/New York, Routledge, 2016

Daniela Huber and Maria Cristina Paciello (eds), '10 Years of Arab Uprisings and the EU's Pragmatist Turn: Grassroots Perceptions from the Mediterranean Space', in *European Foreign Affairs Review*, Vol. 25, Special issue (May 2020)

Elisabeth Johansson-Nogués, 'Gendering the Arab Spring? Rights and (In)security of Tunisian, Egyptian and Libyan Women', in *Security Dialogue*, Vol. 44, No. 5/6 (October-December 2013), p. 393–409

Marc Lynch (ed.), *The Arab Uprisings Explained. New Contentious Politics in the Middle East*, New York, Columbia University Press, 2014

Marc Lynch and Jillian Schwedler, 'Introduction to the Special Issue on 'Islamist Politics After the Arab Uprisings'', in *Middle East Law and Governance*, Vol. 12, No. 1 (April 2020), p. 3–13

MERIP, 'Return to Revolution', in *Middle East Report*, No. 292/293 (Fall/Winter 2019), https://merip.org/magazine/292-3

Yezid Sayigh, *Owners of the Republic. An Anatomy of Egypt's Military Economy*, Washington, Carnegie Endowment for International Peace, 2019, https://carnegieendowment.org/publications/80325

Diane Singerman, 'Youth, Gender, and Dignity in the Egyptian Uprising', in *Journal of Middle East Women's Studies*, Vol. 9, No. 3 (Fall 2013), p. 1–27, https://doi.org/10.2979/jmiddeastwomstud.9.3.1

Rita Stephan and Mounira M. Charrad (eds), *Women Rising. In and Beyond the Arab Spring*, New York, New York University Press, 2020

Andrea Teti, Pamela Abbott and Francesco Cavatorta, *The Arab Uprisings in Egypt, Jordan and Tunisia. Social, Political and Economic Transformations*, Cham, Palgrave Macmillan, 2018

Andrea Teti et al., *Democratisation against Democracy. How EU Foreign Policy Fails the Middle East*, Cham, Palgrave Macmillan, 2020

Sarah Wolff, *Secular Power Europe and Islam. Identity and Foreign Policy*, Ann Arbor, University of Michigan Press, 2021

Hafsa Halawa

Chapter 2: Iraq's Tishreen Movement: A Decade of Protests and Mobilisation

Iraq has endured a turbulent modern history, moulded by the US-led invasion in 2003 that unseated long-time dictator Saddam Hussein and put the country on a transition towards democracy. However, the last 18 years have seen the initial post-Saddam roadmap lose direction, succumb to external influence and violence by non-state actors and eventually become beholden to continued cycles of conflict. While corruption has become an endemic problem, political paralysis has slowly set in, bringing governance to an almost complete halt.

The democratic process has decayed, deflated and flattened into a cyclical empowerment of a political class that reverts to sectarian rhetoric when all else fails, ignores demands for adequate public service delivery and fails to serve communities of changed demographics.

Mobilisation in different forms has been a potent part of a renewed attempt at democratic transition. In Iraq, this has not always been driven by interested citizens who seek to improve their living conditions. Alongside unarmed protest, armed militant insurgents and widespread militias have joined the fray. The largest mobilisation of unarmed citizens, however, remains the October 2019 Tishreen movement (*tishreen* means 'October').

The unrest has massively affected the internal political dynamics and forced through a militarisation of society generally, even if first born out of dissent towards the US occupation of the country. The political and security vacuum during the post-invasion period as well as continued violence provoked the cultivation of Al-Qaeda in Iraq and eventually the rise of the so-called Islamic State in Iraq and Syria (ISIS) and the swift takeover of territory across parts of the country in 2014.

Until the outbreak of the Tishreen revolution, protests had been inherently political in nature and form. With obvious exceptions – notably the Basra protests of 2018 – periodic protests were defined by their political leaning or organisation and remained inherently a tool for political gain in both form and ideology. The 'Sadr protests' of 2016 remain the most obvious of these. All this is not to say that the 2019 protest movement is deeply apolitical; rather that it is the first prolonged movement that has emerged independent of any political party or ideology. While this may not outlast a patient, corrupt and powerful political elite, it has proven a watershed moment for the post-2003 political order. Iraqi domestic dynamics are now being more pertinently scrutinised by the international community, including the European Union and the United States, through the lens of the civilian movement, the moment of revolution and the near-breaking point in the economy that has come with the outbreak of the covid-19 pandemic.

1. Protests in Iraq: 2011 to the present

The outbreak of protests in October 2019 came as a shock to outside observers. The prolonged nature of the movement and its generally non-sectarian message has endured, forcing a domestic reckoning between protestors, citizens and political representatives. However, the movement itself was not a sudden event, but rather a continuation and evolution of mass mobilisation as a form of dissent that has been part of the country's political and social fabric for several years already.

While Iraq did not experience the kind of revolutionary wave seen in other parts of the Arab world in 2011, the Arab Spring by no means bypassed it.[1] The protests that engulfed the region were also present in Iraq, albeit with much less international focus as they did not bring about political change the way they did in Egypt, Tunisia and elsewhere. Ultimately, popular protests in Iraq in 2011 lacked the capacity to endure state-sponsored violence. The political establishment in Iraq was able to contain and dissipate protest anger with little to no concession.

In 2011, Iraq had already been rid of Saddam for almost a decade – removed by force by the US-led invasion and subsequent occupation in 2003 – and protests that decried the leadership of then-Prime Minister Nouri al Maliki lacked the type of single-form unity seen in other countries (like Tunisia, Libya, Yemen, Syria and Egypt), which targeted one single personality as representative of the regime. The protests also remained comparatively small, when viewed in light of the events in Egypt's Tahrir Square or Tunisia's Avenue Habib Bourguiba. In addition, Iraq had already seen continuous forms of conflict since 2003, due to the anti-US insurgency and the formation of armed non-state actors with political influence. The post-2003 order gave significant power to armed militias and political actors that formed armed groups either as an extension of their political power, or in support of it.[2] As a result, the protests that emerged in 2011

[1] Marina Ottaway and Danial Anas Kays, 'Iraq: Protest, Democracy, and Autocracy', in *Carnegie Articles*, 28 March 2011, https://carnegieendowment.org/publications/43306.
[2] Joost Hiltermann, 'Iraq: The Clerics and the Militias', in *The New York Review of Books*, 13 October 2015, https://www.crisisgroup.org/node/1822.

remained powerless and were violently put down, set amid a fatigued conflict narrative, growing Iranian influence and the start of the US retreat.[3]

In the years after 2011, Iraq saw periodic protests waves, most prominently the Sadr protests in 2016 and the Basra protests of 2018, before things came to a head with the October revolution in 2019.

The Sadr protests saw the occupation of the parliament building and parts of the ultra-protected Green Zone in Baghdad in response to parliament inactivity.[4] Led by the powerful Shia cleric/politician/militia leader Muqtada al Sadr, thousands of his supporters descended upon the institutional buildings to protest the decision-making process in the formation of government. As a figure, Muqtada has carefully and coherently manipulated citizens and political elites alike over the years to further his political project and fulfil his own personal ambitions.[5] Buoyed by arguably the largest civilian constituency of any major political group, Sadr has managed to become the most effective spoiler of the political process. This has been exacerbated in recent years as his constituency support translates into more and more representation in parliament.

The protests themselves were driven by growing anger over corruption within the political system and the disconnect between political elites and the general population. While they were without a doubt politically driven, they reflected genuine dissent and dissatisfaction with the political system. This is a sentiment that has only grown over the decade and has expanded beyond political figures and their constituencies to take hold in society.

Further protests that occurred during 2015/16 were overshadowed in large part by the ongoing war against ISIS that had forced the country's population into a form of complete submission: not just to the Iraqi political order and its armed extensions, but also continued and re-emerging foreign intervention and continued proxy wars as well as a strong and mobilised militant insurgency. The war against ISIS saw the formation of an international coalition, led by the United States (including NATO allies), and increasing involvement of Iran's military. By late 2017, when then-PM Haider Abadi declared the war 'over' with the retaking of Mosul from ISIS, the country had emerged from its most violent

---

[3]   James Jeffrey, 'Behind the U.S. Withdrawal from Iraq', in *Washington Institute Policy Analysis*, 2 November 2014, https://www.washingtoninstitute.org/node/4454.

[4]   Jennifer Williams, 'The Political Crisis Rocking Baghdad and Why It Matters for the War on ISIS', in *Vox*, 19 April 2016, https://www.vox.com/2016/4/19/11451550.

[5]   Thanassis Cambanis, 'Can Militant Cleric Moqtada al-Sadr Reform Iraq?', in *The Century Foundation Reports*, 1 May 2018, https://tcf.org/content/report/can-militant-cleric-moqtada-al-sadr-reform-iraq.

conflict in 18 years broken, weak and facing near collapse. At the peak of the war over six million citizens were internally displaced. To date, over 1.5 million people remain (officially) displaced, although the unofficial number is believed to be much higher.[6] Entire towns and cities were almost entirely destroyed and are yet to be rebuilt, including Mosul, the country's second-largest city, as well as major parts of the disputed territories, like Hawija, Sinjar, Ba'quba and many others.[7]

While the 2016 protests were led by Sadr and fuelled by dissatisfaction with Abadi, the 2018 Basra protests following the May 2018 elections were of a very different nature.[8] Arguably resulting in the derailment of Abadi's attempts to secure a second term, the protests that rocked Basra – and the country – for months, would appear (with hindsight) to have set in motion the spark that would later erupt in the 2019 Tishreen movement.

In the summer of 2018, facing excruciating power cuts amid soaring summer temperatures, mass protests broke out across the province.[9] These protests were less politically aligned than the Sadr movement, and the country was unable to contain the sustained anger coming from the protestors, exacerbated by the continuation of the violent response by the state (including tacit support of armed non-state actors) in response to the demonstrations. Mirroring smaller protests that broke out in 2015, rather than the 2016 Sadr movement, the 2018 protests proved to be the tipping point for the use of mobilisation as a political tool harnessed by citizens. Fuelled by testimonies of the suffering in Iraq's poorest province (despite holding over 95 per cent of its oil wealth), videos, reporting and media focus helped bring the plight of citizens to the fore. While during that period anger remained localised to Basra, the sentiment was harnessed across the country, which allowed the protests to remain powerful in the face of government confusion, political paralysis and no leading authority to respond to demands. Similar tactics have been deployed since 2019.

---

[6]   As of 31 December 2020. See Internal Displacement Monitoring Centre (IDMC) website: *Iraq*, https://www.internal-displacement.org/countries/iraq.

[7]   Building Peaceful Futures, *Conflict Analysis. Sinjar and Hawija, Iraq*, Erbil, Save the Children Iraq, 2019, https://www.australianhumanitarianpartnership.org/library-contents/conflict-analysis-sinjar-and-hawija-iraq-2019.

[8]   Isam al Khafaji, 'Iraq 2018 Elections: Between Sectarianism and the Nation', in *Bawader*, 12 July 2018, https://www.arab-reform.net/?p=2948.

[9]   Matthew Schweitzer, 'Protests in Southern Iraq Intensify, Is Instability to Follow?', in *IPI Global Observatory*, 24 July 2018, https://theglobalobservatory.org/?p=18022.

Epitomising the clear angst over the mismanagement of governance and lack of service delivery, powerful images of the effects of contaminated water resources, lack of fuel and electricity and the decrepit state of the province sustained protests throughout the political process of government formation in the months following the 2018 elections.[10] The power of the Basra protests took on new resonance. Whilst protests against a lack of service delivery are not uncommon, notably in the summer owing to increasingly unbearable temperatures, the 2018 movement built from there. That the epicentre of protest was the southern province of the country – heavily Shia-dominated – was not lost on the protestors, and the targets of their anger quickly spread from the government, to Shia political figures, and beyond towards the Iranian regime.[11] Such a message has resonated and grown during the 2019 movement, which has forced a political reckoning for the elite as the South rages.

Following the May 2018 parliamentary elections, the talks over possible government coalitions were officially halted as anger in Basra raged. With immediate support for their plight coming from the most trusted leader, Ayatollah Ali al Sistani, and other 'opposition' politicians, the protests effectively brought down the Abadi government and any opportunity for the suggested Abadi-Sadr coalition to take power.

The moment also set a precedent that has since defined the political process: the appointment of unelected 'technocrats' to top executive positions, as public trust in political representatives has all but disappeared. As political factions could not agree on which party leader should get the opportunity to form a government, and with leaders attempting to distance themselves from protest ire, technocrat Adel Abdel Mahdi (AAM – a former minister of Finance and deputy PM under Maliki), was appointed PM in a negotiated settlement, facilitated by Sistani.[12]

The moment also proved an inflection point for the state institutions, as a civilian-led parliament ceded authority to the religious authority of Ayatollah

[10]   Glada Lahn and Nouar Shamout, 'Basra's Poisonous Water Demands International Action', in *Chatham House Expert Comments*, 14 November 2018 https://www.chath amhouse.org/node/15623.

[11]   'Iraq Protests: Demonstrators in Basra Storm Iran's Consulate', in *Deutsche Welle*, 7 September 2018, https://p.dw.com/p/34W9o.

[12]   Suadad Al-Salhy, 'Rival Iraqi Factions Make Coalition Deal and End Al-Abadi's Prime Minister Hopes', in *Arab News*, 13 September 2018, https://www.arabnews.com/node/1371716.

Sistani, who took on a more overt political role that continues to this day.[13] Sistani's political influence has increased – whether intentionally or as a consequence of events – thereby turning him into a seemingly apolitical kingmaker.

Over the years, the general theme of protests in the country has revolved around poor governance and the lack of job and economic opportunity for Iraqis. Messages centred around poor public service delivery have defined civilian relations with political leaders, mired in sectarianism and corruption. But the 2019 protests that brought about the Tishreen movement have been the least sector-specific wave the country has witnessed in the last decade.[14]

In the period between the summer of 2018 and the outbreak of protests, Iraq witnessed a lack of political direction on a scale not seen in the aftermath of the US invasion and occupation. A new form of government immobility set in, with an unelected prime minister, who had no civilian constituency and lacked any coherent security sector support and religious authority. AAM was effectively a 'sitting duck' PM, nominated by political leaders with the largest majority in parliament – who remained on opposite sides of the political fray – arguably for no other reason than to provide a new scapegoat for Iraq's ills.

As a result, the parliament has failed to address the lack of legitimacy of government in failing to agree on anything from budgetary reform to more consequential social and political reforms. In addition, the transfer of power to Iranian-backed militia groups in parts of the country liberated from ISIS created massive social fractures and remains an unrecognised problem to this day. Arguably, the sentiment of the 2018 protests has never waned – rather paused in the early period of AAM's premiership, and as anger grew the movement expanded, capturing a significant part of the country and exploding in the form of Tishreen.

Viewed as part of the 'Arab Spring 2.0', Iraq's Tishreen revolution has – as noted – been incorrectly viewed by many as a sudden Arab uprising moment. Instead, it has resulted from years of low-level mobilisation in protests against poor governance, lack of democratic progress and armed insurgency. The message of the Tishreen movement has focused much more on the entirety of the political elite, armed non-state actors who now form politically represented

---

[13]   Harith Hasan, 'The Subtle Power of Sistani', in *Diwan*, 14 November 2019, https://carne
       gie-mec.org/diwan/80346.
[14]   National Democratic Institute (NDI), *Iraq: We Want a Homeland. Key Findings of
       Qualitative Research Conducted in Five Provinces in Iraq: Baghdad, Basra, Diyala, Erbil,
       and Nasiriyah. December 2019–February 2020*, September 2020, https://www.ndi.org/
       sites/default/files/Iraqi%20Protests%20Research%20Report_EN.pdf.

militias, continued and increasing influence of Iran on those militia groups[15] (and by extension the political process), all amidst a decaying post-conflict landscape, active drivers of conflict and stagnant development.[16]

The movement has remained largely non-sectarian, despite the fact that protests rage across the majority Shia-populated South and political leaders continue to attempt to infiltrate and co-opt the movement, using sectarianism as a way to break it. Muqtada al Sadr's attempts to do so stand out as the most consequential example of this. The movement has brought together most of Iraq's social classes in a majority youthful movement ranging from school students to young unemployed citizens. Women play a large and consequential part, with female activists forming an integral part of the calls for social change including a domestic violence bill, an early marriage bill, and greater access to education for girls.

Besides the lack of services or poor governance, the message from the movement, 'we want a country', has focused on corruption within the political class and seeks the complete overhaul of the post-2003 political order.[17] Whilst previous iterations focused on a particular manifestation of poor governance (lack of electricity, access to jobs), the defining message from the movement is that citizens want ownership and agency over their country and how it is governed. The broader message of the revolution remains the overhaul of sectarian division of power, the end of institutionalised corruption and the reversal of far-reaching power transfers to armed non-state actors.

In a post-2003 order, where cycles of conflict have ravaged many parts of the country, Iraq's physical infrastructure is literally collapsing. Where it does not exist, millions have been displaced, either into a cycle of UN registration and state-controlled camps or unofficial displacement absorbing themselves into new communities in different parts of the country in an attempt to start over. Physical violence, sexual assault and financial extortion are daily realities for millions – especially women – including at the hands of the state. Homes demolished in 2014 are yet to be rebuilt. Teachers and doctors from war-ravaged cities have disappeared into a self-sufficient cycle of international humanitarian aid support, likely never to return to public sector practice. For those who

---

[15]   Ranj Alaadin, 'Containing Shiite Militias: The Battle for Stability in Iraq', in *Brookings Doha Center Policy Briefings*, December 2017, http://brook.gs/2jZ9CP8.

[16]   Hafsa Halawa, 'The Forgotten Iraq', in *MEI Policy Papers*, No. 2020-7 (March 2020), https://www.mei.edu/node/80974.

[17]   Zahra Ali, 'Iraqis Demand a Country', in *Middle East Report*, No. 292/293 (Fall/Winter 2019), p. 2–5, https://merip.org/?p=79032.

have remained in their areas of origin, or those who attempt to return, parts of the country still resemble the days of the height of conflict against ISIS, almost entirely untouched by state or local authorities. The war has officially been over since 2017, but in reality, war is very much a daily experience for millions of Iraqis.

Protests have been tempered throughout 2020 as the covid-19 pandemic ravaged the country.[18] In the early period of a national curfew, some protestors chose to remain in public squares like Baghdad's Tahrir Square. Protests were sporadic but remained, while a great number of activists moved their activities online. A large part focused on the pandemic and ensuring social awareness of the healthcare risks, supporting civil society, while the online space became a locus for intellectual political debate on the definition of identity, what forms of constitutional principles could be advocated for, and the ongoing debate on whether to participate politically or not. That specific debate has taken on significance with the announcement of early elections, set for October 2021, but possibly delayed to 2022, and has forced decisions on whether to engage and form political parties or remain a potent civilian force through mobilisation.[19] Ultimately, however, the movement remains active, and has become a significant part of the political calculation, with an opportunity to define a new phase for the country's post-Saddam trajectory and democratisation.

2. National political dynamics and the Tishreen movement

The last decade in the country has been widely defined as the decade of increased terrorism – marked by the war against ISIS – and fractured relations with the West (namely the United States), while Iran's influence has increased. However, domestically, the country should be more appropriately viewed from the perspective of a slowly decaying political infrastructure, fuelled by the normalisation of political corruption and the effect of conflict on the impact of sectarian narratives and messages in the public and political space. This has, as a result, provided the space for manifestations of violence and protest that have sadly become routine.

---

[18]   Youssef Cherif, Hafsa Halawa and Özge Zihnioğlu, 'The Coronavirus and Civic Activism in the Middle East and North Africa', in Richard Youngs (ed.), *Global Civil Society in the Shadow of Coronavirus*, Washington, Carnegie Endowment for International Peace, December 2020, p. 21–26, https://carnegieendowment.org/publications/83142.

[19]   Cathrin Schaer, 'Iraq's New Protester Parties Plan to Change the Country', in *Deutsche Welle*, 22 January 2021, https://p.dw.com/p/3oHOz.

The Tishreen movement, however, is a watershed moment for the country.[20] While the movement has remained inherently non-sectarian, the translation into the political space of almost all protest movements/mobilisation since 2011 remains of sectarian nature. The author's own field research in 2018 revealed a fatigued and disenfranchised public neither energised nor driven by sectarian politics or the narrative parroted by politicians in the country, which for the most part has manifested itself in consecutively diminishing voter turnout.

Those invested parts of the electorate clearly lack a desire to make their voices heard at the ballot box. Their right not to vote, however, continues to empower the same political actors who have brought the country to its knees, albeit now depending on much smaller constituencies. It is also an example of the lack of opportunity and diversity in the political landscape, whereby disenfranchised voters have no alternative options.

Voters who do engage with the electoral process, remain loyal – insofar as they vote – to the sectarian divisions that exist. Therefore, it is predicted that not only will any attempts at political formation of the protest movement fail at the ballot box, but that voter apathy and a continued drop in voter numbers will define the post-Tishreen elections.[21] Any failing of political actors formed out of the movement will be capitalised on by the entrenched political parties, even if their predictable failure is a result of the behaviour of the political elite itself in curbing opportunity, outfunding and outmanoeuvring a young movement, and manipulating the process to their benefit, namely electoral legislation and voter education.

Political elites are organising – individually and collectively – to challenge the authority of the protest movement, at the expense of any form of improved governance or progress on the agenda of moving the country forward.[22] Having delegated authority to a second unelected government when it appointed former intelligence chief, Mustafa Al Kadhimi, as prime minister, the political elites continue in their attempts to avert the wrath of watchful protestors and citizens, shifting responsibility to the new prime minister, and by extension culpability for a continued failure to respond to the array of demands and needs.

---

[20]   Hamzeh Al-Shadeedi, Mac Skelton and Zmkan Ali Saleem, 'Why Iraq's Protesters Won't Go Home: 10 Voices from the Movement', in *LSE Middle East Centre Blog*, 3 March 2020, https://wp.me/p3Khxv-2iu.

[21]   Erik K. Gustafson and Omar Al-Nidawi, 'Iraqi Protesters' Perilous Journey to the Ballot Box', in *MEI Policy Analysis*, 22 March 2021, https://www.mei.edu/node/82608.

[22]   Samir Sumaida'ie, 'The Hijacking of Democracy: The Role of Political Parties in Iraq', in *Wilson Center Viewpoints*, 8 April 2021, https://www.wilsoncenter.org/node/105840.

The entrenchment of this political entitlement is lost on a younger civilian population and drives protests made up of large swathes of society who have known little else but the post-2003 political system. For most Iraqis, Saddam Hussein is a leader who defines their parents' and grandparents' lives, but not their own present time. The shifting regional demographics that have seen young adults and teens overtake their seniors as the most representative of society carries with it a disconnect of identity among Iraqi communities.[23] 2003 is no longer just the line in the sand that defines a pre/post-Saddam Iraq politically. It extends into the social fabric, defining political identity and social cohesion factors that now navigate opposition to the current political order.

In other words, young Iraqis are no longer drawn by the argument of how much worse off the country was under Saddam. In some quarters, 'better the devil you know than the devil you don't' does not apply. As a result, within small parts of the protest movement calls for a return to strongman/authoritarian rule can be heard.[24] It is a sign of the level of desperation, frustration and anger harboured towards the current elite. That military rule may steer the country in a better direction is more an indictment of just how colossal the failure of governance is now, than it is proof of any loyalties or love for a bygone dictator (or another one in the future).

And that is not to speak of unchecked militia groups. The protest movement faces violent repercussions in its attempt to organise, with assassinations of young protestors a daily occurrence. Militia groups exercise power, authority and control over massive parts of civilian life in the country. Building on now years of governance and security control in the liberated parts of the country (post-ISIS), militias now thrive, increasing their presence and power across the country. All the while, they remain unchecked.[25] Transparency and accountability are at the heart of protestors' calls for a new country, and yet armed non-state actors have

---

[23]   Asha Amirali, 'The "Youth Bulge" and Political Unrest in Iraq: A Political Economy Approach', in *K4D Helpdesk Reports*, 11 November 2019, https://opendocs.ids.ac.uk/opendocs/handle/20.500.12413/14815.

[24]   Pesha Magid, 'Angry Iraqis Demand New Government', in *Foreign Policy*, 7 October 2019, https://foreignpolicy.com/2019/10/07/angry-iraqis-yearn-for-military-rule-again.

[25]   Hassan Hassan, 'How Iraq's Top ISIS Scholar Became a Target for Shiite Militias', in *Newlines Magazine*, 4 October 2020, https://newlinesmag.com/essays/the-man-who-knew-too-much-why-shiite-militias-killed-iraqs-finest-isis-scholar. At the time of writing, dozens of young male and female activists have been targeted and assassinated by Shiite militias, with no accountability to date for any of the killings.

only furthered their entrenchment in the political system and the state's security architectures.

Civilians have been left unprotected, ungoverned and ignored. The current political class remains ignorant of the ongoing erosion of its power and mandate. For those civilian leaders supportive of or led by militia groups, it remains a myth that they yield significant power or control. Beyond their own direct spheres of economic corruption (and some might argue even within), power has become beholden to violent actors, now that violence has been given the space to direct the political landscape.[26] The country is now led by militia groups and their leaders – whether it be al-Sadr and his civilian movement, which masks his armed militia in the first instance, or the plethora of Iranian-backed militia groups that make up the broadly defined Hashd al Shaabi.

It is a definition that extends, too, to the Kurdistan Regional Government (KRG) and its leadership.[27] Rather than a tussle for influence among militia factions sponsored by proxy states and actors, therein lies a familial war, where armed groups have become an inherent part of the formal security architecture for the autonomous region and illiberal 'democracy' is practised by unsustainable power-sharing agreements between the ruling families.[28]

The Tishreen movement has exposed the ongoing political collapse in a more direct fashion than even the war against ISIS had done. The targeting of young, innocent and unarmed protestors, journalists and academics by Iranian-backed militia groups in the south of Iraq, or the KRG officially in the Kurdistan Region, is merely an example of the 'entitlement to power' concept, upon which the post-2003 order has been built. The movement has also grown beyond the public spaces occupied by protestors. Whether in agreement or not, it has propelled a new discourse amongst the population, and rooted itself at the heart of political discussion. It has also become its own 'catch-all' phrase or response, in the face of continued anger at the lack of development and opportunity in the country.

In response to the movement itself, and the national message that has resonated across all parts of the country, security forces – whether formal or not – have

---

26   Katie Bo Williams, 'Militias in Iraq Provide Security, Wield Political Power, and May Be Tearing the Country Apart', in *Defence One*, 2 March 2021 https://www.defenseone.com/threats/2021/03/militias-iraq-provide-security-wield-political-power-and-may-be-tearing-country-apart/172390.

27   Jenna Krajeski, 'How the War with ISIS Has Exposed Kurdistan's Internal Divisions', in *The Nation*, 6 April 2015, https://www.thenation.com/?p=117302.

28   Kawa Hassan, 'Kurdistan's Politicized Society Confronts a Sultanistic System', in *Carnegie Papers*, August 2015, https://carnegieendowment.org/publications/61026.

engaged in an intense crackdown. In addition, a widespread discrediting campaign continues, and the political elite has emerged from the pandemic seeking to reassert its control over the political system. Amended electoral laws appear nonsensical, and certainly not more equitable or representative than previous laws, the unspoken cloud of constitutional reform remains ignored, while the government attempts to temper daily anger and violence by forming hapless investigation committees.[29] The poor pandemic response and failed attempts at economic reform serve as examples of the failures of the country's political system and its elite, as well as the human toll of continued corruption and securitisation of the state.[30]

Whether or not the Tishreen movement continues in physical form in the same way that it was created is irrelevant. Citizens' opposition towards the ruling class has been a mainstay feature across the entire country for most of the last decade and will continue to be so in the years to come.[31] With little to no humility or political courage among them, the political elites will likely continue to crack down on the movement in a futile attempt to put out the fires of anger and disillusionment, resulting in more violence, continued instability and increased security threats against the population and the government alike.

3. The Tishreen movement and geopolitics

Since the initial taking of territory by ISIS in 2014, Iraq has become awash with weapons and proxy actors. US and allied presence in the country – which had all but disappeared in 2011 following disagreement over a continuation of the State of Forces Agreement between the United States and Iraq – morphed into the 'Global Coalition to Defeat ISIS', while Iranian-backed militia groups gained legitimacy in fighting militants both alongside and independent of the state's security forces. Concurrently, Kurdish PKK-aligned actors in Syria have provoked a Turkish military response in the disputed Ninewah Plains (namely Sinjar), and Israel continues to expand its military response to perceived Iranian threats with periodic attacks in Iraqi territory. Since the war ended and ISIS

---

[29]   Falih Hassan and Jane Arraf, 'Fire at Baghdad Hospital Packed with Covid Patients Kills at Least 82', in *The New York Times*, 25 April 2021, https://nyti.ms/3aEH19i.

[30]   Kirk H. Sowell, 'Iraq's Dire Fiscal Crisis', in *Sada*, 2 November 2020, https://carnegieendowment.org/sada/83108.

[31]   Harith Hasan, 'Iraq Protests: A New Social Movement Is Challenging Sectarian Power', in *Middle East Eye*, 4 November 2019, https://carnegieendowment.org/publications/80256.

territory was regained, continued threats and attacks from militia groups against US outposts leave the threat perception of war between Iran and the United States constantly fluctuating.

Domestically, Baghdad and Erbil remain ideologically split over how to counter the myriad of security threats, leaving a vacuum that has resulted in this new playground for an array of actors. Iraqis continue to bear the toll of these continued stand-offs. As civilian politicians all but cede control to armed non-state actors in the most critical areas of state governance and security architecture, there is little ability to manoeuvre the country out of this quagmire – and certainly not without external support and security prowess.

The defining feature of the geopolitics in Iraq remains the tensions between Washington and Tehran. During the four years of a reactive and unarticulated policy from the Trump administration, Iraq was seen as mere collateral damage in invoking the 'maximum pressure' campaign against the Iranians; the buffer by which direct conflict could be averted but where confrontation between the parties could continue.

The EU played – and still plays – a nominal role, which has perpetuated the general perception of it as a supportive and trusted but powerless ally. EU member states have their own independent foreign policy priorities which determine the level of their engagement militarily in Iraq in support of the broadly defined US mandate. The lack of direct EU representation within the hard security environment also adds to the broader confusion, potent in Iraq, between the authority of member states versus that of Brussels. The United Kingdom (no longer a member of the EU), remains the most ardent of these partners, while other members of the Five-Eyes (Australia, Canada, New Zealand) have joined a number of EU member states in providing support. More recently the NATO mission in Iraq has sought to expand its presence, although this has been widely interpreted as a cover by which the United States can continue its slow withdrawal from the country.

Alongside military engagement, the United Nations has kept an oversized presence in Iraq since 2003. The UN has never sanctioned a peacekeeping operation (DPKO). Nevertheless, the UN's Assistance Mission in Iraq (UNAMI) has been present for over 18 years, has spent and still spends billions of dollars to implement a variety of programmes, geared towards the sustainable development of the country and the success of its democratic transition. UNAMI's presence includes the large presence of over ten UN agencies including UNHCR, UNDP, UNICEF, UN Women, UNEP, UNFPA and others. The civilian form of international intervention has also paved the way for an array of international NGOs, development partners and donors to entrench themselves into the governance of the country. The EU-Iraq strategy alone totals some 600 million euros in aid that includes humanitarian support to immediate conflict zones.

UN political missions of this nature are never intended to last for decades, nor to entrench themselves so deeply in a post-conflict political landscape. Their presence is predicated on an invitation by the host country. Considering its outsized presence and arguably minimal impact, there is an argument to be made that UNAMI (and by extension the plethora of development actors and donors in the country) has itself become an integral part of the government and the post-2003 political order.

The Iraqi government derives its international legitimacy from the continued presence and funds of these international partners, even when the ruling class invoke corruption as a way to bypass the constitution, corrupt the judiciary, divert power to armed non-state actors or use force to crack down on civilian mobilisation. This extensive international presence in Iraq for almost two decades has resulted in the successive evading of criticism for alleged human rights abuses amid a continued shrinking of the civic space that invites parallels with the region's worst perpetrators such as Egypt's military regime, or the Kingdom of Saudi Arabia under the leadership of Crown Prince Mohamed bin Salman.

Yet, the Tishreen movement has still emerged despite all these barriers to its mobilisation. International partners have rightly supported the civilian movement and disavowed the significant state-sponsored violence seen against protests as a result. However, conditional diplomacy or support has not yet figured into any form of material response from international actors.

Meanwhile, the region is shifting towards a more authoritarian and securitised landscape, arguably now bearing the fruits of the US-sponsored, securitised post-9/11 Western foreign policy. While many rightly note that this policy spearheaded the US-led invasion into Iraq in 2003, the long-term effect of the policy writ large has been to securitise foreign policy engagement to the extent that all bilateral engagement in the MENA region became tied to security interests and hard security goals and outcomes. The result in Iraq has been catastrophic, and while there is now a fundamental discussion on the recalibration of that bilateral engagement in Washington, it remains tied to a binary argument of troop withdrawal vs. 'forever wars'. There is little attempt to innovate or shift US foreign policy away from the securitised language and nature of its implementation that has defined it for 20 years. Nor are there any material attempts from the new Biden administration to differentiate security goals and priorities in Iraq, as they relate to its policy towards Iran.

While the Tishreen movement remains an inherently Iraqi movement, it is one that takes place amid the ruins of the Syria conflict and at a moment when regional geopolitics is shifting irreparably in a post-ISIS, post-Trump Middle East. Iran remains in many ways in control of Iraq's hard security (through powerful militias in control of large swathes of the territory), and the international community (which includes both NATO and EU member states) remain beholden to a US policy that cannot decipher the difference between Iran and Iraq.[32] As this ongoing stand-off protracts, Turkey gains further military confidence, building on its presence in Syria and Libya to capture parts of a vacuum in Iraq and expand its regional project.[33]

Furthermore, while deprioritised by many, the heightened suspense brought about by a lack of sustainable peace between Erbil and Baghdad not only plagues the country's development but is a root driver of the instability that exists in the country. The KRG continues to utilise its smartly outsized diplomatic presence to invoke power that it does not, by definition and constitution, have. And Baghdad resorts to exerting its power by force to the detriment of the KRG, for the most part for no other reason than the fact that it can. Constitutional amendments remain the 'bogey-man' that no one wishes to discuss – politicians and intelligentsia alike – and the United States and its allies continue to act upon a non-existent binary logic created by the post-2003 order that pits Erbil against Baghdad, that erodes the sum of Iraq's parts rather than approaching the country as a whole.

Domestic politics and civilian relations therefore play out in a securitised theatre of numerous proxy actors and interests, with little regard to how the country itself may develop. The Tishreen movement is continuously analysed through this lens of proxy involvement and broader geopolitical significance from international and domestic actors, which removes agency from its members and arguably absolves the international community of the need to respond. It can be said that protestors are fighting not only their leaders but also the international community, which implicitly continues to embolden their behaviour.

Of massive implication in these failings is the inability to materially understand the far-reaching impact of Tishreen and its message, which has resonated across the country and embedded itself into the psyche of ordinary Iraqis – whether they support the movement or not. Tishreen has wrongly been deduced as a Southern movement against a Shia-led majority in Baghdad. In truth, the

---

[32] Omar Al-Nidawi, 'The Real Cost of US-Iran Escalation in Iraq', in *MEI Policy Analysis*, 27 January 2020, https://www.mei.edu/node/80824.

[33] Washington Kurdish Institute, *Ending Turkish Occupation of Iraq – It's Now or Never*, 6 October 2020 https://dckurd.org/?p=15944.

movement is inherently about Iraq's identity, the direction of its development and the lack of human security, amid a failure to support democratisation and equitable representation and rule of law in a country now deeply divided as a result.

Conclusion

Over the last 18 years, colossal mistakes have been made in Iraq. The United States has squandered many opportunities to perfect an imperfect path towards successful democratic transition, while the Iraqi political class has stolen, embezzled and thrived on its access to the country's riches. Sectarian divisions, the war against ISIS and the massive influence Iran has over relatively small, but hugely powerful and significantly violent non-state groups have created a vicious cycle of constant instability, human insecurity and national deprivation. The ongoing tussles – political, social and security – between the central government and the KRG have widened the vacuum of power, which has been filled by militias. The country is filled with political elites beholden to no one but themselves and dependent on each other for their own survival. The need to change the country's future is not only urgent, but also growing ever more elusive.

On its current path, in the near-term Iraq is on its way to another conflict. With no international power or actor to directly blame or divert attention to, the risks of a deep, protracted, ugly civil war are very real. Iraq remains deeply scarred by the experience of recent decades – in conflict or under sanctions – and is now governed by the power of a gun. The country is awash with weapons, with civilian communities now armed to the teeth. Conflict that would likely see militia groups pitted against their own people, coupled with a dramatic economic collapse, could define dynamics in Iraq for many years to come, and preclude any positive development away from the 2003 political order and towards a more orderly democratic transition.

Iraqis' grievances are so many, so common and so relentless that they continue to overtake each other. There has never been an independent or internationally sanctioned peace process in the country, and the need for one is urgent. The result of this continued instability and lack of progress on any form of reconciliation is millions of Iraqis displaced through war and marginalisation, and a shifting demographic that is more a result of conflict and security threats than it is a youth bulge. It is a complete failure to provide services from running water, to schools, to human security. It is human rights abuses on a daily basis, including the violent assassination of young, unarmed civilians. It is cracks in the social fabric that run so deep, with layers of grievances from different communities – all just as valid, all superseded by the newest grievance – that have created a never-ending cycle of distrust, 'red-flag' conflict drivers and disenfranchisement on the part of all citizens.

The international community – those who seek the positive and sustainable development of Iraq – requires a desperate and prioritised reset. This means a deeper, positive and supportive approach to Tishreen and its members, alongside an obvious and clear acknowledgment of the failings of the government and its international partners in recent years. The governance and public service delivery issues remain papered over through the support of hundreds of local and international NGOs, international donors and billions of dollars in development aid, but this approach is insufficient and only aiding the negative trajectory of the country.

The Tishreen movement should be openly and actively supported. This can be achieved through material support to its organisation, activity and awareness raising or education. Impartial media, created by this younger generation that is mobilising, should be harnessed, and promoted through the support provided to civil society actors. Its expansion and the carrying of its message should be emboldened by international partners who should never fail to ensure that the protection of civic space, gender equality and rights, and governance are the priority discussion points in bilateral engagements.

Here the EU, having less military investment in the country, can act first, pushing the international community to consider and impose sanctions against a broad swathe of political and security actors in response to human rights abuses, corruption and the subversion of democratic development. UNAMI should revisit its mandate, reduce its presence and reconstitute its development assistance in the wake of continued corruption. The United States and its NATO allies should condition security support on the political courage of politicians to confront and address militia activity in the country. While the international community cannot themselves change the country and Iraqi politics, their presence and outsized power mean that domestic pressures will not fall solely on the shoulders of a young, civilian protest movement or religious figures such as Ayatollah Sistani.

To say the current political system has failed may seem sensationalist. But the country's trajectory is one that denies Iraqis their civil and human rights and legal and physical protection. The international lens by which Iraq is viewed, in a post 9/11 securitised landscape, itself denies civilians a right to self-determination, marginalises minority communities, imposes risks of deadly proportion on those who seek to actively be engaged, and eventually will destroy a country of millions. If the moral duty and values-based agenda purportedly promoted by the international community to ally with the Tishreen movement, support the country and engage in meaningful reconciliation is not a sufficient call to action, then the drivers of new conflict should act as a powerful warning of what is to come if no action is taken.

References

Ranj Alaadin, 'Containing Shiite Militias: The Battle for Stability in Iraq', in *Brookings Doha Center Policy Briefings*, December 2017, http://brook.gs/2jZ9CP8

Zahra Ali, 'Iraqis Demand a Country', in *Middle East Report*, No. 292/293 (Fall/Winter 2019), p. 2–5, https://merip.org/?p=79032

Isam al Khafaji, 'Iraq 2018 Elections: Between Sectarianism and the Nation', in *Bawader*, 12 July 2018, https://www.arab-reform.net/?p=2948

Omar Al-Nidawi, 'The Real Cost of US-Iran Escalation in Iraq', in *MEI Policy Analysis*, 27 January 2020, https://www.mei.edu/node/80824

Suadad Al-Salhy, 'Rival Iraqi Factions Make Coalition Deal and End Al-Abadi's Prime Minister Hopes', in *Arab News*, 13 September 2018, https://www.arabnews.com/node/1371716

Hamzeh Al-Shadeedi, Mac Skelton and Zmkan Ali Saleem, 'Why Iraq's Protesters Won't Go Home: 10 Voices from the Movement', in *LSE Middle East Centre Blog*, 3 March 2020, https://wp.me/p3Khxv-2iu

Asha Amirali, 'The "Youth Bulge" and Political Unrest in Iraq: A Political Economy Approach', in *K4D Helpdesk Reports*, 11 November 2019, https://opendocs.ids.ac.uk/opendocs/handle/20.500.12413/14815

Building Peaceful Futures, *Conflict Analysis. Sinjar and Hawija, Iraq*, Erbil, Save the Children Iraq, 2019, https://www.australianhumanitarianpartnership.org/library-contents/conflict-analysis-sinjar-and-hawija-iraq-2019

Thanassis Cambanis, 'Can Militant Cleric Moqtada al-Sadr Reform Iraq?', in *The Century Foundation Reports*, 1 May 2018, https://tcf.org/content/report/can-militant-cleric-moqtada-al-sadr-reform-iraq

Youssef Cherif, Hafsa Halawa and Özge Zihnioğlu, 'The Coronavirus and Civic Activism in the Middle East and North Africa', in Richard Youngs (ed.), *Global Civil Society in the Shadow of Coronavirus*, Washington, Carnegie Endowment for International Peace, December 2020, p. 21–26, https://carnegieendowment.org/publications/83142

Erik K. Gustafson and Omar Al-Nidawi, 'Iraqi Protesters' Perilous Journey to the Ballot Box', in *MEI Policy Analysis*, 22 March 2021, https://www.mei.edu/node/82608

Hafsa Halawa, 'The Forgotten Iraq', in *MEI Policy Papers*, No. 2020–7 (March 2020), https://www.mei.edu/node/80974

Harith Hasan, 'Iraq Protests: A New Social Movement Is Challenging Sectarian Power', in *Middle East Eye*, 4 November 2019, https://carnegieendowment.org/publications/80256

Harith Hasan, 'The Subtle Power of Sistani', in *Diwan*, 14 November 2019, https://carnegie-mec.org/diwan/80346

Falih Hassan and Jane Arraf, 'Fire at Baghdad Hospital Packed with Covid Patients Kills at Least 82', in *The New York Times*, 25 April 2021, https://nyti.ms/3aEH19i

Hassan Hassan, 'How Iraq's Top ISIS Scholar Became a Target for Shiite Militias', in *Newlines Magazine*, 4 October 2020, https://newlinesmag.com/essays/the-man-who-knew-too-much-why-shiite-militias-killed-iraqs-finest-isis-scholar

Kawa Hassan, 'Kurdistan's Politicized Society Confronts a Sultanistic System', in *Carnegie Papers*, August 2015, https://carnegieendowment.org/publications/61026

Joost Hiltermann, 'Iraq: The Clerics and the Militias', in *The New York Review of Books*, 13 October 2015, https://www.crisisgroup.org/node/1822

James Jeffrey, 'Behind the U.S. Withdrawal from Iraq', in *Washington Institute Policy Analysis*, 2 November 2014, https://www.washingtoninstitute.org/node/4454

Jenna Krajeski, 'How the War with ISIS Has Exposed Kurdistan's Internal Divisions', in *The Nation*, 6 April 2015, https://www.thenation.com/?p=117302

Glada Lahn and Nouar Shamout, 'Basra's Poisonous Water Demands International Action', in *Chatham House Expert Comments*, 14 November 2018 https://www.chathamhouse.org/node/15623

Pesha Magid, 'Angry Iraqis Demand New Government', in *Foreign Policy*, 7 October 2019, https://foreignpolicy.com/2019/10/07/angry-iraqis-yearn-for-military-rule-again

National Democratic Institute (NDI), *Iraq: We Want a Homeland. Key Findings of Qualitative Research Conducted in Five Provinces in Iraq: Baghdad, Basra, Diyala, Erbil, and Nasiriyah. December 2019–February 2020*, September 2020, https://www.ndi.org/sites/default/files/Iraqi%20Protests%20Research%20Report_EN.pdf

Marina Ottaway and Danial Anas Kays, 'Iraq: Protest, Democracy, and Autocracy', in *Carnegie Articles*, 28 March 2011, https://carnegieendowment.org/publications/43306

Cathrin Schaer, 'Iraq's New Protester Parties Plan to Change the Country', in *Deutsche Welle*, 22 January 2021, https://p.dw.com/p/3oHOz

Matthew Schweitzer, 'Protests in Southern Iraq Intensify, Is Instability to Follow?', in *IPI Global Observatory*, 24 July 2018, https://theglobalobservatory.org/?p=18022

Kirk H. Sowell, 'Iraq's Dire Fiscal Crisis', in *Sada*, 2 November 2020, https://carnegieendowment.org/sada/83108

Samir Sumaida'ie, 'The Hijacking of Democracy: The Role of Political Parties in Iraq', in *Wilson Center Viewpoints*, 8 April 2021, https://www.wilsoncenter.org/node/105840

Washington Kurdish Institute, *Ending Turkish Occupation of Iraq –It's Now or Never*, 6 October 2020 https://dckurd.org/?p=15944

Jennifer Williams, 'The Political Crisis Rocking Baghdad and Why It Matters for the War on ISIS', in *Vox*, 19 April 2016, https://www.vox.com/2016/4/19/11451550

Katie Bo Williams, 'Militias in Iraq Provide Security, Wield Political Power, and May Be Tearing the Country Apart', in *Defence One*, 2 March 2021 https://www.defenseone.com/threats/2021/03/militias-iraq-provide-security-wield-political-power-and-may-be-tearing-country-apart/172390

Mattia Giampaolo

Chapter 3: The Two Souls of the Egyptian Revolution and Its Decline. A Socio-Political Perspective

On 25 January 2011, some 15,000 people gathered in Maidan al-Tahrir, the main square of Cairo, shouting for the removal of long-term president Muhammad Hosni Mubarak. The large protests that were sparked in Cairo soon swept to other Egyptian cities and instilled unity among different societal layers: from the educated middle class to the working class, students, the unemployed and women's movements. During the 18 glorious days of Tahrir, it seemed as if Egypt, after 30 years of authoritarian rule, could turn into a different country, free from despotism, corruption and poverty. Unsurprisingly, the slogan of the protests in Tahrir and in the whole country was *'aish, hurriyya 'adala ijtima'iyya* (bread, freedom and social justice).

Looking back today, if on the one hand the protests of 2011 triggered a deep change in the Egyptian society, on the other they have been unable to generate enduring political change. The capacity of Tahrir to mobilise millions of citizens from different social classes and areas has not produced an organic political organisation that could challenge the Egyptian *deep state*.

This is even the more surprising given that the forces gathering in Tahrir had been accumulating for more than ten years. There were new political movements, born in 2000 during the mobilisation in solidarity with the Palestinian Intifada. There were university unions, human rights organisations and the workers' movement, with women active in all of them. All these components, to different extents, were victims of more than 30 years of autocracy. Workers spent more than eight years protesting against the privatisation of the national industries and seeking better working conditions. Students and youth were denouncing the high rate of unemployment and the violence of the police within campuses. Women demanded equal rights and spoke out against daily harassment. Political forces that were not part of the formal opposition – victims of the lack of political freedom – were calling for free and fair elections.

How can the lack of political change be explained? One reason lies in the hostility of some political and social movements in Egypt towards political organisation, similar to social movements that had evolved in the last decade across the globe such as the early 2000s No Global Movement,[1] the International Peace Movement[2] or movements in Europe and Latin America established after the 2008 global financial crisis among youth, industrial and public sector workers. Despite the broad mobilisation, these initiatives did not culminate in any kind of organisation, and ended up, in some cases, supporting reactionary movements (far-right and populist parties in Europe) or leaving the political arena without any alternative.[3] Indeed, all those movements, including the Egyptian ones, formed in a period in which the idea of political party and ideology was in decline at the global level.

As Asef Bayat has outlined in his latest book, *Revolution without Revolutionaries*, those who animated Tahrir Square were 'rich in tactics of mobilization but poor in vision and strategy of transformation; they adopted loose, flexible, and horizontal organization but one that suffered from fragmentation.'[4] These movements were characterised by the lack of vertical structure, preferring a horizontal organisation without leadership and a clear political ideology, animated by the idea of changing the world without taking power.[5] This allowed them, on one side, to bypass the capillary repression power of the regime but, on the other, made them miss the chance, in the aftermath of Mubarak's downfall, to develop a political path for the transition, leaving the field to counterrevolutionary and more organised forces such as the Egyptian army and the Muslim Brotherhood.

---

[1] In Egypt also activists established the Anti-Globalization Egyptian Group linked to the World Social Forum, see Gianni Del Panta, *Rivoluzione e controrivoluzione in Egitto. Da Piazza Tahrir al colpo di stato di una borghesia in armi*, Bologna, il Mulino, 2019.

[2] John Chalcraft, 'Horizontalism in the Egyptian Revolutionary Process', in *Middle East Report*, No. 262 (Spring 2012), p. 6–11, https://merip.org/?p=6541.

[3] Francesco Scanni, 'Populismo reattivo: un contro-eccesso alla crisi del modello di integrazione europeo' [Reactive Populism: A Counter-Excess to the Crisis of the European Integration Model], in *Europea*, Vol. 4, No. 1 (May 2019), p. 75–112.

[4] Asef Bayat, *Revolution without Revolutionaries. Making Sense of the Arab Spring*, Stanford, Stanford University Press, 2017, p. 18.

[5] John Foran, 'Beyond Insurgency to Radical Social Change: The New Situation', in *Studies in Social Justice*, Vol. 8, No. 1 (June 2014), p. 5–25, https://doi.org/10.26522/ssj.v8i1.1036.

1. Revolution and revolutionaries: The social and political souls of the Egyptian revolution

The Egyptian revolution did not occur overnight. It was the result of more than ten years of accumulation of revolutionary energy among different social layers, which can be divided into two 'souls' that rarely met in the aftermath of Mubarak downfall: political and social. These two souls reflected the main demands of the protesters in 2011. On one side, there were the political movements of the early 2000s, animated by the urban middle-class, with specific demands for political freedom and the respect of human rights; on the other side, the workers' movement which, since 2004, had initiated a long wave of struggling for better working conditions and against the privatisation of national industries.

The origins of the political movements which animated Tahrir Square on 25 January 2011 are rooted in the early 2000s, when thousands of Egyptians took to the streets to support the second Palestinian Intifada and, in 2003, the international peace movement against the US-led invasion of Iraq. These protests were sparked by extra-parliamentary forces, notably left-wing activists, who constituted the Egyptian Popular Committee in Solidarity with Palestinian Intifada (EPCSPI) with Tahrir Square as the epicentre of the protests.[6]

Although the protests did not directly target the Egyptian regime, they represented the base for a first catalysation of revolutionary demands. According to Hossam El-Hamalawy (a prominent revolutionary and activist in the Egyptian revolution), the protests in supporting Palestinian Intifada 'soon gained an antiregime dimension, and police showed up to quell the peaceful protests'.[7] The movement empowered when the US invaded Iraq in 2003 and furthered by the EPCSPI turned into an anti-war movement which was swelled by the return of the student movement after years of silence.

This slow but increasing incubation of demands culminated with the first political attempts to reunite youth, activists and extra-parliamentary political parties under a unique umbrella. The first political experiment, which emerged in 2003, was the Egyptian Movement for Change, known as *Kifaya* (Enough!), which counted political and intellectual figures amongst its ranks.[8] This movement was an alliance of 300 public personalities and political party leaders who

---

[6]   Gianni Del Panta, *Rivoluzione e controrivoluzione in Egitto*, cit., p. 135.

[7]   Hossam El-Hamalawy, 'Egypt's Revolution Has Been 10 Years in the Making', in *The Guardian*, 2 March 2011, https://www.theguardian.com/p/2ne5v.

[8]   Manar Shorbagy, 'Understanding Kefaya: The New Politics in Egypt', in *Arab Studies Quarterly*, Vol. 29, No. 1 (Winter 2007), p. 39–60, at p. 43.

aimed to counter the regime through street politics and political initiatives against the emergency law and the chronic corruption within high echelons of the regime.

If the protests in the early 2000 rarely targeted President Mubarak, *Kifaya* demonstrations were a direct attack against him.[9] From this movement other committees and organisations were established in other cities both linked to and separated from *Kifaya* itself. These included the Youth Committee for Change, the Lawyers' Committee for Change, the Doctors' Committee for Change and the Workers' Committee for Change.[10]

Due to the strong presence of Egyptian youth and students within the satellite organisations around *Kifaya*, this political front split in two. While the old generation of activists preferred to combine mobilisation with a reconstruction of the institutions 'from below' with the aim of gaining a role in the national political arena, the young generation of activists were more inclined to continue the mobilisation and civil disobedience against the regime.[11] These new political initiatives soon clashed due to internal divisions and the regime's repression, which picked up especially after the 2005 parliamentary elections when the largest oppositional force, the Muslim Brotherhood, by filing independent candidates gained 20 per cent of the seats.

Thus, even if the political demands fell into the void due to internal splits and regime repression tactics, in 2006, given the regime's implementation of neoliberal policies, the other soul of the 25 January revolution came to the surface with huge waves of strikes within both the industrial and public sectors. As Joel Beinin outlined, 'workers were by far the largest component of the burgeoning culture of protest in the 2000s that undermined the legitimacy of the Mubarak regime'.[12] The entry on the political scene of the workers' movement signalled a turning point in that 'decade-long molecular process of accumulation of antiregime energies'.[13]

---

9   Ibid.
10   See transcript of a workshop on the strike movement in Egypt that took place at the sixth Cairo antiwar conference, held 27–30 March 2008: 'Class Struggle in Egypt', in *International Socialist Review*, No. 59 (May-June 2008), https://isreview.org/issue/59/class-struggle-egypt.
11   Manar Shorbagy, 'Understanding Kefaya', cit.
12   Joel Beinin, 'The Rise of Egypt's Workers', in *Carnegie Papers*, June 2012, p. 1, https://carnegieendowment.org/publications/48689.
13   Gianni Del Panta, 'The Role of the Egyptian Working Class in Mubarak's Ouster', in *Partecipazione e conflitto*, Vol. 9, No. 2 (2016), p. 615–639, at p. 615, https://doi.org/10.1285/i20356609v9i2p614.

The loss of purchasing power, the worsening of labour conditions and the privatisation of historical national industries increased workers' discontent towards the regime.[14] Between July 2004 and March 2006, 80 public industries were sold and 200 industries were privatised.[15] Worker mobilisation peaked in December 2006 when more than 20,000 workers of the Misr Spinning and Weaving Company in Mahalla al-Kubra went on strike after the government did not keep its promise of an annual bonus.[16] The government eventually did pay the bonuses, and the success of the workers pushed other textile sectors to stage similar protests in the following months: between December and March, more than 30,000 workers participated in strikes and protests.[17]

Despite the strong opposition to the regime's privatisation and liberalisation plans, workers at that time did not engage in direct political demands. This, however, does not mean that the strikes did not have political effects. They represented a political challenge to the regime. The great wave of strikes was, *inter alia*, a direct assault on the Egyptian Trade Union Federation (ETUF), which was the only labour organisation permitted by the regime (since the Nasser era) and fully co-opted.[18] In this context, workers openly criticised the trade union and started to call, despite the strong police assaults, for the removal of the old ETUF representatives within the organisation. In Mahalla, for example, workers collected more than 14,000 signatures demanding that the state-controlled union step down.[19] The workers' mobilisation was political also in terms of challenging the regime's structures and *modus operandi* since even the 'simplest expression of discontent [was] severely forbidden'.[20]

Women's defence groups also played a central role in this wave of protests representing, perhaps, the only political actor able to combine civil and social

---

[14]   Joel Beinin, 'Civil Society, NGOs, and Egypt's 2011 Popular Uprising', in *South Atlantic Quarterly*, Vol. 113, No. 2 (2014), p. 396–406.

[15]   Nadia Ramsis Farah, *Egyptian Political Economy. Power Relations in Development*, Cairo/New York, The American University in Cairo Press, 2009.

[16]   Ann Alexander and Mostafa Bassiouny, *Bread, Freedom, Social Justice. Workers and the Egyptian Revolution*, London, Zed Books, 2014.

[17]   Joel Beinin and Hossam El-Hamalawy, 'Egyptian Textile Workers Confront the New Economic Order', in *Middle East Report Online*, 25 March 2007, https://merip.org/?p=1314.

[18]   Ibid.

[19]   'Class Struggle in Egypt', cit.

[20]   Gianni Del Panta, 'The Role of the Egyptian Working Class in Mubarak's Ouster', cit., p. 620.

rights. In many factories, notably textile production, women accounted for 15 per cent of the total labour force.[21] Women were also at the forefront of the *Kifaya* movement as well as of the workers' strikes.[22] The struggle for women's rights was backed by many civil society organisations such as Al-Nadeem Centre (Centre for Rehabilitation of Victims of Violence and Torture) or by the Egyptian Initiative for Personal Rights, which supported victims of violence and harassment with legal and psychological services. The increasing violence of police against women's defence groups as well as against those who took part in the strikes augmented the discontent towards the regime. This rage increased the consciousness that women's emancipation could be reached only through the struggle against the regime and its patriarchal structure.

Despite this great mobilisation of the social and political souls of the Egyptian revolution, these two sides rarely converged either before or in the aftermath of the Mubarak downfall. On the workers' side, the labour movement rarely advanced political demands and it always 'mistrusted the opposition [political] intelligentsia as outsiders who sought to impose their own agenda'.[23] This was very visible in the attempt of the newly born 6 April Movement during the strikes in Mahalla in 2008 to support workers in their demand for political reform. In 2008, the 6 April Movement started launching a solidarity campaign on Facebook for workers protesting in the Delta industrial city of Mahalla al-Kubra. The workers, however, did not welcome the 6 April Movement's support especially due to their fear of the regime's reaction.[24] Indeed, as Nadine Abdalla outlined: 'Hosni Mubarak's regime carefully distinguished between peoples' demands – those referring to their socioeconomic situations and those touching on political issues. Any kind of linkage was considered a red line not to be crossed'.[25]

On the political side, the extra-parliamentary political forces, such as *Kifaya* and other political parties or movements, did not regard workers as social and political change actors. This was mainly due to the elitist character of the

---

[21]   Adam Hanieh, *Lineages of Revolt. Issues of Contemporary Capitalism in the Middle East*, Chicago, Haymarket Books, 2013, p. 59.

[22]   Rabab El-Mahdi, 'Does Political Islam Impede Gender-Based Mobilization? The Case of Egypt', in *Totalitarian Movements and Political Religions*, Vol. 11, No. 3–4 (September-December 2010), p. 379–396.

[23]   Joel Beinin, 'The Rise of Egypt's Workers', cit., p. 6–7.

[24]   Nadine Abdalla, 'Egypt's Workers – From Protest Movement to Organized Labor', in *SWP Comments*, No. 32 (October 2012), https://www.swp-berlin.org/en/publication/egypts-workers.

[25]   Ibid., p. 2.

political parties within *Kifaya* and, as for the youth movements, due to the difference in terms of mobilisation tools (for the youth movement, the new social networks) and scant trust in the new political actors in the country.[26] Only on a few occasions did political figures of the left such as Khaled Ali, director of the Egyptian Centre for Economic and Social Rights, attempt to link 'workers' economic demands to political demands toward the very end of the Mubarak era'.[27] This disenchantment towards the political parties and forces, not only by workers but at a broader social level, was the effect of the political legacy of the traditional political forces and the presence of another strong actor: the Muslim Brotherhood. As will be outlined in the next paragraph, the polarisation of the political forces (the so-called traditional secular forces and the Muslim Brotherhood and Islamists in general) and their electoral competition within the Mubarak regime kept up, on the one hand, the facade of democracy and, on the other hand, weakened the political forces by pitting them against each other.[28]

2. From Mubarak to al-Sisi: Playing with traditional oppositions

People on the eve of the 25 January revolution were disenchanted with political forces in Egypt due to their strict relations with the ruling party and regime. Among those who called for demonstrations there was not, formally, any opposition force. On that day, the Tagammu' Party closed its headquarters in respect for the police forces,[29] and the Wafd Party stayed out of the protests.[30] This was different for the Muslim Brotherhood (MB). While the organisation officially refused to participate in the protests, a majority of its youth activists did take to the streets and were among the demonstrators.

This reluctant behaviour of the traditional political forces was mainly due to their relationship with the regime. Their presence within the political arena was useful to maintain and legitimate the façade of democracy, which made them pawns and therefore, agents of the regime.[31] They were pawns because they

---

[26] Holger Albrecht, *Raging Against the Machine. Political Opposition under Authoritarianism in Egypt*, Syracuse, Syracuse University Press, 2013, p. 89.

[27] Joel Beinin, 'The Rise of Egypt's Workers', cit., p. 6.

[28] Maye Kassem, *Egyptian Politics. The Dynamics of Authoritarian Rule*, Boulder/London, Lynne Rienner, 2004, p. 141–145.

[29] 25 January was originally the police celebration.

[30] Gianni Del Panta, *Rivoluzione e controrivoluzione*, cit., 159–160.

[31] Holger Albrecht, *Raging Against the Machine*, cit.

passively legitimised the fake democracy of the regime through their participation in elections, while also making agreements on parliamentary seats. They
were agents because they used the regime's capacity to repress opposition if one
of the two main rivalries (secularists and Islamists) demonstrated a supremacy
in terms of presence within professional associations or in electoral turnouts.[32]
If the traditional secularist forces maintained their political presence within the
political arena thanks to the regime's support, the Muslim Brotherhood developed during the 1980s and 1990s a gradual capillary penetration of the society.

The MB, since the 1970s, has been characterised by two internal currents. One
was the conservative wing, linked to the Guidance Council, which led them for
example speak about religion in ideological terms and depict the installation of
an Islamic state as major goal. The other, born within university campuses, self-
defined as reformist and was more active and inclined to penetrate the society,
notably the unions and professional organisations.[33]

The crisis of Nasserism and the initial liberalisation under Anwar al-Sadat in
the 1970s and 1980s witnessed a rapid decline of all the social services, which
were gradually replaced with charity associations run by the Brotherhood. These
activities went in parallel with political engagement, especially within the professional associations where they were able to guarantee services. Insurance,
benefits and social protection were the backbone of the popularity of the MB
among public workers and middle-class professionals.[34]

If during the 1990s the movement maintained a conservative vision of the
power, starting from the 2000s it shifted towards more secular issues such as
political rights, socioeconomic policies and human rights violations.[35] This
corresponded also to the ambition of the MB to form its own political party. The
key moment was the 2005 elections when the MB won 20 per cent of the parliament seats. From this moment on the organisation pushed for political reform,
especially related to the political freedoms.[36] The Egyptian regime responded by

---

[32] Hesham Al-Awadi, *The Muslim Brothers in Pursuit of Legitimacy. Power and Political
      Islam in Egypt Under Mubarak*, London/New York, I.B. Tauris, 2014.

[33] Barbara Zollner, 'The Brotherhood in Transition: An Analysis of the Organization's
      Mobilizing Capacity', in Peter Lintl, Christian Thuselt and Christian Wolff (eds),
      Religiöse Bewegungen als politische Akteure im Nahen Osten, Baden-Baden, Nomos,
      2016, p. 43–70.

[34] Ibid., p. 51.

[35] Amr Hamzawi and Nathan J. Brown, 'The Egyptian Muslim Brotherhood: Islamist
      Participation in a Closing Political Environment', in *Carnegie Papers*, No. 19 (March
      2010), https://carnegieendowment.org/publications/40318.

[36] Ibid.

pushing through constitutional amendments that would limit political parties linked to religious ideology and by repressing all those who were opposing the regime.[37]

The National Security (*Amn al-Marzkazi*) and the police became more and more violent towards anyone who expressed hostility to the regime. The assassination by the police forces of an innocent youth, Khaled Said, in Alexandria in 2010 fuelled the rage of millions of Egyptians after his tormented body was published by his family on Facebook. Discontent grew especially after the fraudulent nature of the parliamentary elections in November 2010 and after Muhammed Bouazizi set himself on fire in Tunisia, kicking off the Tunisian revolution in December 2010.

The downfall of the Mubarak regime was possible thanks to several factors, which combined altogether during the glorious 18 days of Tahrir. All political forces together with the urban proletariat and the workers contributed to putting an end to three decades of authoritarian rule. Although the final say was in the hands of the army, which refused to crack down on workers and common Egyptians, the huge wave of mass protests led to Mubarak's resignation and to the start of the political transition.

In addition, the move of the army came after talks with the US administration which called, through the then President Obama, on the military to make concrete steps towards the transition.

The army in Egypt symbolised for both the people and some political parties a progressive body which could direct the transition.[38] Indeed, the army, notably in the last decade before the revolution, remained a relatively distant partner of the Mubarak regime and this sheltered it from the people's rage.[39] The target of the Tahrir demonstrations was the old dictator and his inner circle represented by his son Gamal and the National Democratic Party (NDP). Furthermore, the choice of the army to support the removal of the long-standing president was due to Mubarak's attempts to discriminate against it in favour of the police and to diminish its economic weight by favouring the emergence, since the early 2000s, of a super-capitalist class[40] sponsored by Mubarak's son Gamal. Gamal's intent was to create his own inner circle to engage support for his future presidency,

---

[37]   Ibid.
[38]   Gianni Del Panta, *Rivoluzione e controrivoluzione*, cit., p. 192.
[39]   Ibid.
[40]   Daniela Pioppi, 'Playing with Fire. The Muslim Brotherhood and the Egyptian Leviathan', in *The International Spectator*, Vol. 48, No. 4 (December 2013), p. 51–68.

while limiting the role of the old guard of the regime represented partly by figures linked to the army who could obstruct his ambition to be the new president.

> Before the revolution two main factions have been fighting within the regime: on one
> side, the old guard which considered the State capitalism, even in a neo-liberal form, a
> stronghold to be maintained; on the other, the new guard, led by Gamal Mubarak more
> opened to the West, and other global powers.[41]

The platform to realise this project was the NDP which, since the 1980s, gave
the regime the political base within both the institutions and the society. The
party, in addition, was a vehicle to promote Gamal Mubarak's aspirations as his
father's successor. This political move weakened the NDP especially after Gamal
Mubarak created, in 2002, the 'Future Generation' project within the party with
the aim of promoting himself as the new leader and the 'natural successor' of his
father for the presidency.[42]

This was one of the main reasons which led the Egyptian military and part
of the old guard of the regime to abandon Mubarak and back his downfall from
above, as the protesters were demanding. The objective of the army was to protect its huge economic interests, prevent any civilian force from controlling the
defence budget, and avoid a dangerous power vacuum. Indeed, the decision not
to repress the protests earned the army the title of 'saviour of the nation' and led
some groups to launch the slogan in Tahrir 'al-gaish w al-sha'ab yid wahda' (the
army and the people are one thing).

Beyond this narrative, what legitimated the leading role of the army was the
rapid splitting of the Square protesters and the marriage between the military
and the Muslim Brotherhood. With Mubarak's resignation, the movements
which animated the revolution were divided between those who wanted to continue to occupy the Square (6 April Movement, leftist parties and other youth
movements) and those who expressed their willingness to initiate the political
transition (liberals, Islamists and right- wing parties).[43]

The lack of political experience of these new political actors and their internal
disorganisation favoured the rise of the Muslim Brotherhood. The downfall of
Mubarak gave the MB the possibility to build its own political party, *Hizb al-
hurriya wa al-'adala* (the Freedom and Justice Party, FJP) and formally enter the

---

[41]   Gennaro Gervasio interview, 'Uno sguardo sull'Egitto', in *Potere al Popolo*,
       16 October 2019, https://poterealpopolo.org/?p=45577.
[42]   Gianni Del Panta, *Rivoluzione e controrivoluzione*, cit., p. 127.
[43]   Brecht de Smet, *Gramsci on Tahrir. Revolution and Counter Revolution in Egypt*,
       London, Pluto Press, 2016.

political arena.[44] Despite the MB being prevented from creating its own political party, the organisation, since its return to the social-political scene in 1970s, was able to build and develop what many scholars defined as *al-Tanzim* (the organisation),[45] namely a rigid and vertical structure that enabled the MB to penetrate the whole fabric of the Egyptian society, from neighbourhoods to governorates and economic sectors. This rigid structure and the experience acquired in the last decade within the political institution under Mubarak allowed the MB to deal with the politics of the transition.

The 'arranged marriage' between the MB and the Egyptian army[46] (more precisely the Supreme Council of the Armed Forces, or SCAF) was of the result of these two actors seizing the opportunity that the revolution had given them. The arrangement would give the military the political platform to lead the transition and avoid the revolutionary movements, while the MB was given the chance to establish a real party in the political context[47] and to extend its cultural and moral views within the society.[48] This alliance, however, declined at the end of 2011 and in 2012 during the parliamentary and presidential elections, when the Muslim Brotherhood conquered the majority of seats in the parliament and the presidency with Mohamed Morsi.

In the first phase of his presidency, Morsi had limited powers (the SCAF was still in control), but things changed as the newly elected president fired all top brass and appointed General Abd al-Fattah al-Sisi as minister of defence. Matters worsened as the economic crisis increased. In 2012, the unemployment rate reached a peak of 12.6 per cent (the highest since 1995), and prices increased by 36 per cent in 2013. In addition, national reserves decreased from 36 billion dollars in January 2011 to 15 billion dollars in 2012, while the annual deficit skyrocketed to 30 billion dollars in the same year.[49] The last straw was the constitutional declaration in November 2012, when President Morsi assumed full powers and put himself above any control from other institutions.[50]

---

[44]   Daniela Pioppi, 'Playing with Fire', cit., p. 57.

[45]   Hesham Al-Awadi, *The Muslim Brothers in Pursuit of Legitimacy*, cit.

[46]   Gennaro Gervasio, 'Egitto, la transizione interrotta', in *Critica marxista*, Vol. 43, No. 2–3 (2015), p. 72–78.

[47]   Ibid.

[48]   Gianni Del Panta, *Rivoluzione e controrivoluzione*, cit., p. 193.

[49]   For figures, see: Macrotrends: *Egypt Unemployment Rate 1991–2021*, https://www.macrotrends.net/countries/EGY/egypt/unemployment-rate; Philip Marfleet, *Egypt. Contested Revolution*, London, Pluto Press, 2016, p. 136–137.

[50]   Gennaro Gervasio, 'Egitto, la transizione interrotta', cit., p. 73; Daniela Pioppi, 'Playing with Fire', cit., p. 61.

Morsi's move provoked a wrathful response from the opposition parties, which constituted the *Jabhat al-inqadh al-watani* (National Salvation Front). This political initiative was constituted by the traditional opposition forces, among them al-Wafd, al-Tagammu', Free Egyptians Party (led by the businessmen Sawaris) and the Constitution Party (led by former head of the International Atomic Energy Agency and Nobel Peace Prize laureate Mohamed ElBaradei). The aim of the National Salvation Front was to restore the democratic transition in Egypt and avoid the 'Brotherisation' of the country.

Protests and marches spread all over the country. In April 2013, five activists formed *Tamarrud* (Rebellion), which brought together traditional political forces, youth movements, the former members of the so-called *Fulul* (figures linked to the ancient regime) and also embittered MB supporters, with the aim of bringing Morsi down.[51] *Tamarrud* culminated with General al-Sisi's coup on 3 July 2013, which marked the end of the revolutionary process and the triumph of the counterrevolutionary phase. The unpopular political decision of Morsi pushed the army to intervene in order to preserve their own interests and avoid a perennial unstable situation.

Al-Sisi was able to present himself to the people as their saviour from the barbarity of the Islamist forces. The worker leader Kamal Abu Aita (a prominent figure and leader of the Egyptian Federation of the Independent Trade Unions) became Labour Minister while the Socialist Hamdin Sabbahi (former presidential candidate and one of the most popular figures in Tahrir) and Mohamed ElBaradei (the first figure to challenge the Mubarak regime in 2010 as presidential candidate) were appointed as vice-presidents of the first presidency of Adly Mansour.

The support of those political figures, who were protagonists in the Square, provoked a gradual de-mobilisation of the movements and the Square itself. Only few continued to mobilise but the rise in power of al-Sisi marked the capitulation of the revolutionary movements. The increasing political polarisation of the country between Islamist and non-Islamist forces exacerbated the social and political contradictions. The revolution and revolutionaries, from that moment on, were but agents of external powers, such as Turkey or Qatar (sympathetic to the MB), while the new regime elevated itself as the unique force to avoid a 'Syria scenario' and the spread of radical groups. Many who supported the protests and had been protagonists of the great popular movements in 2011 now felt in the hands of the counterrevolutionary forces.

---

[51]   Daniela Pioppi, 'Playing with Fire', cit., p. 74.

3. The US, EU and regional powers in the transition

The Egyptian uprising took Europe by surprise. Catherine Ashton, the former High Representative of the European Union for Foreign Affairs and Security Policy, issued the EU's first declaration on Egyptian events only on 27 January 2011, claiming:

> I call on the Egyptian authorities to fully respect and protect the rights of their citizens to manifest their political aspirations by means of peaceful demonstrations. The voices calling for the full respect of their political, social and economic rights should be listened to carefully.[52]

This was due to the Union's tendency to look first at what the US would do. The Council Conclusions on Egypt, in which the EU called for a political transition, came only after the Obama administration decided, after talks with the high ranks of the army, to sideline Mubarak and his inner circle.[53]

The victory of the Muslim Brotherhood in parliamentary and presidential elections represented both a continuity and a rupture with the past in terms of foreign policy and international relations. Morsi's presidency was characterised by a rapprochement with Iran, marked by the president's visit to Tehran in 2012, the first since 1979,[54] and the tight relations with the Palestinian branch of the MB, Hamas. At the same time, even though the Iranian-Egyptian rapprochement alarmed the US administration, Morsi maintained strong links with then President Barak Obama who saw the Muslim Brotherhood as an actor which could deliver reforms.[55] Furthermore, in his 2009 speech in Cairo Obama underlined the change, at least on paper, in the approach of the US to the Middle East and more particularly in terms of democracy:

> I know there has been controversy about the promotion of democracy in recent years, and much of this controversy is connected to the war in Iraq. [. . .] No system of

52 European External Action Service (EEAS), *Statement by the EU High Representative Catherine Ashton on the Events in Egypt*, 27 January 2011, https://www.consilium.eur opa.eu/uedocs/cms_Data/docs/pressdata/EN/foraff/118963.pdf.

53 Edmund Blair and Samia Nakhoul, 'Obama Demands Change as Mubarak Meets Army', in *Reuters*, 30 January 2011, https://www.reuters.com/article/us-egypt-idUSTR E70O3UW20110130.

54 Azzurra Meringolo, 'From Morsi to Al-Sisi: Foreign Policy at the Service of Domestic Policy', in *Insight Egypt*, No. 8 (March 2015), p. 3, https://www.iai.it/en/node/3965.

55 Alain Gresh, 'Barack Obama, 'Lackey' of Egypt's Muslim Brotherhood', in *Orient XXI*, 13 September 2018, https://orientxxi.info/magazine/barack-obama-lackey-of-egypt-s-muslim-brotherhood,2623.

government can or should be imposed by one nation by any other. That does not lessen my commitment, however, to governments that reflect the will of the people.[56]

Things also improved as Morsi mediated a ceasefire between Hamas and Israel in 2012. This move was welcomed by Washington, representing the green light for the external legitimisation that Morsi needed. At the same time, this US endorsement created discontent, and even rage, in the conservative regimes in the Gulf, which have always considered the MB as a threat to their dynastic security.[57] Headed by the Kingdom of Saudi Arabia (KSA) and the United Arab Emirates (UAE), the Gulf countries accused the Obama administration of being a lackey of the MB.[58] This rhetoric, along with the one whereby Morsi wanted to transform Egypt into an Islamic Republic, was then reinforced by the centralisation of powers by the MB President, which opened the way, as we have seen above, to the huge wave of protests followed by the coup of the Minister of Defence al-Sisi in July 2013. In the eyes of the Gulf monarchies, al-Sisi represents the stabilising figure that has prevented the rise of Islamism (i.e., the MB) in Egypt.

On the regional level, the July 2013 massacre of Rabaa al-Adawiyya, in which about 900 pro-Morsi protesters were killed by the Egyptian security forces, was one followed by al-Sisi's attacks against Qatar and Turkey, which, in the eyes of the regime, were plotting against Egypt by supporting the MB. In this context, the Egyptian internal polarisation was deeply influenced by the regional split among the 'conservative bloc' (the KSA and the UAE) and the Islamist one.

This does not mean that the actual regime is a champion of laicism. This is demonstrated by the presence among the government's supporters of Salafi *Hizb al-Nur* (The Light Party), which serves on one side as an internal legitimator in the eyes of the conservative portions of society and on the other represents accountability towards the Gulf states where Salafists have their roots.[59] Not surprisingly, the Gulf monarchies became the main sponsors of the new regime

---

[56]   US Presidency, *Remarks by the President on a New Beginning*, Cairo University, 4 June 2009, https://obamawhitehouse.archives.gov/the-press-office/remarks-presid ent-cairo-university-6-04-09.

[57]   Eric Trager, 'The Muslim Brotherhood Is the Root of the Qatar Crisis', in *The Atlantic*, 2 July 2017, https://www.theatlantic.com/international/archive/2017/07/muslim-brotherhood-qatar/532380; Alexey Khlebnikov, 'The New Ideological Threat to the GCC: Implications for the Qatari-Saudi Rivalry', in *Strategic Assessment*, Vol. 17, No. 4 (January 2015), p. 17–28, https://www.inss.org.il/?p=62216.

[58]   Alain Gresh, 'Barack Obama, 'Lackey' of Egypt's Muslim Brotherhood', cit.

[59]   Azzurra Meringolo, 'From Morsi to Al-Sisi: Foreign Policy at the Service of Domestic Policy', cit., p. 5.

by pledging billions of dollars and investments in Egypt.[60] Indeed, since 2015 Saudi Arabia and the UAE have been the two main partners of al-Sisi. In 2015, Saudi Arabia signed an agreement with the Egyptian regime for 30 billion rials (8 billion dollars) to be invested in infrastructure and a free trade zone in Sinai,[61] while in the same year the UAE contributed to the reinvigoration of the Egyptian economy with a 4 billion dollars investment in Sharm al-Shaykh and in the new administrative capital.[62]

On the international level, despite the initial cold reaction by the EU and the US, the period following the coup was characterised by their full recognition of the regime. The Obama administration did not recognise it as a coup. Former Secretary of State John Kerry claimed that the military intervention was taken to restore democracy in the country.[63] As for the EU, its reaction was similar. The Union did not recognise the army manoeuvre as a military coup but something more complex especially due to the huge mobilisation of the people against the Morsi presidency.[64]

Furthermore, the real watershed came with the 2014 presidential elections, when the EU and the US fully recognised al-Sisi as president despite fraud, violence and a drastic reduction of political freedom during the electoral period. This legitimisation of al-Sisi needs to be seen in the context of the effects of 'instability' on Europe. The transformation of the Libyan revolution into a civil war, the increasing polarisation between Turkey and Qatar (supporters of the MB) and Saudi and the UAE, mounting flows of migrants landing on European shores, as well as the spread of terrorism and non-state actors in Syria and Libya, pushed Western powers to support the new regime.

Egypt became one of the watchdogs of the EU in terms of migration and security. Its fight against radical Islamists and its commitment to avoiding flows of migrants permitted al-Sisi to acquire the external legitimacy he needed. His

---

[60] Ibid., p. 4.

[61] Ali Abdelaty, 'Egypt, Saudi Arabia Sign 60 Billion Saudi Riyal Investment Fund Pact', in *Reuters*, 9 April 2016, https://www.reuters.com/article/us-egypt-saudi-idUSKC N0X60VQ.

[62] Mary Sophia, 'UAE to Build Egypt's New Capital City', in *Gulf Business*, 15 March 2015, https://gulfbusiness.com/?p=65619.

[63] 'Egypt Army 'Restoring Democracy', Says John Kerry', in *BBC News*, 1 August 2013, https://www.bbc.com/news/world-middle-east-23543744.

[64] Luis Doncel, 'Lo ocurrido en Egipto es más complejo que un golpe de Estado', in *El País*, 20 August 2013, https://elpais.com/internacional/2013/08/20/actualidad/137701 2594_718800.html.

capacity to maintain 'order' within the country through capillary repression of every form of opposition has allowed him to become a central partner for the EU member states. However, while Egypt could appear in the eyes of many as a strong country, it is extremely weak. The chronic economic crisis affecting it keeps fuelling deep discontent. Indeed, in the last two years the country has witnessed, although limited in numbers and duration, two waves of protests due to economic crisis and the government policies that have disrupted the already weakened public sector. The loans from the IMF in 2016 and 2020 provoked a series of structural reforms that triggered a cut to public services and a rise in the cost of living.

Despite the IMF's enthusiasm about the Egyptian government's performance in terms of economic reforms,[65] poverty has skyrocketed. According to the World Bank, poverty in Egypt accounted for 32.5 per cent (30 million Egyptians) in 2020,[66] while since 2019 the government has been liquidating some historical national industries, provoking the rage of thousands of workers.[67] These moves by the regime are the result of the failure of neo-liberal policies. While such policies permitted the country to avoid default, they have also generated great discontent among impoverished social classes, over whom authoritarian rule has strengthened.

Conclusion

The Egyptian 2011 revolution did not happen overnight, but was the outcome of more than a decade of an accumulation process which engaged, as outlined, both the social and political sides of the Egyptian society. Demonstrations against the Mubarak regime, the organisation of different political platforms (separated from the traditional parties) and the great waves of strikes in the factories and in the public sector constituted the political and the social souls of the revolution. However, despite mass participation in the protests, the Square has not been

---

[65]   International Monetary Fund (IMF), *IMF Executive Board Approves US$2.772 Billion in Emergency Support to Egypt to Address the COVID-19 Pandemic*, 11 May 2020, https://www.imf.org/en/News/Articles/2020/05/11/pr20215-egypt-imf-executive-board-approves-us-2-772b-in-emergency-support-to-address-the-covid19.

[66]   World Bank, *Poverty & Equity Brief: Arab Republic of Egypt*, April 2021, http://datab ank.worldbank.org/data/download/poverty/987B9C90-CB9F-4D93-AE8C-75058 8BF00QA/AM2020/Global_POVEQ_EGY.pdf.

[67]   Beesan Kassab, 'Explainer: Too Much Steel? What Are the Market Conditions Behind the Decision to Liquidate Egyptian Iron and Steel', in *Mada Masr*, 15 February 2021, https://www.madamasr.com/en/?p=320980.

able to create an alternative political project to challenge the Egyptian deep state. Three reasons explain this disappointing outcome.

First, the incapacity of both souls of the revolution to unite their demands under a political umbrella opened the doors to counterrevolutionary forces, namely the MB and the Egyptian army.

Second, far from being victims of the army, the MB proved incapable of dealing with democracy (at least in its procedural aspects), reflecting partly its authoritarian nature. The army, which in Egypt is still considered the protector of the country, did not want to appear as part of this instability. In this context, the removal of Morsi from the presidency was aimed at safeguarding the role of the army in the Egyptian political scene.

Third, the nightmare of a Syrian or Libyan scenario in Egypt has strengthened the perception that the army is the sole actor capable of challenging terrorism and avoiding the worst. This has been strengthened by the support of regional and international powers which, in order to preserve their interests, have preferred to restore old approaches and forms of government rather than to support a real democratic transition.

References

Nadine Abdalla, 'Egypt's Workers –From Protest Movement to Organized Labor', in *SWP Comments*, No. 32 (October 2012), https://www.swp-berlin.org/en/publication/egypts-workers

Ali Abdelaty, 'Egypt, Saudi Arabia Sign 60 Billion Saudi Riyal Investment Fund Pact', in *Reuters*, 9 April 2016, https://www.reuters.com/article/us-egypt-saudi-idUSKCN0X60VQ

Hesham Al-Awadi, *The Muslim Brothers in Pursuit of Legitimacy. Power and Political Islam in Egypt Under Mubarak*, London/New York, I.B. Tauris, 2014

Holger Albrecht, *Raging Against the Machine. Political Opposition under Authoritarianism in Egypt*, Syracuse, Syracuse University Press, 2013

Ann Alexander and Mostafa Bassiouny, *Bread, Freedom, Social Justice. Workers and the Egyptian Revolution*, London, Zed Books, 2014

Asef Bayat, *Revolution without Revolutionaries. Making Sense of the Arab Spring*, Stanford, Stanford University Press, 2017

Joel Beinin, 'Civil Society, NGOs, and Egypt's 2011 Popular Uprising', in *South Atlantic Quarterly*, Vol. 113, No. 2 (2014), p. 396–406

Joel Beinin, 'The Rise of Egypt's Workers', in *Carnegie Papers*, June 2012, https://carnegieendowment.org/publications/48689

Joel Beinin and Hossam El-Hamalawy, 'Egyptian Textile Workers Confront the New Economic Order', in *Middle East Report Online*, 25 March 2007, https://merip.org/?p=1314

Edmund Blair and Samia Nakhoul, 'Obama Demands Change as Mubarak Meets Army', in *Reuters*, 30 January 2011, https://www.reuters.com/article/us-egypt-idUSTRE70O3UW20110130

John Chalcraft, 'Horizontalism in the Egyptian Revolutionary Process', in *Middle East Report*, No. 262 (Spring 2012), p. 6–11, https://merip.org/?p=6541

Gianni Del Panta, *Rivoluzione e controrivoluzione in Egitto. Da Piazza Tahrir al colpo di stato di una borghesia in armi*, Bologna, il Mulino, 2019

Gianni Del Panta, 'The Role of the Egyptian Working Class in Mubarak's Ouster', in *Partecipazione e conflitto*, Vol. 9, No. 2 (2016), p. 615–639, https://doi.org/10.1285/i20356609v9i2p614

Brecht de Smet, *Gramsci on Tahrir. Revolution and Counter Revolution in Egypt*, London, Pluto Press, 2016

Luis Doncel, 'Lo ocurrido en Egipto es más complejo que un golpe de Estado', in *El País*, 20 August 2013, https://elpais.com/internacional/2013/08/20/actualidad/1377012594_718800.html

Hossam El-Hamalawy, 'Egypt's Revolution Has Been 10 Years in the Making', in *The Guardian*, 2 March 2011, https://www.theguardian.com/p/2ne5v

Rabab El-Mahdi, 'Does Political Islam Impede Gender-Based Mobilization? The Case of Egypt', in *Totalitarian Movements and Political Religions*, Vol. 11, No. 3–4 (September-December 2010), p. 379–396

European External Action Service (EEAS), *Statement by the EU High Representative Catherine Ashton on the Events in Egypt*, 27 January 2011, https://www.consilium.europa.eu/uedocs/cms_Data/docs/pressdata/EN/foraff/118963.pdf

Nadia Ramsis Farah, *Egyptian Political Economy. Power Relations in Development*, Cairo/New York, The American University in Cairo Press, 2009

John Foran, 'Beyond Insurgency to Radical Social Change: The New Situation', in *Studies in Social Justice*, Vol. 8, No. 1 (June 2014), p. 5–25, https://doi.org/10.26522/ssj.v8i1.1036

Gennaro Gervasio, 'Egitto, la transizione interrotta', in *Critica marxista*, Vol. 43, No. 2–3 (2015), p. 72–78

Gennaro Gervasio, 'Uno sguardo sull'Egitto', in *Potere al Popolo*, 16 October 2019, https://poterealpopolo.org/?p=45577

Alain Gresh, 'Barack Obama, 'Lackey' of Egypt's Muslim Brotherhood', in *Orient XXI*, 13 September 2018, https://orientxxi.info/magazine/barack-obama-lackey-of-egypt-s-muslim-brotherhood,2623

Amr Hamzawi and Nathan J. Brown, 'The Egyptian Muslim Brotherhood: Islamist Participation in a Closing Political Environment', in *Carnegie Papers*, No. 19 (March 2010), https://carnegieendowment.org/publications/40318

Adam Hanieh, *Lineages of Revolt. Issues of Contemporary Capitalism in the Middle East*, Chicago, Haymarket Books, 2013

International Monetary Fund (IMF), *IMF Executive Board Approves US$2.772 Billion in Emergency Support to Egypt to Address the COVID-19 Pandemic*, 11 May 2020, https://www.imf.org/en/News/Articles/2020/05/11/pr20215-egypt-imf-executive-board-approves-us-2-772b-in-emergency-support-to-address-the-covid19

Beesan Kassab, 'Explainer: Too Much Steel? What Are the Market Conditions Behind the Decision to Liquidate Egyptian Iron and Steel', in *Mada Masr*, 15 February 2021, https://www.madamasr.com/en/?p=320980

Maye Kassem, *Egyptian Politics. The Dynamics of Authoritarian Rule*, Boulder/London, Lynne Rienner, 2004

Alexey Khlebnikov, 'The New Ideological Threat to the GCC: Implications for the Qatari-Saudi Rivalry', in *Strategic Assessment*, Vol. 17, No. 4 (January 2015), p. 17–28, https://www.inss.org.il/?p=62216

Philip Marfleet, *Egypt. Contested Revolution*, London, Pluto Press, 2016, p. 136–137

Azzurra Meringolo, 'From Morsi to Al-Sisi: Foreign Policy at the Service of Domestic Policy', in *Insight Egypt*, No. 8 (March 2015), https://www.iai.it/en/node/3965

Daniela Pioppi, 'Playing with Fire. The Muslim Brotherhood and the Egyptian Leviathan', in *The International Spectator*, Vol. 48, No. 4 (December 2013), p. 51–68

Francesco Scanni, 'Populismo reattivo: un contro-eccesso alla crisi del modello di integrazione europeo' [Reactive Populism: A Counter-Excess to the Crisis of the European Integration Model], in *Europea*, Vol. 4, No. 1 (May 2019), p. 75–112

Manar Shorbagy, 'Understanding Kefaya: The New Politics in Egypt', in *Arab Studies Quarterly*, Vol. 29, No. 1 (Winter 2007), p. 39–60

Mary Sophia, 'UAE to Build Egypt's New Capital City', in *Gulf Business*, 15 March 2015, https://gulfbusiness.com/?p=65619

Eric Trager, 'The Muslim Brotherhood Is the Root of the Qatar Crisis', in *The Atlantic*, 2 July 2017, https://www.theatlantic.com/international/archive/2017/07/muslim-brotherhood-qatar/532380

US Presidency, *Remarks by the President on a New Beginning*, Cairo University, 4 June 2009, https://obamawhitehouse.archives.gov/the-press-office/ remarks-president-cairo-university-6-04-09

World Bank, *Poverty & Equity Brief: Arab Republic of Egypt*, April 2021, http:// databank.worldbank.org/data/download/poverty/987B9C90-CB9F-4D93- AE8C-750588BF00QA/AM2020/Global_POVEQ_EGY.pdf

Barbara Zollner, 'The Brotherhood in Transition: An Analysis of the Organization's Mobilizing Capacity', in Peter Lintl, Christian Thuselt and Christian Wolff (eds), *Religiöse Bewegungen als politische Akteure im Nahen Osten*, Baden-Baden, Nomos, 2016, p. 43–70

Carmen Geha

Chapter 4: From Revolt to Community-Driven Resistance: Beirut's Year of Hell

More than a decade has passed since the Arab uprisings sparked a wave of discontent and created political, social and security ripple effects across the region. The trajectories of these protests, their composition and responses from Arab regimes were distinctly different but their narratives had elements of great similarity including freedom, gender equality, economic opportunity, and social justice.

Until 2019, Lebanon had seemingly escaped this mass wave of popular mobilisation. In fact, a literature was growing to explain why it was nearly impossible for Lebanon to witness a nation-wide revolution. The forces of deeply entrenched sectarianism and widespread clientelism were often used as rationales for why a revolution in the Lebanese context was not possible. The discontent that sparked a wave of great hope and exuberance in October 2019 created a rupture from the bleak history of war and post-war sectarian politics in Lebanon. A great deal of hope and potential were riding on this revolution. Could it finally put enough pressure for reform and an end to corruption? We will never know. The events that followed, from financial collapse to the covid-19 pandemic leading up to the Beirut port explosion on 4 August 2020, crushed the spirit and momentum of revolt, at least in that version.[1]

This chapter traces the evolution of anti-regime protests in Lebanon – overshadowed by the port explosion as a disastrous critical juncture – and argues that community-driven resistance is emerging as a means for collective action and self-preservation. In doing so, the chapter seeks to advance the literature on abeyance by showing what people do to create an alternative to the regime when they are not protesting, transcending the constraints of national and regional geo-politics within which the regime is seated. The chapter expands the critique of studying movements as linear modalities of mobilisation and abeyance, arguing that emergence of new actors is not spontaneous but displays continuity

---

[1]   The chapter is based on personal activist experience embedded in a critical examination of literature and key events that led up to this analysis.

of networks and shared experiences.[2] It shows that contestation of political systems does not always take place on the street in the form of revolt but can take the shape of solidarity movements, creation of new institutions and experiencing alternative realities, far from the street and from electoral politics. This form of contestation, particularly in times of disaster, enables us to recognise local community actors' role in resistance.

1. Hell explained: Sectarian warlords and the politics of exclusion

The year 2020 will be remembered as one of the most difficult human experiences for people across the world. But for people residing in Lebanon, 2020 unleashed a hell on earth. The President of the Republic, Michel Aoun, had announced this unleashing in a press conference on 1 September when asked what might happen if no government was formed; his reply was, 'We are on our way to hell.'[3] At the time of writing, ten months following the explosion of the Beirut port on 4 August, Lebanese politicians have yet to form a government. The investigation has not yet led to any results nor have any public officials been questioned or detained. Meanwhile, a caretaker government is in charge at a time when the compounded crises of the coronavirus pandemic, financial collapse and security unrest have paralysing effects on people's wellbeing. The year 2020 was the final nail in the coffin for the dignity of the Lebanese people, who had lived near tons of explosives for six years without knowing it.[4]

The port explosion which claimed the lives of 200 people, wounded 6,000 others and rendered around 300,000 people homeless within moments, epitomises Lebanon's endemic problems. A combination of corruption and negligence led to the storage of 2,750 tons of ammonium nitrate near people's homes, schools, hospitals, and shops.[5] The explosion exposed a criminally culpable regime where

[2]   See for instance Cristina Flesher Fominaya, 'Debunking Spontaneity: Spain's 15-M/ Indignados as Autonomous Movement', in *Social Movement Studies*, Vol. 14, No. 2 (2015), p. 142–163.

[3]   Alain Daou et al., 'Breaking the Cycle: Issue 2: It Starts with Us', in *Khaddit Beirut* portal, last modified 7 December 2020, https://khadditbeirut.com/?p=810.

[4]   Julie Ray, 'Political, Economic Strife Takes Emotional Toll on Lebanese', in *Gallup News*, 19 November 2020, https://news.gallup.com/poll/325715/political-economic-str ife-takes-emotional-toll-lebanese.aspx.

[5]   See Sam E. Rigby et al., 'Preliminary Yield Estimation of the 2020 Beirut Explosion Using Video Footage from Social Media', in *Shock Waves*, Vol. 30, No. 6 (September 2020), p. 671–675, https://doi.org/10.1007/s00193-020-00970-z.

public officials had known about the existence of explosive material for over six years, but had done nothing about it.[6] Traced back to individuals affiliated with the Syrian regime, the explosive material exposed how Lebanon's political system and instability is deeply rooted in a geopolitical context. The main player in this context is Hezbollah, which has been involved in the war in Syria alongside the Assad regime overtly since 2013, despite early attempts by the Lebanese government at the time to disassociate Lebanon from the conflict.[7] This policy of disassociation proved impossible and dragged Lebanon into an open border policy all the way up to the present where Lebanese goods and services including fuel continue to be smuggled to fund the ongoing conflict in Syria.[8] The explosion exacerbated the long history of a political system that thrives on exclusion and is organised around sectarian and regional fault lines. How did Beirut get to this explosive event?

Even though there is evidence and critique of the Lebanese model as failing to introduce democratic reforms and achieve peace, recent analysis still contends that the Lebanese model could be successfully applied to end conflicts in Yemen, Iraq and Libya. Stephan Rosiny, for instance, hails the Lebanese model as one of co-existence from which Syria can learn.[9] This is a dangerous assertion because it overlooks the fact that the power-sharing system in Lebanon gave legitimacy to a handful of sectarian leaders who participated in the civil war and then divided the spoils of the state among themselves. There was no opportunity for state-building in the Lebanese case. Instead, consociationalist representation came at

---

6   See Reuters, 'Lebanon's Leaders Warned in July about Explosives at Port, Say Documents', in *The National*, 10 August 2020, https://www.thenationalnews.com/world/mena/lebanon-s-leaders-warned-in-july-about-explosives-at-port-say-documents-1.1062000.

7   Waleed Hazbun, 'Assembling Security in a "Weak State:" The Contentious Politics of Plural Governance in Lebanon since 2005', in *Third World Quarterly*, Vol. 37, No. 6 (2016), p. 1053–1070.

8   Mayssa Awad and James André, 'Lebanon and Syria: Smuggling and Sanctions, the New Front Line' (podcast), in *France 24*, 16 April 2021, https://www.france24.com/en/tv-shows/reporters/20210416-lebanon-syria-smuggling-and-sanctions-the-new-front-line.

9   Stephan Rosiny, 'A Quarter Century of "Transitory Power-Sharing": Lebanon's Unfulfilled Ta'if Agreement of 1989 Revisited', in *Civil Wars*, Vol. 17, No. 4 (2015), p. 485–502.

the expense of civil society, national interests and shared identity.[10] Now a century later, we can capture three recurrent dimensions of exclusionary politics that manifest in such a system.

To understand the dynamics of national and regional politics at the time of the explosion, we need to historicise the political system. The Ottoman Empire and French mandate that followed it laid the foundation for the 1926 constitution which established the sectarian power-sharing political system.[11] The constitution guaranteed equal representation for sectarian communities in public posts. Lebanon's independence from the French in 1943 ushered in the National Pact, an unwritten agreement to share power disrupted only in 1975 by the outbreak of the civil war. On 22 October 1989, Lebanese deputies met in the city of Ta'if in Saudi Arabia and reached a US-backed agreement to end the war. The resulting treaty was known as the Ta'if Agreement or the National Accord Document (*Wathiqat al-wifaq al-watani*) and represented the outcome of a negotiated deal supported by the Syrian government and the international community. On paper, the Ta'if Agreement included mechanisms that would lead to a transition, but the post-war system turned former sectarian warlords into politicians, while allowing Hezbollah's armed militia to grow.[12]

For thirty years, unobstructed by the US and Europe, the government of Syrian president Hafiz al-Assad tampered with election results to ensure Lebanon's legislature had a pro-Syrian majority, violently suppressed any opposition and controlled public resources.[13] Popular protests in the spring of 2005, which became known as the Cedar Revolution, pushed for the withdrawal of Syrian troops in April 2005. But even in withdrawing, Syria remained a polarising actor in Lebanese politics with the March 8 Hezbollah-led movement thanking the regime and vowing loyalty, and the March 14 camp holding Syria responsible for the assassination of Prime Minister Rafiq Hariri. In effect, the polarisation was over seats and cabinet positions but neither March 8 nor 14 March 14 sought

[10] See Janine A. Clark and Bassel F. Salloukh, 'Elite Strategies, Civil Society, and Sectarian Identities in Postwar Lebanon', in *International Journal of Middle East Studies*, Vol. 45, No. 4 (November 2013), p. 731–749.

[11] See Samir Khalaf, *Civil and Uncivil Violence in Lebanon. A History of the Internationalization of Communal Conflict*, New York, Columbia University Press, 2002.

[12] See Roger Mac Ginty, 'Reconstructing Post-war Lebanon: A Challenge to the Liberal Peace? Analysis', in *Conflict, Security & Development*, Vol. 7, No. 3 (2007), p. 457–482.

[13] See Raymond Hinnebusch, 'Pax Syriana? The Origins, Causes and Consequences of Syria's Role in Lebanon', in *Mediterranean Politics*, Vol. 3, No. 1 (Summer 1998), p. 137–160.

to reform the sectarian system or combat corruption.[14] Instead, after 2005, Lebanese politics became further divided among sectarian lines and the 2009 elections were manipulated and reported to have had the highest rates of corruption and documented bribery in Lebanon's history.[15]

This disappointed a generation of activists who had gained collective consciousness around the time of the Cedar Revolution. They emerged as activists emboldening civil society to take on key reform issues including access to information, electoral reform and gender equality.[16] These groups used advocacy strategies, campaigning and mobilising to push state institutions and parliamentary representatives to amend laws and policies, mainly to no avail.[17] Good governance was largely lacking after 2005, and this left a large percentage of youth disenfranchised from the political elite both in the March 8 and March 14 camps.

Broadly speaking between 2005 and 2011, activists organised themselves around a range of political reform issues but were met with neglect and lack of response. A case in point was the long history of feminist organising around a range of discriminatory laws and practices facing women in Lebanon. Women's rights organisations campaigned for women's right to pass nationality to their children, protection from violence, reproductive health and representation in politics – all to no avail.[18] Instead, the Lebanese sectarian system monopolised the space through the National Commission for Lebanese Women, which failed to produce any reform that would address the structural barriers women face. Another key area was electoral reform: despite the efforts of the Lebanese Association for Democratic Elections and a coalition of civil society actors, the electoral system continued to be marked by violence, corruption and districting with no oversight from an independent Commission.[19] It was instead managed by the Ministry of Interior, headed by a minister who has often run for election.

---

[14]   See Ohannes Geukjian, *Lebanon after the Syrian Withdrawal. External Intervention, Power-Sharing and Political Instability*, London/New York, Routledge, 2017.

[15]   Daniel Corstange, 'Vote Trafficking in Lebanon', in *International Journal of Middle East Studies*, Vol. 44, No. 3 (August 2012), p. 483–505.

[16]   For a history on these groups see Carmen Geha, *Civil Society and Political Reform in Lebanon and Libya. Transition and Constraint*, London/New York, Routledge, 2016.

[17]   Janine A. Clark and Bassel F. Salloukh, 'Elite Strategies, Civil Society, and Sectarian Identities in Postwar Lebanon', cit.

[18]   See Lina Khatib, 'Gender, Citizenship and Political Agency in Lebanon', in *British Journal of Middle Eastern Studies*, Vol. 35, No. 3 (2008), p. 437–451.

[19]   Daniel Corstange, 'Clientelism in Competitive and Uncompetitive Elections', in *Comparative Political Studies*, Vol. 51, No. 1 (January 2018), p. 76–104.

Through all of these years, the absence of reform was happening right under the oversight of international donors, including the European Union.

Lebanon's political system remained non-reformist but showed resilience, especially after 2011 and the outbreak of civil war in Syria. Despite the expectations that Syria's conflict would spill over into Lebanon and despite the massive influx of Syrian refugees, the political system remained intact.[20] After 2011, Lebanese politicians postponed by consensus parliamentary elections three times. Lebanon was also without a president for over two years, a vacuum that Hezbollah-backed Michel Aoun eventually filled. The October 2016 election of Aoun as president created a tipping point; this was the first time since the civil war that Hezbollah, with its allies, had a majority grip over parliament and government. This was followed by a decline in civil liberties and economic recession which planted the seeds for the emergence of mass mobilising and political opposition, which extended beyond civil society activists to the country as a whole in October 2019. This mass organising was focused against the regime's network or machinery of sectarianism and corruption (al-manzoumeh).

There are three dimensions of continuity from the history of the regime that represent politics of exclusion. The first dimension is *exclusion based on impunity* and its manifestation in the institutions and political practices of post- civil war Lebanon. The modern roots of impunity lie in the amnesty agreement for crimes committed in the war. There is evidence in the literature that power-sharing is a means to achieve a pragmatic political agreement among divided parties, with relative success in the cases of Northern Ireland and South Africa.[21] But in the Lebanese case, the lack of justice after the war enshrined governance through impunity. Months can go by with no functional government, years can go by with no elections, and scores can be assassinated without justice ever being served. This impunity is also greatly gendered and intersects with class and sectarian identities. Women are treated differently by the system depending on what sect they are born into. Laws that regulate child marriage, divorce and inheritance differ because Lebanese personal status is governed by fifteen religious courts and no civil status code exists, although women's rights organisations have

[20]   Carmen Geha, 'Resilience through Learning and Adaptation: Lebanon's Power-Sharing System and the Syrian Refugee Crisis', in *Middle East Law and Governance*, Vol. 11, No. 1 (May 2019), p. 65–90.

[21]   Joanne McEvoy and Brendan O'Leary, eds, *Power Sharing in Deeply Divided Places*, Philadelphia, University of Pennsylvania Press, 2013.

demanded this reform for decades.[22] This results in a system where gender-based violence is prevalent and for instance a rapist could escape trial if he proposes to marry his victim.

The second of the dimensions of exclusion which shaped the protest movements is the *formality of informality*. State institutions, parliament and cabinet are not the places where decisions are made. Real power and capacity to deliver services lie outside the state. Backdoor dealing is the norm at the National Dialogue Table where a group of fifteen men meet to discuss strategic issues in times of crisis, or choose not to meet, thereby rendering all political institutions irrelevant and paralysing the state.[23] This formal informality is what we can describe as a powerful but weak state, which Mouawad and Bauman showed as a state complicating the daily experience of citizens, and not a weak state removed from daily life.[24] It is difficult to overthrow or hold accountable someone who is not in an official government position or has not been elected to office, which is the case for several powerful *zu'ama* (sectarian leaders) or party leaders, including Samir Geagea of the Lebanese Forces, Sleiman Frangieh of the Marada Party and Hassan Nasrallah of Hezbollah. Because power-sharing rests on the acquiescence of politicians, it is their approval and consensus that facilitates or obstructs the work of state institutions, a phenomenon that has resulted in months-long deadlock or in missing constitutional deadlines for the sake of maintaining consensus. It is impossible for citizens or civil society actors to advocate for reform,[25] ask for information or ensure transparency because state institutions have no power to make decisions; strategic decisions are in the hands of sectarian warlords.

The third of dimension of the politics of exclusion is *widespread corruption*. The state's resources were the incentive used to get warlords to agree to peace in 1990. They indeed treat public positions and resources as their own and use them for clientelism. Countless attempts to combat corruption and ensure equity in services failed miserably. The politicians have the final say in hiring the civil

---

[22] See Dima Dabbous, 'Legal Reform and Women's Rights in Lebanese Personal Status Laws', in *CMI Reports*, No. 3 (September 2017), https://www.cmi.no/publications/6341.

[23] See Henrik Hartmann, 'National Dialogues and Development', in *National Dialogue Handbook Conceptual Studies*, February 2017, https://berghof-foundation.org/library/national-dialogues-and-development.

[24] Jamil Mouawad and Hannes Bauman, 'In Search of the Lebanese State', in *The Arab Studies Journal*, Vol. 25, No. 1 (Spring 2017), p. 60–65.

[25] See Paul W.T. Kingston, *Reproducing Sectarianism. Advocacy Networks and the Politics of Civil Society in Postwar Lebanon*, Albany, State University of New York Press, 2013.

service and they also manage the portfolios of health and education, treating these services as favours and benefits granted to their supporters. Corruption in the electricity sector alone has cost 40 billion US dollars in debt.[26] A Ponzi scheme run by the Central Bank fell through in 2020 and depositors lost all their money while the local currency collapsed – rising from 1,500 to 13,000 to the dollar at the time of writing. Successive governments after the civil war piled up public debt to international donors that were in acquiescence with maintaining the role of the Lebanese elite at any cost. Largely a remittance economy, Lebanon also borrowed from Arab Gulf states that began to retreat with the increased power of Hezbollah after 2016.[27] Corruption coupled with negligence and lack of competence in state institutions meant that ammonium nitrates and picric acid were stored under sweltering heat for more than six years at the Beirut port. Warlords have set up an intricate web of services to their loyalists including healthcare, education and jobs.[28] Clientelism exacerbates gendered discrimination, with women making up less than 5 per cent of the parliament on average, despite years of funding from EU and other donors for women's supposed empowerment.[29] Women are almost absent from decision-making roles and are disproportionally affected by unemployment and lack of public services. These networks of institutions mean that politicians have no interest in, nor would they benefit from, any attempt for reform.[30] France is leading international efforts to support Lebanon and for the first time collectively donors have conditioned aid on reforms. The Arab Gulf states, and especially Saudi Arabia, have distanced themselves from Lebanon due to Hezbollah's growing influence over national

---

[26] Bassem Mroue, 'Minister, No Investor for Lebanon's Ailing Power Sector', in *AP News*, 16 July 2020, https://apnews.com/article/d8ca48aa2eddc1bd7075feabfd725a88.

[27] Edmund Blair, 'Explainer: Lebanon's Financial Meltdown and How it Happened', in *Reuters*, 17 September 2020, https://reut.rs/2H0aPkL.

[28] For a comprehensive and definitive view of sectarian welfare and its connection to corruption see: Melani Cammett, *Compassionate Communalism. Welfare and Sectarianism in Lebanon*, Ithaca/London, Cornell University Press, 2014.

[29] Carmen Geha, 'The Myth of Women's Political Empowerment within Lebanon's Sectarian Power-Sharing System', in *Journal of Women, Politics & Policy*, Vol. 40, No. 4 (2019), p. 498–521.

[30] For example, politicians have parallel sectarian charities such as the Hariri Foundation, Makhzoumi Foundation, Sadr Foundation, Moawad Foundation and Azm and Saadeh Foundation.

politics. The International Monetary Fund has made numerous attempts at pushing for reform in exchange for a bailout, to no avail.[31]

2. From protests to revolution: Three major waves

The three aforementioned dimensions – namely impunity, informality and corruption – reinforce each other and create a deeply entrenched politics of exclusion. They also shape the narrative and strategy of activists and the regime's responses of co-optation and oppression leading up to the 2019 October uprisings.

The discontent against the politics of exclusion and sectarianism enabled the long-time demands of activists to reach the mainstream media and create a ripple effect through protests against the whole political class. The protests rejected the polarised politics of March 8 and March 14, and framed Lebanon's problems as endemic and protected by the entire political elite.

The first wave of protests is known as the *Isqat al-Nizam al-Ta'ifi* (bringing down the sectarian regime) inspired by the uprisings in Egypt and Tunisia in January-February 2011. The movement was much smaller than in Egypt and Tunisia but organisers were able to articulate a Lebanese version of bringing down the system that mobilised people to the streets.[32] This Lebanese movement was confronted with the reality that there was not one dictator to be removed but an entire system to be toppled. The movement organisers chanted slogans calling for the end of the regime 'and its symbols' (*wa-rumuzih*), referring to powerful political leaders who were not actually part of formal state institutions, meaning they could not resign, but who protected and supported the sectarian system. Women were at the forefront of these protests, as bringing down the sectarian system would inevitably ensure gender equality under the law. The top demand under eradicating the sectarian system would be a unified status code and so several women's rights groups joined these protests and held public sessions to make demands for citizenship, civil marriage and civil status.

In classic co-optation fashion, the speaker of parliament Nabih Berri was the first to claim that he and his movement also wanted to change the sectarian

---

[31]   International Monetary Fund (IMF), *Statement by the Managing Director at the International Conference in Support of the Lebanese People*, 2 December 2020, https://www.imf.org/en/News/Articles/2020/12/02/sp120220-statement-by-the-managing-director-international-conference-in-support-of-lebanese-people.

[32]   Sami Hermez, 'On Dignity and Clientelism: Lebanon in the Context of the 2011 Arab Revolutions', in *Studies in Ethnicity and Nationalism*, Vol. 11, No. 3 (December 2011), p. 527–537.

system, calling for youth members of his party, the Amal Movement, to join the protests. The then Head of the Free Patriotic Party Michel Aoun saluted the protesters, claiming that his party was a pioneer in fighting sectarianism since its 2005 charter stated the need to separate politics from religion. Walid Jumblatt, a Druze leader and head of the Progressive Socialist Party, also openly took part in supporting the demands of the protesters. Many politicians embraced the famous 2009 quote of Maronite patriarch Nasrallah Boutros Sfeir, who had stepped down the day before the first protest: 'We must first eradicate sectarianism from [our] souls (*al-nufus*) and not from [legal] texts (*al-nusus*).'

For activists, this co-optation of the movement's demands by traditionally sectarian leaders was confusing. The people paying lip service to anti-sectarianism were the very same warlords and leaders who were in power, who kept sectarianism in the texts (*nusus*) in a way that discriminated against women and ensured that elections are performed so as to keep them in power. After April 2011, the organisers did not call for another protest, and Lebanon entered a phase of political deadlock. But the aftermaths of these protests included a narrative adopted by a generation of activists, especially young women, who were realising that advocacy and demanding change from this system were ineffective. Lebanon would need radical change because those in power simply have no interest in shaking the pillars of what keeps them in power: the triangle of impunity, informality and corruption.

Then in the summer of 2015, a combination of hot weather electricity problems and governmental deadlock following the second postponement of parliamentary elections triggered a next wave of protest in Lebanon. A trash crisis began because people living near the Na'ama landfill protested and refused to let garbage dumpsters into their area due to overflow of garbage. The landfill which opened in 1997 was intended to be a temporary solution for trash in Beirut and Mount Lebanon. The solution, supposedly an interim one, was still in place almost two decades later despite numerous smaller protests by affected residents of Na'ama.[33] Trash immediately started piling up and anger on the part of residents of the peripheral town Na'ama reached Beirut, leading a group of activists to mobilise with the slogan *tol'it rihitkum* literally meaning 'your stench has emerged' – rendered in English as 'You Stink'.[34]

---

[33] See Human Rights Watch, '*As If You're Inhaling Your Death*'. *The Health Risks of Burning Waste in Lebanon*, November 2017, https://www.hrw.org/node/311168.

[34] See Carmen Geha, 'Politics of a Garbage Crisis: Social Networks, Narratives, and Frames of Lebanon's 2015 Protests and Their Aftermath', in *Social Movement Studies*, Vol. 18, No. 1 (2019), p. 78–92.

The protest organisers of You Stink identified the garbage crisis as a political crisis, a failure and a result of corruption and negligence. Protesters claimed that political corruption was starting to reek, just like the stench of garbage, and the group staged marches towards government agencies and threw bags of garbage over security barricades into government compounds. Immediately thousands of people began rallying behind You Stink, as the movement resonated not only with demands to clean the streets but also to 'clean' the government of sectarian leaders. The protests became known as the *hirak* ('movement'), which grouped together various movements that demonstrated against the political system. This was a first mass articulation of trash, electricity, unemployment and inflation as resulting from political failure and corruption. Women were also at the forefront of this movement; young feminists joined the protests carrying the slogan 'Feminist Block'. They articulated a vision for the protests that was intersectional: garbage was corruption, and corruption and sectarianism were the same forces endangering the lives and bodies of women.

The summer *hirak* uncovered how long corruption can go unpunished and how the sectarian warlords were still able to meet over dialogue, but not to regulate the sector and create a solution to the mounting trash. The media reported that more than 100,000 citizens attended, making it one of the largest street protests in Lebanon's recent history. Following the protests, the Beirut *Madinaty* (Beirut My City) electoral campaign was founded by a group of activists, professionals, artists and university professors. For this group, there was the need for a political opposition group to take the momentum from the streets to the competition for the seats of the Beirut municipality. It included 50 per cent women candidates and once more women emerged as founders and spokespersons. Beirut *Madinaty* won 30 per cent of the votes but no seats due to the majoritarian electoral system, but it gave birth to subsequent movements in other areas such as Baalbeck, and created a precedent encouraging other opposition groups to run for parliament in 2018. Contestation had now moved from street politics to electoral campaigning, and many activists had begun to win support from constituencies.[35]

The 2019 October revolution was by far the most historical juncture for anti-regime protests and sentiments. The revolution opened up the space of political participation that had thus far been monopolised by sectarian parties. Because the revolution was not hierarchal, once again women emerged at the centre of not only every protest but every public dialogue, media appearance and police

---

35   Ibid.

station where activists were illegally detained or arrested. They succeeded in putting forward, to a large extent, an intersectional narrative that was inclusive of migrant workers, refugees and members of the LGBTQ community.[36]

The revolution was a major precedent in three ways. First, it broke taboos that the Lebanese psyche had stored so deeply from the civil war and its aftermath. The phrase *'kellon yaaneh kellon'* (all means all of them) that became a mainstream slogan and approach to holding all politicians accountable is a sign of social transformation unlike any other in the country's history. Different groups that would protest or demand reform saw their own leader (*za'im*) as untouchable. But this time the protestors cursed all politicians and showed their faces and names across the city. Second, the intensity, longevity and decentralised nature of the revolution showed that it was not only urban elite and 'civil society' in and around the Beirut area who wanted to confront the system and *zu'ama*, there was a national outcry and demand for new political leadership.[37] The movement was also purposeful in that it attacked parliament, banks and politicians' homes – bringing out salient corruption patterns in the public education system, media, health, environment but mainly corruption that uses violence to silence dissent. Third, the revolution was gendered not only in terms of women's leading participation and main roles as mobilisers, spokespersons and advocates, but also in putting the issues of gender equality on the table.[38] There was a clear and deliberative narrative against the version of state feminism that had produced and protected sectarian political parties leaving women's voices out of the spaces where decisions about their lives and wellbeing are made. Historically women needed a sectarian patriarch to adopt them on his list, and they would then have to reinforce his policies and act as his representative. The revolutionaries contested this and even as the protests entered abeyance, there was a rise for a new form of inclusive politics through new political parties and platforms that focused on women's representation and gender-inclusive policies.

---

[36] Lebanese law still criminalises homosexuality.
[37] For analysis on the protests see Lebanese Center for Policy Studies, 'Why Did the October 17 Revolution Witness a Regression in Numbers?', in *Setting the Agenda*, 31 October 2020, https://www.lcps-lebanon.org/agendaArticle.php?id=199.
[38] See Carmen Geha, 'Our Personal Is Political and Revolutionary', in *Al-Raida Journal*, Vol. 44, No. 1 (2020), p. 23–28, http://alraidajournal.com/index.php/ALRJ/article/view/1818.

3. The explosion and its aftermath: Community-driven resistance

By early 2020, the collapsing currency and economic recession caused poverty to plunge to record highs. In March, the covid pandemic reached Lebanon with an already crumbling and ill-equipped health sector. In that same month, Lebanon defaulted. Even before the explosion, the numbers of protestors had regressed largely due to co-optation and state violence. The politics of exclusion and power-sharing explained above had stifled the revolution. First, it was impossible to hold accountable whoever was responsible for the faltering currency and the loss of depositors' money. Second, it was impossible to ask for the resignation of the main powers, national and regional, who were not officially part of the government created in January 2020. The formal informality of the system had trumped any demands for reform and accountability. Finally, widespread corruption meant that people relied on goods and services; they suddenly stopped cursing and chanting, and retreated to a victim position. The revolution had started to create solid social networks of solidarity, mobilisation and even new friendships which sustained beyond the streets. But nothing could have prepared anyone for the port explosion on 4 August 2020.

To say the least, the port explosion was a rupture, which destroyed the last shred of people's connection and trust in the state. At the same time, it was the ultimate enabling factor for sectarian leaders to resort to their evil patterns of impunity, informal back-door dealing (or the lack thereof) and corrupt clientelism. The tragic aftermath of the explosion led to waves of local and international mobilisation like never before. In the midst of massive destruction and devastation, people came together to sweep streets, fundraise, rebuild homes and confront a political class notorious for impunity. Instead of protesting a system widely understood as corrupt, people organised and rallied so that aid would go directly to homes, schools, people in need, and to civil society associations or independent political groups. As opposed to a negligent and corrupt political system, people and communities were resisting by doing well and building networks of solidarity. This time it seemed that the international community, given the magnitude of the disaster, could not go back to propping up a political class and void national institutions. It heeded the call of the people and refused to provide any aid to the government without structural reforms, a condition that remains unmet at the time of writing.

People in Lebanon – not only the Lebanese but diaspora, civil society and international donors –geared up all that they knew and had first to call the culprits by their name: *'kellon yaaneh kellon'*. Five days after the explosion, a mass mourning protest was held and organisers declared that they would not wait for a verdict. They knew who was responsible. In an unprecedented scene, protestors set up hanging gallows with puppets of all the politicians (*all of them*) in downtown Beirut. But the regime responded, as unhinged and resilient as ever, with tear gas, live bullets and impunity. It is safe to say that by August 2020, the revolution and people's souls had been crushed. Although the revolutionaries called for a symbolic protest in October 2020, at which thousands showed up, the revolutionary moment itself was gone. The people of Lebanon were facing a new reality.

Constructive resistance literature defines the term as people coming together to create alternative realities, to experience a world they wish to live in and to co-create solutions for common problems. After the explosion, it was clear that people were living under the mercy of murderers; but despite all the international condemnation, the Macron initiative and local outcry, no government was formed and eight months later no investigation has been completed. President Macron had flown into Lebanon days after the explosion demanding that the political class enact immediate reforms and appoint a functional government; he would later say that the politicians lied and are a disgrace because until today Lebanon is without a government. Juxtaposed to this stagnation and continued violence, actors all over Beirut were launching community-driven initiatives, using new tools to help victims restore some sense of dignity and autonomy. Indeed, what happened was a transformation of social relationships in everyday life, where people came together not only to show solidarity but to co-create and find an alternate path to survive and persist.[39] Constructive resistance occurs when people begin to build the society and polity that they desire independently from the structures that govern their live.[40] Rejecting '*all of them*', the organisers of this movement may have started out spontaneously over a shared pain but slowly exhibited patterns of similarity and of deliberative action to resist the prevalent dimensions of exclusion, and replace them with a new politics of inclusion and resistance for the collective good.

The political contention, after the protest on 9 August that was met by violence, had transformed into a community-driven mode of resistance. Almost

[39] Sean Chabot and Stellan Vinthagen, 'Decolonizing Civil Resistance', in *Mobilization: An International Quarterly*, Vol. 20, No. 4 (December 2015), p. 517–532.

[40] Majken Jul Sørensen, 'Constructive Resistance: Conceptualising and Mapping the Terrain', in *Journal of Resistance Studies*, Vol. 2, No. 1 (2016), p. 49–78, https://resistance-journal.org/wp-content/uploads/2021/04/Volume-2-Number-1.-Majken.pdf.

opposite to the passive notion of resilience which can be critiqued as covering up injustice and pushing people to adapt without change,[41] this resistance movement after the explosion is aimed at demanding accountability and uncovering the corruption as well as the negligence that caused the corruption, while lifting up the most vulnerable and providing basic services. This is an important theoretical and political distinction. The resilience of the state is apparent in the case of Lebanon which is able to survive shocks,[42] whereas what people are doing and organising are actually acts of resistance and confrontation.

While it is impossible, due to the absence of data so far, to map out all of the initiatives, I propose a typology to be able to conceptualise the different ways in which these new movements are mobilising with and for the community. In terms of a typology, it is possible to identify a range of movements whose networks pre-existed before the explosion but had to get more organized and active the wake of the crisis. This conceptual typology of a community-driven resistance is based on the movement's strategies which need not be mutually exclusive. The four-fold typology selected for illustration and analysis here uses an approach that emphasises intersectionality in the Lebanese context. I call it resistance because it cuts across the fault lines of historical exclusion to offer a different way of working with people, for people, in the face of continued impunity, informality and corruption. This intersectionality is evident in that women are at the forefront of this movement, but also in that the internal ways of organising are gender inclusive. These movements also target historically marginalised people and communities, including migrants and refugees. In the wake of the explosion, 'all of them means all of them' has turned into 'all of us means all of us'. It was a call to put into action the slogans of a crushed revolution, as all over Beirut volunteers of different nationalities rushed to pull out bodies, people attended mass funerals and candlelight vigils were held in most major cities across the world. This typology may include movements with different strategies but the frame and narrative were similar: the politicians were the culprits, nobody is coming to save the people, the people had to do this themselves for 'all of the people'.

---

41   See Rima Majed, 'Interview: Beirut Blast Exposed a Global System', in *rs21*, 30 August 2020, https://www.rs21.org.uk/2020/08/30/interview-beirut-blast-exposed-a-global-system.

42   Carmen Geha, 'Resistance not Resilience: A Proposal for Collective Action', in *An-Nahar*, 17 May 2021, https://tinyurl.com/yfftjxn7.

The first type is the *relief and humanitarian aid organisations or groups*, such as Offre Joie which mobilised 6,000 volunteers to rebuild hundreds of homes in weeks. The significance of Offre Joie lies in the model of volunteer-based service and collaboration it led in the heavily damaged Karantina and Mar Mikhael neighbourhoods. By contrast to a totally absent government and weak state institutions, Offre Joie mobilised resources and people to lift up a community in need. In the face of polarised politics and inefficient government institutions, Offre Joie brought youth from across the country, from different backgrounds, and organised them into shifts to work on cleaning and fixing homes. Relying only on in-kind donations, Offre Joie's offices were flooded with support from all over the world and in just a matter of weeks, they had helped rebuild hundreds of homes. Another example is *'Beit el Baraka'* (the house of blessing) which today has rebuilt 3,100 homes offering housing to the forgotten and vulnerable. Beit el Baraka also opened a free supermarket and helps families with medicine, committing to human dignity and social security for all. Nusaned is another local organisation rebuilding shops in the devastated areas of Gemayzeh and Mar Mikhael, seeking to restore the local social fabric and dynamism of an area crushed to pieces.

The second type is *advocacy and human rights organisations* including legal activists, such as Legal Agenda or the Beirut Bar Association, defending the rights of the victims' families or the marginalised groups in the most affected areas. Both these organisations existed before the explosion and turned their focus to aiding the homeless and the vulnerable. The Kafala system in Lebanon puts migrant workers into a situation of modern slavery. Abused by their employers, many of these workers were left on the side of the road after the explosion. Legal Agenda as well as the Anti-Racism Movement (ARM) dedicate their resources and expertise to advocate for migrant workers' rights.[43] The Beirut Bar Association (BBA) is leading a volunteer lawsuit on behalf of the families of the victims, presenting a unique case of judges and lawyers serving the community while the actual government-led investigation stalls.[44] The BBA is not only providing legal services but also speaks against corruption in the judiciary. This

---

[43] See Laure Ayoub, 'Foreign Workers Revolt Against the "Republic's Contractor" in Lebanon', in *Legal Agenda*, 21 April 2021, https://english.legal-agenda.com/?p=23972.

[44] After making some progress, the politicians interfered to remove the judge in the middle of the investigation, see AFP, 'Lebanon Judge Removed from Beirut Blast Probe: Judicial Source', in *France 24*, 18 February 2021, https://www.france24.com/en/live-news/20210218-lebanon-judge-removed-from-beirut-blast-probe-judicial-source.

advocacy movement is also coupled with a rise in journalists uncovering violence, corruption and negligence daily on the news.[45]

The third type is *fundraising platforms*, whether local or international, focused on raising funds for Beirut and condemning corruption and incompetence at the government level, such as Xpatria in Switzerland. Xpatria's mission is to channel diaspora funding to initiatives based in Beirut, whether to individual households or trusted NGOs. In contrast with the government being a black-box of funding where millions go missing over the years, Xpatria and other similar platforms commit to transparency and accountability. Impact Lebanon is a UK-based organisation that existed before the explosion and that also launched a fundraiser providing direct aid to those affected by the disaster. Impact Lebanon also resists the usual ineffectiveness of the state by partnering with a quality assurance company as well as using a strategy to vet NGOs and ensure that local needs are met. Several crowd-funding websites have also mushroomed, dedicating their platforms to not only channelling aid but also matching donors with local trusted associations and families.

Some organisations and movements can *combine more than one of these strategies*. A case in point is *Khaddit Beirut* (Beirut Shake-Up) created on 5 August, the day after the explosion, as a movement of activists, business owners, academics and experts that channelled their activism to meet the needs of the community. Khaddit Beirut (KB) adopts an agile, evidence-based, inclusive and holistic approach that is informed by local needs, accountable to people and focused on sustainable solutions in the areas of communities' health, education, environmental health and local business. In terms of the typology of strategies described here, KB operates in the nexus of advocacy and providing services.

KB is a network of 200-plus activists and experts implementing interventions around Community Health, Community Education, Environmental Health and Inclusive Businesses. Its members embedded themselves with the community in the devastated areas for several weeks and months to identify what institutional models were destroyed in the blast and how they can be rebuilt in an inclusive sustainable way. It mobilises the diaspora to provide its expertise and goodwill to advocate for the needs of the community. KB's main strategy aims at creating scalable models which – in theory – can be adopted by the government at some point, but the end result is not policy change or governmental reform.

---

[45]   See for example Timour Azhari, 'No More COVID Jabs in Parliament, Says Lebanon's Deputy Speaker After Scandal', in *Reuters*, 12 March 2021, https://reut.rs/3tdzOnv.

By working with constituencies and communities, KB is able to both confront the political class but also support state-building by undertaking four different models of engagement. The first is transforming a primary healthcare
centre in the devastated community of Karantina into a community healthcare
centre. Where Lebanon's health services are either private or used as a web of
clientelism, KB nurses and doctors volunteer to help a community serve its own
needs by training health agents and partnering with the staff at the Karantina
hospital. Rather than turning away people for not affording healthcare or for
the colour of their skin, KB's aspiration for a model of health is inclusive, free
and community-led. The second is transforming schools into communities of
active citizenship and solidarity in a time of crisis. KB partners with teachers,
principals and parents to understand the needs of students and develop solutions
collaboratively. This is an act of resistance to the mainstream state policy that
has depleted the education sector of its resources, defunded public schools and
segregated students based often on their nationality. The third is modelling a
process for inclusive business recovery. The small shops, restaurants and cafes
that defined the social fabric of the devastated area for so long were destroyed.
Rebuilding businesses is not about securing equipment to reopen but partnering
with business owners to rethink their long-term plans. This is also an act of resistance to a government that is completely absent from this sector and imposes
structural barriers. Finally, the environmental team at KB is implementing
models of community mobilising to address local waste management issues and
raise awareness on environmental hazards. The explosion left people paranoid
and afraid of the air they breathe and the water they drink. By teaming up with
activists and local committees, KB is able to present a model of engaged citizens
putting their environmental wellbeing first, as a strategy to resist what the state
has done for them.

Conclusion: A call to action

It has only been ten months since the port explosion and it may be too soon to
assess the real impact on the lives of people and communities, but there has been
a shift in Beirut from revolutionary politics to a community-driven resistance.
This has been sparked by several factors emanating not only from the stagnation
in national politics but also the international and regional context. The longer
reforms stall, the longer aid and foreign investment will have to wait. Meanwhile
the financial crisis, the pandemic and a city in ruins are all factors that appear
to have pushed activists to shift their strategies. This form of resistance is aimed
at the long term but can create an experience that the people of Lebanon have

so far been deprived of, an experience aimed not at 'all the politicians' but at 'all of the people' – leaving nobody behind because of their gender, race or class. Community mobilisation and solidarity is now a mode of everyday resistance in Beirut and it deserves support.

If the EU wants to play a positive role in Lebanon, it should not ask about the funds that were dispersed with little to show in the last thirty years. The Lebanese government has received funding for EU projects on state restructuring, e-government, environment and gender reform, with little or nothing to show. The EU has started and should continue partnering with local institutions in education, health, civil society and also businesses, on identifying their needs. The activists may have turned their attention to devastated streets but the demand for political reform and the end of the politics of exclusion have never been stronger, and the EU should also push for political reform that ensures the representation of women, new political parties and competent individuals who are able not only to support a community in disaster but draw a vision for future resistance based on equal rights and the participation of 'all' the people to challenge 'all' the politicians.

References

AFP, 'Lebanon Judge Removed from Beirut Blast Probe: Judicial Source', in *France 24*, 18 February 2021, https://www.france24.com/en/live-news/20210218-lebanon-judge-removed-from-beirut-blast-probe-judicial-source

Mayssa Awad and James André, 'Lebanon and Syria: Smuggling and Sanctions, the New Front Line' (podcast), in *France 24*, 16 April 2021, https://www.france24.com/en/tv-shows/reporters/20210416-lebanon-syria-smuggling-and-sanctions-the-new-front-line

Laure Ayoub, 'Foreign Workers Revolt Against the "Republic's Contractor" in Lebanon', in *Legal Agenda*, 21 April 2021, https://english.legal-agenda.com/?p=23972

Timour Azhari, 'No More COVID Jabs in Parliament, Says Lebanon's Deputy Speaker After Scandal', in *Reuters*, 12 March 2021, https://reut.rs/3tdzOnv

Edmund Blair, 'Explainer: Lebanon's Financial Meltdown and How it Happened', in *Reuters*, 17 September 2020, https://reut.rs/2H0aPkL

Melani Cammett, *Compassionate Communalism. Welfare and Sectarianism in Lebanon*, Ithaca/London, Cornell University Press, 2014

Sean Chabot and Stellan Vinthagen, 'Decolonizing Civil Resistance', in *Mobilization: An International Quarterly*, Vol. 20, No. 4 (December 2015), p. 517–532

Janine A. Clark and Bassel F. Salloukh, 'Elite Strategies, Civil Society, and Sectarian Identities in Postwar Lebanon', in *International Journal of Middle East Studies*, Vol. 45, No. 4 (November 2013), p. 731–749

Daniel Corstange, 'Clientelism in Competitive and Uncompetitive Elections', in *Comparative Political Studies*, Vol. 51, No. 1 (January 2018), p. 76–104

Daniel Corstange, 'Vote Trafficking in Lebanon', in *International Journal of Middle East Studies*, Vol. 44, No. 3 (August 2012), p. 483–505

Dima Dabbous, 'Legal Reform and Women's Rights in Lebanese Personal Status Laws', in *CMI Reports*, No. 3 (September 2017), https://www.cmi.no/publications/6341

Alain Daou et al., 'Breaking the Cycle: Issue 2: It Starts with Us', in *Khaddit Beirut* portal, last modified 7 December 2020, https://khadditbeirut.com/?p=810

Cristina Flesher Fominaya, 'Debunking Spontaneity: Spain's 15-M/Indignados as Autonomous Movement', in *Social Movement Studies*, Vol. 14, No. 2 (2015), p. 142–163

Carmen Geha, *Civil Society and Political Reform in Lebanon and Libya. Transition and Constraint*, London/New York, Routledge, 2016

Carmen Geha, 'The Myth of Women's Political Empowerment within Lebanon's Sectarian Power-Sharing System', in *Journal of Women, Politics & Policy*, Vol. 40, No. 4 (2019), p. 498–521

Carmen Geha, 'Our Personal Is Political and Revolutionary', in *Al-Raida Journal*, Vol. 44, No. 1 (2020), p. 23–28, http://alraidajournal.com/index.php/ALRJ/article/view/1818

Carmen Geha, 'Politics of a Garbage Crisis: Social Networks, Narratives, and Frames of Lebanon's 2015 Protests and Their Aftermath', in *Social Movement Studies*, Vol. 18, No. 1 (2019), p. 78–92

Carmen Geha, 'Resilience through Learning and Adaptation: Lebanon's Power-Sharing System and the Syrian Refugee Crisis', in *Middle East Law and Governance*, Vol. 11, No. 1 (May 2019), p. 65–90

Carmen Geha, 'Resistance not Resilience: A Proposal for Collective Action', in *An-Nahar*, 17 May 2021, https://tinyurl.com/yfftjxn7

Ohannes Geukjian, *Lebanon after the Syrian Withdrawal. External Intervention, Power-Sharing and Political Instability*, London/New York, Routledge, 2017

Henrik Hartmann, 'National Dialogues and Development', in *National Dialogue Handbook Conceptual Studies*, February 2017, https://berghof-foundation.org/library/national-dialogues-and-development

Waleed Hazbun, 'Assembling Security in a "Weak State:" The Contentious Politics of Plural Governance in Lebanon since 2005', in *Third World Quarterly*, Vol. 37, No. 6 (2016), p. 1053–1070

Sami Hermez, 'On Dignity and Clientelism: Lebanon in the Context of the 2011 Arab Revolutions', in *Studies in Ethnicity and Nationalism*, Vol. 11, No. 3 (December 2011), p. 527–537

Human Rights Watch, 'As If You're Inhaling Your Death'. *The Health Risks of Burning Waste in Lebanon*, November 2017, https://www.hrw.org/node/311168

Raymond Hinnebusch, 'Pax-Syriana? The Origins, Causes and Consequences of Syria's Role in Lebanon', in *Mediterranean Politics*, Vol. 3, No. 1 (Summer 1998), p. 137–160

International Monetary Fund (IMF), *Statement by the Managing Director at the International Conference in Support of the Lebanese People*, 2 December 2020, https://www.imf.org/en/News/Articles/2020/12/02/sp120220-statement-by-the-managing-director-international-conference-in-support-of-lebanese-people

Samir Khalaf, *Civil and Uncivil Violence in Lebanon. A History of the Internationalization of Communal Conflict*, New York, Columbia University Press, 2002

Lina Khatib, 'Gender, Citizenship and Political Agency in Lebanon', in *British Journal of Middle Eastern Studies*, Vol. 35, No. 3 (2008), p. 437–451

Paul W.T. Kingston, *Reproducing Sectarianism. Advocacy Networks and the Politics of Civil Society in Postwar Lebanon*, Albany, State University of New York Press, 2013

Lebanese Center for Policy Studies, 'Why Did the October 17 Revolution Witness a Regression in Numbers?', in *Setting the Agenda*, 31 October 2020, https://www.lcps-lebanon.org/agendaArticle.php?id=199

Roger Mac Ginty, 'Reconstructing Post-war Lebanon: A Challenge to the Liberal Peace? Analysis', in *Conflict, Security & Development*, Vol. 7, No. 3 (2007), p. 457–482

Rima Majed, 'Interview: Beirut Blast Exposed a Global System', in *rs21*, 30 August 2020, https://www.rs21.org.uk/2020/08/30/interview-beirut-blast-exposed-a-global-system

Joanne McEvoy and Brendan O'Leary, eds, *Power Sharing in Deeply Divided Places*, Philadelphia, University of Pennsylvania Press, 2013

Jamil Mouawad and Hannes Bauman, 'In Search of the Lebanese State', in *The Arab Studies Journal*, Vol. 25, No. 1 (Spring 2017), p. 60–65

Bassem Mroue, 'Minister, No Investor for Lebanon's Ailing Power Sector', in *AP News*, 16 July 2020, https://apnews.com/article/d8ca48aa2eddc1bd7075feabf d725a88

Julie Ray, 'Political, Economic Strife Takes Emotional Toll on Lebanese', in *Gallup News*, 19 November 2020, https://news.gallup.com/poll/325715/political-economic-strife-takes-emotional-toll-lebanese.aspx

Reuters, 'Lebanon's Leaders Warned in July about Explosives at Port, Say Documents', in *The National*, 10 August 2020, https://www.thenationalnews.com/world/mena/lebanon-s-leaders-warned-in-july-about-explosives-at-port-say-documents-1.1062000

Sam E. Rigby et al., 'Preliminary Yield Estimation of the 2020 Beirut Explosion Using Video Footage from Social Media', in *Shock Waves*, Vol. 30, No. 6 (September 2020), p. 671–675, https://doi.org/10.1007/s00193-020-00970-z

Stephan Rosiny, 'A Quarter Century of "Transitory Power-Sharing": Lebanon's Unfulfilled Ta'if Agreement of 1989 Revisited', in *Civil Wars*, Vol. 17, No. 4 (2015), p. 485–502

Majken Jul Sørensen, 'Constructive Resistance: Conceptualising and Mapping the Terrain', in *Journal of Resistance Studies*, Vol. 2, No. 1 (2016), p. 49–78, https://resistance-journal.org/wp-content/uploads/2021/04/Volume-2-Number-1.-Majken.pdf

Aurora Ianni

Chapter 5: Hirak's Trajectory and the 'New Algeria'

In February 2019, the so-called 'revolution of smiles' spread throughout Algeria. President Abdelaziz Bouteflika's announcement that he would seek a fifth term in office triggered an unprecedented popular mobilisation calling for the removal of the old political system. Although the country's recent history was marked by social and political 'unrests', Algeria was spared by the so-called first wave of Arab uprisings that rocked the Middle East and North African region in 2011.

Indeed, even though protests did occur in Algeria as well, they did not bring changes in the system of power. The popular demands for more freedoms and socio-economic opportunities (although they also included calls for social justice and democracy)[1] were soothed particularly through an expansion of social benefits. The government increased public spending and wages, granted loans for enterprises run by young entrepreneurs as well as for housing, all paid for by oil and gas exports' revenues. In addition, in 2012, in a speech that was considered historic, Bouteflika called on the youth to take charge of the country and asked the old guard to take a step back,[2] while announcing a series of reforms including a constitutional revision. The government also increased women's representation in parliament, setting a 30 per cent quota of seats for female deputies. While these openings were more cosmetic than substantial, both legislative and local elections confirmed the majority of votes and seats of the National Liberation Front (FLN) and the National Rally for Democracy (RND). Furthermore, public concerns about instability in neighbouring Libya and the threat of terrorism, together with the very much persistent legacy of destruction of the 1990s civil war, helped the regime keep control of the situation. Such 'Algerian exceptionalism' was not going to last, however.

---

[1] For a broader analysis see Andrea Dessì, 'Algeria at the Crossroads, between Continuity and Change', in *IAI Working Papers*, No. 11|28 (September 2011), https://www.iai.it/en/node/3379.

[2] Gian Paolo Calchi Novati and Caterina Roggero, *Storia dell'Algeria indipendente. Dalla guerra di liberazione a Bouteflika*, Milano, Bompiani, 2018, p. 398.

1. The revolution of smiles

The socio-economic situation of Algeria has been deteriorating since 2014, when hydrocarbon prices started to decline. As a result, in the following years, due to the fall and mismanagement oil revenues and to a lack of investment in diversification, the government has not been able to strengthen its welfare system. On the eve of the protest movement, the high rate of youth (aged 15–24) unemployment, which oscillated around 30 per cent in both 2018 and 2019, the state of public services (particularly education and health) and the level of corruption[3] were major factors of social anger.

The hallmark of Bouteflika's twenty-year rule (1999–2019) was a system of power marked by corruption and patronage towards business groups, ministers, officials and other authorities to secure his power and that of his entourage (main governmental political parties, economic elites, among the others). Massive clientelism typically deriving from rentier economies, the lack of government transparency and the low independence of the judiciary contributed to the high level of internal corruption. In 2019 Freedom House classified Algeria as 'not free' and the Corruption Perceptions Index ranked Algeria 106th out of 180 countries.[4] Bouteflika's seeking re-election – despite his debilitating stroke in 2013 and his sporadic appearances in public since then – was seen a manoeuvre to keep this system in place. However, in 2019 the deep economic crisis made it overly difficult for this rentier system to win over domestic unrest. Furthermore, the insistence on the 'provision of security,' a claim used by the political class to legitimate itself since the end of the civil war, seemed to have lost sway. Young generations do not have living memories of these events. In addition, support to the Hirak from popular figures from the time of the battle of Algiers[5] during Algeria's struggle for independence, delegitimised the claim to revolutionary legacy that former governments used to remain in power.[6]

---

[3] Michael Robbins, *The 2019 Algerian Protests*, Arab Barometer, August 2019, https://www.arabbarometer.org/wp-content/uploads/ABV_Algeria_Protests_Public-Opinion_Arab-Barometer_2019.pdf.

[4] Transparency International, *Corruption Perceptions Index 2019*, 2020, p. 3, https://www.transparency.org/en/publications/corruption-perceptions-index-2019.

[5] See as an example, the participation of Djamila Bouhired, hero of the battle of Algiers.

[6] For a broader anlysis see Yahia Zoubir, 'The Algerian Crisis: Origins and Prospects for a "Second Republic"', in *Al Jazeera Centre for Studies Reports*, 21 May 2019, https://studies.aljazeera.net/en/node/1620.

The Hirak started its marches with a broad social base, involving people from all walks of lives regardless of social, ethnic, religious and political backgrounds. Remarkably, the percentage of women's participation in the street demonstration was high – this does not come as a surprise considering the long tradition of women's activism in Algerian history. In March 2019, numerous Algerian feminists from the civil society organisations as well as students and intellectuals developed and shared a declaration underlining the need for full equality between citizens, regardless of gender, class, religion or beliefs for constructing a common future, while paving the way for their participation in the Hirak's weekly demonstrations with the set-up of the 'feminist square' (*Carré féministe*).[7]

Slogans such as '*No à le mandate de la honte*' (No to the term of shame) and '*Karama*' (Dignity) were campaigned during weekly marches against the fifth term of Bouteflika and for the removal of all the figures associated with him. Regime change was the main demand cementing the mobilisation of the Hirak, which however went further in asking for a real civilian-run state, the independence of the judiciary, the rule of law and freedom of the media, among other things. In addition, the presence of women also favoured an intra-Hirak debate in terms of gender equality demands.[8]

Core successful strategies of the Hirak were both its peaceful nature, to which the presence of women seems to have contributed,[9] and its use of humour. Memes and jokes directed to Bouteflika and his affiliates, comedically twisted public official speeches, as well as political caricatures were among the means used to express discontent towards those in power.[10] In addition, the leaderless nature of the Hirak favoured its capacity to gain massive participation. The choice of not linking protests to any ideology and focusing on regime change helped to bring together a great number of people.

---

[7] Saadia Gacem et al., 'Femmes algériennes pour un changement vers l'égalité', in *El Watan*, 21 March 2019, https://www.elwatan.com/?p=565017.

[8] Some activists preferred avoiding ideological divisions to keep the movement united around the central aim of regime change. Some others, especially feminists and members of progressive associations/parties, considered the 2019 uprising to be the right time for putting gender equality issues on the table. See Tin Hinane el Kadi, 'Women's Role in Algerian Pro-Democracy Movement', in Lorenzo Coslovi et al., 'Women in Transition: The Role of Women and the Arab Springs 2.0', in *CeSPI Research Reports*, December 2020, p. 35–42, https://www.cespi.it/en/node/1646.

[9] Ibid.

[10] Hiyem Cheurfa, 'The Laughter of Dignity: Comedy and Dissent in the Algerian Popular Protests', in *Jadaliyya*, 26 March 2019, https://www.jadaliyya.com/Details/38495.

Unlike what happened in 2010–2011, protests were now more linked to political demands 'over the social and economic ones previously made'.[11] The main
target of the Hirak was directly the system of power. In addition, it seems that the
strength of this movement was to have learnt from the mistakes that occurred in
neighbouring countries after the 2011/12 uprisings: together with the removal
of the ruling elite, the Hirak asked for the end of military interference in politics. Furthermore, some analysts noted that most Islamists who took part in
the protests did so in a national function, rather than as Islamists,[12] united in
the demands for regime change. The regime has tried to foment identity-based
fractures within the movement, for instance by arresting demonstrators holding
the Amazigh flag under charges of undermining national unity,[13] but the Hirak
remained united. The inclusiveness of this uprising thus made those in power
unable to apply a *divide et impera* approach to weaken or co-opt some of its
various segments. The decentralised organisation of marches through Facebook
pages spreading messages throughout Algeria and avoiding government-con-
trolled media channels, made the movement hard to be discredited or controlled,
at least until the covid-19 pandemic spread throughout the country.

Rallies were continuously held until covid-19 started to become a challenge
for street demonstrations. The decision to stop rallies in March 2020 was due,
apart for governmental bans, to a request coming from different actors taking
part in the protests, to avoid the spread of the virus. During the pandemic, the
Hirak switched to online activism, through Facebook groups and web platforms.
This virtual version was also supported by many representatives of the Algerian
diaspora. Among them were Algerian columnists from all over the world who
work with the *Radio Corona Internationale* station, founded to deal with the
evolution of protests in the face of the covid-19.[14] Furthermore, the movement

[11]   Inès Osman, 'Algeria: The Arab Spring's Late Bloomer?', in *Tahrir Institute for Middle
       East Policy Analysis*, 9 February 2021, https://timep.org/commentary/analysis/alge
       ria-the-arab-springs-late-bloomer.
[12]   Aili Mari Tripp, 'Beyond Islamist Extremism: Women and the Algerian Uprisings
       of 2019', in *CMI Briefs*, No. 2019:09 (October 2019), https://www.cmi.no/publicati
       ons/6983.
[13]   Mahpari Sotoudeh, 'Successes and Shortcomings: How Algeria's Hirak Can Inform
       Lebanon's Protest Movement', in *Middle East Institute Articles*, 3 June 2020, https://
       www.mei.edu/node/81308.
[14]   Sara Zanotta, 'Hirak Behind Closed Doors. The Evolution of Algerian Protest
       Movement while Facing Coronavirus', in *NAD*, 24 April 2020, http://nad.unimi.it/
       ?p=3597.

reinvented itself also in the role of 'service provider' during the pandemic, mobilising supplies for hospitals trying to cope with the shortcomings of the Algerian health infrastructures. In addition, it was involved in raising awareness campaigns on the risks of covid-19 and promoting phone-based medical consultations with doctors to reduce hospital visits.[15]

Meanwhile, (online) initiatives such as Nida 22 were launched to both keep the mobilisation alive and open an intra-Hirak debate for coordinating different activists of the movement. The collective advocated for the full sovereignty of the people within the framework of a civil, democratic and civilian system, the respect for human and citizens' rights, individual and collective freedoms, equality between citizens, a state governed by the rule of law, independence of the judiciary, and the separation and balance between powers, among other claims.[16]

2. Domestic political dynamics during the Hirak uprisings

The military apparatus has played a fundamental role in arbitrating internal political dynamics and favouring presidential appointments since Algeria's independence. 2019 was no exception. With social tensions emerging, the generals put political representatives aside to temporarily take control, in the attempt to safeguard their economic and political privileges effectively managing the interim phase leading to the presidential elections.

Indeed, in March 2019, the chief of staff of Algeria's armed forces, Ahmed Gaïd Salah, demanded the immediate resignation of Bouteflika referring to article 102 of the constitution, which allows for 'the president's removal on grounds of ill health'.[17] The presidential removal in April was arguably a way for the military to maintain power by meeting people's demands. But this move did not translate into a halt of the Hirak. The resignation of President Bouteflika was considered just a half victory by the people, who kept on asking for regime change. With slogans such as 'Dawla madaniyya mashi askariyya' (civil and not military state), demonstrators strived for the establishment of a truly democratic state run by

---

[15]   Elizia Wolkmann, 'Algeria's Protesters Say Covid-19 Will Not Kill Movement, Just Transform It', in Al-Monitor, 3 April 2020, https://www.al-monitor.com/node/25371.

[16]   Abdelghani Aichoun, '"Nida 22", une initiative pour une concertation autonome intra-hirak', in El Watan, 22 October 2020, https://www.elwatan.com/?p=681461.

[17]   James McDougall, 'How Algeria's Army Sacrificed a President to Keep Power', in BBC News, 6 April 2019, https://www.bbc.com/news/world-africa-47821980.

civilians rather than a feckless civilian-led government that is managed by the military.

The response to social turmoil of the ruling elite in the past two years has relied on four pillars: the holding of presidential elections, the revision of the constitution, early legislative elections and the repression of opposition activists.

Due the massive boycott by the Hirak, elections were postponed from April to July but due to the lack of viable candidates they were held only in December. Although protesters were asking to postpone the vote until the military and the old guard had quit politics,[18] the five candidates who ran for the presidency in December either supported Bouteflika or had participated in his government. These elections were thus seen by both the Hirak and many political opposition forces as a fraudulent way to restore the old power.

This raises the question as to why the Hirak, which had the support (to varying degrees) of many opposition parties, did not transform into a politically more structured organisation. One reason is the nature of the movement. The inclusiveness of the Hirak has been an asset in terms of mass mobilisation, but has also brought challenges in terms of representation. In addition, the Hirak uprising represented for many protesters the first time they became interested and invested in political issues, as mistrust towards politics was widespread during the Bouteflika era. Such mistrust was extended to politics at large, which may explain why the transition from movement to party for the Hirak was anything but natural. Nor was the incorporation of the Hirak into the existing opposition a goal the movement was really eager for.

Many opposition figures were systematically co-opted by the regime and their interests seemed more linked to accessing benefits deriving from parliamentary participation (high salaries, parliamentary seats, etc.) than the struggle for democracy.[19] Their participation in elections – except for some occasional boycotts – in the past two decades to some extent validated the process they were trying to oppose. The fact that the February 2019 protests were not organised by

---

[18]   Joane Serrieh, 'Algeria Holds Presidential Election as Thousands Demonstrate against Vote', in *Al Arabiya*, 12 December 2019, https://ara.tv/y5hyg.

[19]   Dalia Ghanem, 'Limiting Change through Change: The Key to the Algerian Regime's Longevity', in *Carnegie Reports*, April 2018, https://carnegieendowment.org/publicati ons/76237.

any of the political entities in Algeria in some way attests to 'the rift between the people and the political elite'.[20]

When Abdelmadjid Tebboune, former prime minister in the Bouteflika era, won the elections with the lowest turnout ever (around 40 per cent), it was clear that he lacked popular legitimacy. Nevertheless, he soon declared his readiness to 'extend a hand to the Hirak' for the making of a 'New Algeria' and promised an amended constitution.[21] The promise of both political reforms and constitutional amendments usually follows internal crises in Algeria and shows similarities with the agenda that Bouteflika implemented to cope with the 2010/11 protests. This time, however, the movement did not recognise the new president, and relations further worsened when the pandemic spread throughout the country forcing the protests to halt physically. Tebboune's open hand towards the Hirak was thus soon replaced by a more robust counter reaction.

Initially, the authorities presented restrictions to public gatherings as a temporary measure, but they soon opened the way to repression, especially of activists. According to Human Rights Watch, courts sentenced and jailed leading Hirak figures between March and April 2020 on charges of harming national unity, excluding them from the pardon that freed around 5,000 inmates to reduce overcrowding of prisons during the pandemic.[22] In addition, in April 2020 a bill was approved to criminalise the breaking of lockdown measures and the spreading of 'fake news' harming national unity.[23] As a result, privately owned news and radio websites were blocked.

The constitutional revision was announced while the repression was going on. Presented as a flagship initiative by Tebboune's government to meet the Hirak's demands, people were called to vote on 1 November 2020. The date was symbolic as it was the anniversary of the start of Algerian war of independence against France. Again, due to a boycott championed by the Hirak, participation was at a

---

[20]   Ismail Yaylaci and Muhammad Amasha, *Islamist Movements and Parties in the Algerian Uprising*, Istanbul, Al-Sharq Strategic Research, 10 July 2020, p. 18, https://research.sharqforum.org/?p=16188.

[21]   'Algérie. Le nouveau président Tebboune "tend la main" au mouvement de contestation', in *Ouest France*, 13 December 2019, https://www.ouest-france.fr/monde/algerie/algerie-le-nouveau-president-tebboune-tend-la-main-au-mouvement-de-contestation-6653266.

[22]   Eric Goldstein, 'During Pandemic, Algeria Tightens Vise on Protest Movement', in *HRW Dispatches*, 19 April 2020, https://www.hrw.org/node/341495.

[23]   Committee to Protect Journalists, *Algeria Blocks 3 News Websites and Criminalizes False News*, 22 April 2020, https://cpj.org/?p=37342.

record low (around 24 per cent), a proof the Hirak had not lost its mobilisation strength.

The government presented the new provisions as a 'radical change in the system of governance' aimed at preventing corruption, reinforcing both transparency in the management of public funds and separation of powers, and giving social justice and freedom of the press a solid legal basis.[24] Yet, these changes did not go so far. For instance, while the president can stay in office for two terms maximum, he retains considerable influence over the judiciary.[25] In addition, widespread repression against activists confirms that the guarantees around the freedom of the press remain on paper only. Interestingly, however, as had already happened in 2012 following internal turmoil, the Algerian government opened up to women's rights. The November 2020 constitution contains provisions to improve women's protection as well as women's political participation. Experts note, however, that these steps are more smokescreen than anything else considering that the constitutional reform was approved in a repressive context and that the regressive Family Code – which reduces women's social status to the one of minors – is still in force.[26]

As for the commitment to transparency, the fact that the health status of Tebboune, who contracted covid-19 at the end of October 2020, was not made public brought back memories of the concealment of Bouteflika's illness.[27] After two months of treatment in Germany, President Tebboune announced his recovery on Twitter and ordered the preparation of a new election law 'to begin the post constitution phase'.[28] At the end of February 2021, Tebboune called for the dissolution of the parliament, early legislative elections and a government reshuffle while announcing a pardon for dozens of jailed Hirak activists.[29] These provisions, however, seemed just a tool to undermine renewed Hirak street protests. In the same period an attempt was also made to target the Algerian diaspora, which has played an important role in maintaining the 'flame of the

---

[24] 'Algerian Parliament Adopts Draft of Constitutional Reforms', in *Al Jazeera*, 10 September 2020, https://aje.io/txpdn.

[25] Sofian Philip Naceur, 'Call for Genuine Democracy', in *D+C*, December 2020, p. 16–17, https://www.dandc.eu/en/node/4516.

[26] Tin Hinane el Kadi, 'Women's Role in Algerian Pro-Democracy Movement', cit.

[27] Dalia Ghanem, '"New Algeria" Same as the Old Algeria', cit.

[28] Abd al-Razzaq bin Abdullah, 'Algeria: President Announces Recovery, New Election Law', in *Anadolu Agency*, 13 December 2020, http://v.aa.com.tr/2075649.

[29] 'Algeria's President Calls for Dissolution of Parliament, Elections', in *Arab News*, 18 February 2021, https://arab.news/467np.

Hirak'[30] particularly during the pandemic. A draft law was announced at the beginning of March 2021 that would have revoked the citizenship of Algerians if found perpetrating, outside the national territory, acts against state interests and national security.[31] The draft law was then withdrawn, due to widespread criticism from civil society organisations.[32] Ahead of the legislative elections, crackdown measures on the Hirak continued and validated concerns about the untrustworthiness of the government. The decision taken by the authorities in May to obtain prior authorisation for demonstrations[33] as well as the mounting repression that followed confirm that the government has undertaken more efforts to undermine the movement and its marches than to meet its demands.

Following the largely successful boycott of both the elections and the constitutional referendum, the 'New Algeria' promised by the government is hardly in line with the Hirak's requests and, most importantly, does not break with the past. The constitutional amendments as well as the early legislative elections seem to be perceived by the movement as 'adjustments' for maintaining the status quo.

A predominant question about whether this impasse may be overcome relates to the actions the Hirak will undertake to make its requests heard. Over the last months there has been a kind of divide between those who consider negotiations with authorities without preconditions and 'within the pre-existing institutional framework'[34] as the expected solution to the current stalemate, and those who think that the only way to establish the rule of law is 'a consensual yet radical institutional makeover'. Another interesting issue regards the position of the Islamists within the Hirak. Some actors call for a depoliticised approach to facilitate dialogue among the different souls of the movement and avoid fragmentation.[35] Others are worried about the endorsement of the protests by Rachad, an exile group of Islamist militants,[36] fearing a potential Islamist takeover. But

---

[30]   'In France the Algerian Diaspora Mantains "the Hirak Flame" ', in *The Maghreb Times*, 24 October 2020, https://themaghrebtimes.com/?p=20743.

[31]   'Draft Law on Forfeiture of Citizenship Presented', in *Algeria Press Service*, 4 March 2021, https://www.aps.dz/en/algeria/38333.

[32]   Layne Emery, 'Algeria's Multiprolonged Crackdown on the Hirak', in *Tahrir Institute for Middle East Policy Explainers*, 17 August 2021, https://timep.org/explainers/algerias-multipronged-crackdown-on-the-hirak.

[33]   'Algeria to Ban Unauthorised Protests', in *Al Jazeera*, 9 May 2021, https://aje.io/xm64j.

[34]   Thomas Serres, 'Is Algeria's Hirak Dead?', in *Al Jazeera*, 22 February 2021, https://aje.io/hab5h.

[35]   Ibid.

[36]   Rachad is charged by the Algerian government with gathering former militants from the Islamic Salvation Front (FIS) to infiltrate the Hirak and to harm national unity.

this appears more like a 'threat' fuelled by those in power[37] rather than a real risk in Algeria today. This is due both to the fact that Rachad 'has no monopoly on Islamic discourse in Algeria'[38] and that Islamists, in general terms, are far from being the unanimous emblem of political opposition. During the last twenty years, although strongly present culturally and socially, at least moderate Islamists have been politically co-opted by the government, becoming in some cases part of it, even if relegated to a marginal role. This has caused these parties to lose mass public support and to be considered as part of the corrupt system.[39]

To conclude, in an echo of earlier events the government has tried to present itself in a renewed version open to elections and reforms, including constitutional amendments and improvements in women's rights protection. However, the Hirak's calls for boycotting the various election rounds suggest the movement cannot be co-opted with ambivalent openings made 'from the top', while its activists remain major targets of arrests and repression.

3. Continuity for stability

While the military has engaged in unfounded charges of foreign-backed support for the movement, the predominant tendency of the Hirak has been, in fact, that of rejecting rather than embracing contributions from abroad.

Indeed, foreign powers seem to look favourably to the Tebboune government. The intensification of the president's diplomatic activity towards his foreign partners suggests Algerian willingness to demonstrate his reliability as well as the international partners' apparent preference for maintaining (or improving) ties with the country's existing leadership. While showing solidarity with the Hirak and its demands for democracy, economic and security interests linked to Algeria's stability prevail in foreign actors' calculations.

See 'Algeria Issues "Terrorism" Warrants for Islamist Activists', in *The Arab Weekly*, 22 March 2021, https://thearabweekly.com/node/52044.

[37] In May 2021 both Rachad and the Movement for the Authonomy of Kabile (MAK) were labelled as terrorist organisations by the Algerian authorities. See 'Algeria Labels Opposition Movements As Terrorist Groups', in *Africa News*, 20 May 2021, https://www.africanews.com/2021/05/19/algeria-labells-opposition-movements-as-terrorist-groups.

[38] Moussa Acherchour, 'Algeria's Hirak: Between Concerns of Division and Betting on Unity', in *Bawader*, 19 August 2021, https://www.arab-reform.net/?p=19508.

[39] For a broader analysis see Dalia Ghanem, 'The Shifting Foundations of Political Islam in Algeria', in *Carnegie Papers*, April 2019, https://carnegieendowment.org/publications/79047.

The position of the European Union is emblematic in this sense. In a November 2019 resolution, the European Parliament called for a solution to the crisis in Algeria 'based on a peaceful and inclusive political process', while condemning 'the arbitrary and unlawful arrests, detainment and intimidation of and attacks on journalists, trade unionists, lawyers, students, human rights defenders and civil society and all peaceful protesters taking part in the peaceful Hirak demonstrations'.[40] Again, in November 2020 the European Parliament condemned the deteriorating situation of human rights in the country expressing its 'full solidarity' with the Hirak's demands and calling on the Algerian government to release the detainees sentenced for 'exercising their right to freedom of expression'.[41] However, the EU's general policy position on Algeria seems to be that of subordinating democratic values to economic and security interests.

The EU is Algeria's biggest trading partner, with total bilateral trade in goods amounting to 24.9 billion euro in 2020.[42] Last December, the EU-Algeria Association Council pledged 75 million euros to Algeria to reduce the economic impact of the pandemic crisis.[43] On the same occasion, members of the Association Council discussed 'how to strengthen stability in the region and reviewed important issues in their relations such as governance and human rights, economic cooperation and trade, the environment, energy and migration'. The EU also supports the implementation of the peace agreement in Mali signed in Algiers in 2015 following an Algerian-led mediation effort, and is aligned with Algerian diplomatic support for a UN-brokered national reconciliation process in Libya. Indeed, in January 2020 Tebboune took part in the Berlin Conference over the future of Libya and after a few days gathered the foreign ministers of Chad, Egypt, Mali, Niger, Sudan and Tunisia in Algiers to discuss a

---

[40] European Parliament, *Resolution on the Situation of Freedoms in Algeria* (P9_ TA(2019)0072), 28 November 2019, https://www.europarl.europa.eu/doceo/docum ent/TA-9-2019-0072_EN.html.

[41] European Parliament, *Resolution on the Deteriorating Situation of Human Rights in Algeria, in Particular the Case of Journalist Khaled Drareni* (P9_TA(2020)0329), 26 November 2020, https://www.europarl.europa.eu/doceo/document/TA-9-2020-0329_EN.html.

[42] European Commission, *European Union, Trade in Goods with Algeria*, 2 June 2021, https://webgate.ec.europa.eu/isdb_results/factsheets/country/details_algeria_en.pdf.

[43] Council of the European Union, *Press Release on the Occasion of the Video Conference of the Members of the EU-Algeria Association Council*, 7 December 2020, https://eur opa.eu/!Yk37mH.

settlement of the crisis.[44] A series of high-level meetings with key Libyan leaders indicated Algeria's support for a UN-backed solution that would involve all warring camps. After the approval of the new Libyan government in March 2021, Tebboune expressed full support to the transition process.[45]

The positive role of Algeria for regional stability is also appreciated not just by the EU but by the United States too. In spite of US decreasing attention to North Africa, Washington's economic and security relations with the region have not diminished. Algeria has for years played an important, even critical role in counter-terrorism, especially since the 9/11 terrorist attacks. In addition, the US is one of the top trading partners of Algeria and conversely Algeria is one of the top US trading partners in the MENA region, with the hydrocarbon sector being the main target of US direct investment.[46] The visit of the head of Africom, the Africa Command of the US Armed Forces, to Algeria in September 2020[47] can be seen as a commitment to strengthening relations, especially in the fight against radical, armed Islamist groups and the pursuit of stability in Libya and the Sahel, the latter also recalled by the new US Secretary of State.[48]

France, the European country with which Algeria has the deepest, but also the most complex, relationship due to legacy of French colonial rule, has also opted to support Tebboune's government. President Emmanuel Macron expressed the hope for a successful political transition after the November 2020 constitutional referendum,[49] a position that has remained unchanged after Algeria's complaints about the so-called Stora report, a study on France's rule in Algeria

[44] 'Libya's Neighbours Meet in Algiers in Bid to Diffuse Crisis" in *France 24*, 23 January 2020, https://www.france24.com/en/20200123-libya-s-neighbours-meet-in-algiers-in-bid-to-diffuse-crisis.

[45] Omar Al-Othmani, 'Arab States Welcome Approval of the New Libyan Government', in *Anadolu Agency*, 11 March 2021, http://v.aa.com.tr/2171937.

[46] US Department of State, *U.S. Relations with Algeria*, 20 January 2021, https://www.state.gov/u-s-relations-with-algeria.

[47] 'Le Soudan et l'Algérie, nouveaux centres d'intérêt de la diplomatie américaine en Afrique', in *Le Monde*, 24 September 2020, https://www.lemonde.fr/afrique/article/2020/09/24/le-soudan-et-l-algerie-nouveaux-centres-d-interet-de-la-diplomatie-americaine-en-afrique_6053411_3212.html.

[48] 'US Secretary of State: Washingthon and Algeria Hope to See Stability in Libya', in *The Libya Observer*, 2 May 2021, https://www.libyaobserver.ly/node/18440.

[49] 'Macron Backs Algeria's Tebboune for a Successful Political Transition', in *Asharq Al-Awsat*, 21 November 2020, https://english.aawsat.com/node/2637976.

commissioned by Macron and released at the beginning of 2021.[50] Macron has accepted the report's recommendation to establish a 'reconciliation and truth commission' but refrained from apologising for France's colonial past, whereas Tebboune has said the Algerian government expects nothing short of a 'total recognition of all crimes' committed by France.

Months before, at the end of May 2020, the airing by French public television of two documentaries on the Hirak protests resulted in a kind of diplomatic crisis, as Algeria recalled its ambassador to France for consultation, arguing that documentaries were attacks on the Algerian people and institutions.[51] The crisis was however resolved a week later thanks to a call between the two presidents, in which they agreed to coordinate efforts in restoring security and stability in the region.[52]

Macron's stance after the November referendum has led some members of the Hirak to come out with harsh statements against France. As an example, Karim Tabbou, a prominent Hirak figure, has contended that Macron's backing of his Algerian counterpart was 'in defiance of all the values of justice, freedom and democracy' France claims to represent and support.[53]

Hence, the attitude of foreign powers towards Algeria seems to be that of preferring continuity to avoid instability. This is due to many strategic interests, including the need to manage migration, fend off terrorist threats and preserve economic exchanges. In recent years, the Mediterranean has become a stage for shifting geopolitical balances, with Russia, Turkey, the Arab Gulf states and even China all taking steps to penetrate the area. China's presence in Algeria, in particular, has been gradually growing thanks to investments, such as the port of El-Hamdania in the framework of the Belt and Road Initiative. Furthermore, during the covid-19 crisis China has been carrying out soft power measures to further expand its influence through vaccine diplomacy and offers of health

---

[50] In 2020, French President Macron tasked historian Benjiamin Stora to write a report aimed at reconciliating memories between France and Algeria in an attempt to help the two countries coming to terms with the legacy of French colonisation in Algeria and of the war that ended it.

[51] 'Algeria Recalls France Envoy after Protest Films, Rejects Journalist's Bail Plea', in *Arab News*, 27 May 2020, https://arab.news/guh3a.

[52] 'France, Algeria Pledge to Relaunch Relations after Rift over Hirak Protest Movement', in *The New Arab*, 3 June 2020, https://english.alaraby.co.uk/node/133425.

[53] Madjid Makedhi, 'Karim Tabbou répond au président français Emmanuel Macron: "Votre soutien au pouvoir algérien est une insupportable moquerie"', in *El Watan*, 25 November 2020, https://www.elwatan.com/?p=687028.

and infrastructure assistance, including the construction of a covid hospital in Algeria.[54]

Conclusion

The Hirak mobilisation represented an unprecedent event in Algeria's recent history. Neither the fear of violent spillovers from Libya nor the legacy of the bloody civil war have smothered the spread of this mobilisation. Inclusiveness, unity, peacefulness and the absence of an established leadership have been the key features of this mass popular movement that demanded regime change in February 2019. As usually happens to rentier states facing economic crises, the inability to buy social peace has increased the saliency of paying (façade) attention to popular demands to avoid undermining internal stability.

The regime's roadmap out of the political impasse – made up of presidential elections, constitutional amendments and early legislative elections – has resulted in a failed attempt to restore the legitimacy of a political system discredited in the eyes of society.[55] 'Adjustments' that do not fulfil the Hirak's demands for meaningful political change and that are made in parallel with a repressive campaign targeting the movement's activists will make it harder for those in power to gain popular recognition. This is evident considering both the massive boycott of the various election rounds and the restored street modality of the protests in February 2021. Since then, the authorities have escalated their crackdown on the Hirak through many actions including the requirement of prior authorisation for marches, the deployment of police in the streets and the arrest of civil society activists, reporters, students and members of political parties.[56]

While external players have shown some solidarity towards the Hirak (most notably the European Parliament), foreign powers are likely to keep supporting the Algerian government for both economic and security reasons. Thus, the outcome of the game is in the hands of internal actors. To date, the prospect for a regime change in Algeria remains distant. Amidst repression and the challenges related to the pandemic, it is to be seen what strategies the Hirak will put forward

---

54 'Coronavirus, China to Build Hospital in Algeria', in *The North African Post*, 31 March 2020, https://northafricapost.com/?p=39508.

55 Saïd Djaafer, 'Un Hirak résilient, un régime autiste: pourquoi il faut urgemment changer de paradigme', in 24H Algerie, 23 February 2021, https://www.24hdz.com/?p=16966.

56 See Ilhem Rachidi, 'Repression in Algeria Could It End the Hirak Movement?', in *Sada*, 29 July 2021, https://carnegieendowment.org/sada/85060.

to carry its activism on. Indeed, the road towards a real transition to democracy and the establishment of the rule of law also runs through the Hirak, if the movement ever manages to build an organisational structure and put forward a detailed programme to implement its requests without falling into the trap of divisions.

References

Moussa Acherchour, 'Algeria's Hirak: Between Concerns of Division and Betting on Unity', in *Bawader*, 19 August 2021, https://www.arab-reform.net/?p=19508

Abdelghani Aichoun, ' "Nida 22", une initiative pour une concertation autonome intra-hirak', in *El Watan*, 22 October 2020, https://www.elwatan.com/?p=681461

Omar Al-Othmani, 'Arab States Welcome Approval of the New Libyan Government', in *Anadolu Agency*, 11 March 2021, http://v.aa.com.tr/2171937

Abd al-Razzaq bin Abdullah, 'Algeria: President Announces Recovery, New Election Law', in *Anadolu Agency*, 13 December 2020, http://v.aa.com.tr/2075649

Gian Paolo Calchi Novati and Caterina Roggero, *Storia dell'Algeria indipendente. Dalla guerra di liberazione a Bouteflika*, Milano, Bompiani, 2018

Hiyem Cheurfa, 'The Laughter of Dignity: Comedy and Dissent in the Algerian Popular Protests', in *Jadaliyya*, 26 March 2019, https://www.jadaliyya.com/Details/38495

Committee to Protect Journalists, *Algeria Blocks 3 News Websites and Criminalizes False News*, 22 April 2020, https://cpj.org/?p=37342

Council of the European Union, *Press Release on the Occasion of the Video Conference of the Members of the EU-Algeria Association Council*, 7 December 2020, https://europa.eu/!Yk37mH

Andrea Dessì, 'Algeria at the Crossroads, between Continuity and Change', in *IAI Working Papers*, No. 11|28 (September 2011), https://www.iai.it/en/node/3379

Saïd Djaafer, 'Un Hirak résilient, un régime autiste: pourquoi il faut urgemment changer de paradigme', in *24H Algerie*, 23 February 2021, https://www.24hdz.com/?p=16966

Tin Hinane el Kadi, 'Women's Role in Algerian Pro-Democracy Movement', in Lorenzo Coslovi et al., 'Women in Transition: The Role of Women and the Arab Springs 2.0', in *CeSPI Research Reports*, December 2020, p. 35–42, https://www.cespi.it/en/node/1646

European Commission, *European Union, Trade in Goods with Algeria*, 2 June 2021, https://webgate.ec.europa.eu/isdb_results/factsheets/country/details_algeria_en.pdf

European Parliament, *Resolution on the Deteriorating Situation of Human Rights in Algeria, in Particular the Case of Journalist Khaled Drareni* (P9_TA(2020)0329), 26 November 2020, https://www.europarl.europa.eu/doceo/document/TA-9-2020-0329_EN.html

European Parliament, *Resolution on the Situation of Freedoms in Algeria* (P9_TA(2019)0072), 28 November 2019, https://www.europarl.europa.eu/doceo/document/TA-9-2019-0072_EN.html

Saadia Gacem et al. 'Femmes algériennes pour un changement vers l'égalité', in *El Watan*, 21 March 2019, https://www.elwatan.com/?p=565017

Dalia Ghanem, 'Limiting Change through Change: The Key to the Algerian Regime's Longevity', in *Carnegie Reports*, April 2018, https://carnegieendowment.org/publications/76237

Dalia Ghanem, ' "New Algeria" Same as the Old Algeria', in *Diwan*, 6 November 2020, https://carnegie-mec.org/diwan/83154

Dalia Ghanem, 'The Shifting Foundations of Political Islam in Algeria', in *Carnegie Papers*, April 2019, https://carnegieendowment.org/publications/79047

Eric Goldstein, 'During Pandemic, Algeria Tightens Vise on Protest Movement', in *HRW Dispatches*, 19 April 2020, https://www.hrw.org/node/341495

Madjid Makedhi, 'Karim Tabbou répond au président français Emmanuel Macron: "Votre soutien au pouvoir algérien est une insupportable moquerie" ', in *El Watan*, 25 November 2020, https://www.elwatan.com/?p=687028

James McDougall, 'How Algeria's Army Sacrificed a President to Keep Power', in *BBC News*, 6 April 2019, https://www.bbc.com/news/world-africa-47821980

Sofian Philip Naceur, 'Call for Genuine Democracy', in *D+C*, December 2020, p. 16–17, https://www.dandc.eu/en/node/4516

Inès Osman, 'Algeria: The Arab Spring's Late Bloomer?', in *Tahrir Institute for Middle East Policy Analysis*, 9 February 2021, https://timep.org/commentary/analysis/algeria-the-arab-springs-late-bloomer

Ilhem Rachidi, 'Repression in Algeria Could It End the Hirak Movement?', in *Sada*, 29 July 2021, https://carnegieendowment.org/sada/85060

Michael Robbins, *The 2019 Algerian Protests*, Arab Barometer, August 2019, https://www.arabbarometer.org/wp-content/uploads/ABV_Algeria_Protests_Public-Opinion_Arab-Barometer_2019.pdf

Thomas Serres, 'Is Algeria's Hirak Dead?', in *Al Jazeera*, 22 February 2021, https://aje.io/hab5h

Joane Serrieh, 'Algeria Holds Presidential Election as Thousands Demonstrate against Vote', in *Al Arabiya*, 12 December 2019, https://ara.tv/y5hyg

Mahpari Sotoudeh, 'Successes and Shortcomings: How Algeria's Hirak Can Inform Lebanon's Protest Movement', in *Middle East Institute Articles*, 3 June 2020, https://www.mei.edu/node/81308

Transparency International, *Corruption Perceptions Index 2019*, 2020, https://www.transparency.org/en/publications/corruption-perceptions-index-2019

Aili Mari Tripp, 'Beyond Islamist Extremism: Women and the Algerian Uprisings of 2019', in *CMI Briefs*, No. 2019:09 (October 2019), https://www.cmi.no/publications/6983

Elizia Wolkmann, 'Algeria's Protesters Say Covid-19 Will Not Kill Movement, Just Transform It', in *Al-Monitor*, 3 April 2020, https://www.al-monitor.com/node/25371

Ismail Yaylaci and Muhammad Amasha, *Islamist Movements and Parties in the Algerian Uprising*, Istanbul, Al-Sharq Strategic Research, 10 July 2020, https://research.sharqforum.org/?p=16188

Sara Zanotta, 'Hirak Behind Closed Doors. The Evolution of Algerian Protest Movement while Facing Coronavirus', in *NAD*, 24 April 2020, http://nad.unimi.it/?p=3597

Yahia Zoubir, 'The Algerian Crisis: Origins and Prospects for a "Second Republic"', in *Al Jazeera Centre for Studies Reports*, 21 May 2019, https://studies.aljazeera.net/en/node/1620

Theodore Murphy

Chapter 6: Sudan's Transition in the Balance

The success of the 2018–19 Sudanese revolution hinged on a decentralised pro-test movement structure that achieved unprecedented mass mobilisation while evading state suppression. This strategy eschewed organisation into hierarchical political party structures even after the regime was toppled. However, the second phase of the revolution, which required the new civilian component at the head of the Transitional Government to deliver on reforms, necessitated coherently organised political power.

The absence of such capacity handicapped the civilian component, both in terms of its inability to represent the protest movement that had ushered it into power and in the civilians' competitive relationship with the military component of the Transitional Government. While the protest movement engineered the ouster of President Omar al-Bashir, the security apparatus remained, comprising the Sudanese Armed Forces (SAF), the para-military Rapid Support Forces (RSF) and the National Intelligence and Security Service (NISS). The schism between the SAF and the RSF was a key defining feature of the Sudanese post-2019 trajectory. The protest movement directed its anger at the President not the security apparatus as such. So after the President's ouster, the security apparatus remained, portraying itself as the servant of the people (and the peoples' will in the form of the protest movement), and entered into a tricky power-sharing arrangement with the civilian component.

Champions of each component – military and civilian – formed interna-tionally. Sudan's more autocratic partners supported the military component while the Western democracies embraced the civilians. Since a basis of common interest was never established, the transition period, which was envisaged as car-rying out key reforms and making peace with Sudan's armed opposition groups, was infused with tension. Objectives that ought to have been of national interest transformed into political opportunities to advance the strength of one compo-nent or the other. For example, negotiations with the armed groups were viewed by some within the military component as a chance to improve their status as peacemakers and create military strategic depth by incorporating the armed opposition groups into their extended camp.

While Europe and the European Union identified the change in Sudan as a historic opportunity to advance a liberal and more stable Sudan, two areas of policy intervention were lacking: engagement to create a coherent political power out of the protest movement that could align behind the civilian component; and successfully convincing the autocratic governments behind the military component – Egypt and the United Arab Emirates – to back the civilian component (or at least a modus vivendi).

1. The outbreak of the Sudanese revolution

The Sudanese protest movement emerged in December 2018, triggered by President Bashir's decision to cut subsidies to key economic staples: bread and fuel. The spark was struck when, on 19 December 2018, an office of the ruling National Congress Party was set afire in a small city nestled in the traditional support base of President Bashir's regime of Atbara.[1] The protests quickly spread to 28 cities before honing in on the capital Khartoum where an Egyptian-Maidan moment coalesced.

Unlike earlier protests in 2013, these linked the declining economic situation to a political demand: Bashir stepping down. Although the subsidy cuts represented the proximate cause, Sudan had experienced deep-rooted economic and political problems for years. High military spending – consuming up to 70 per cent of the national budget –, loss of revenue following the secession of oil-rich South Sudan in 2011, international sanctions, as well as corruption and nepotism plagued the country.[2]

It would later emerge that the United Arab Emirates (UAE) and the Kingdom of Saudi Arabia (KSA) took the decision to pull the financial support that had been critical to propping up Sudan's economy in response to President Bashir's decision to allow their rival Turkey to build a naval base at Port Suakin. The naval base represented only the latest in a long string of President Bashir's arbitrage between middle eastern rivals, playing Iran off against Saudi Arabia for example, but it was the straw that broke the camel's back. At the time not recognised for its significance, KSA's failure to renew a financial lifeline forced Bashir into the austerity measures that sparked the revolution; while the withholding of an emergency financial injection once unrest started tipped the scales against the former president.

[1]   Mai Hassan and Ahmed Kodouda, 'Sudan's Uprising: The Fall of a Dictator', in *Journal of Democracy*, Vol. 30, No. 4 (October 2019), p. 89–103, https://www.journalofdemocracy.org/?p=5964.
[2]   'Several Killed in Sudan as Protests over Rising Prices Continue', in *Al Jazeera*, 21 December 2018, https://aje.io/frbvu.

Discerning the winds of change, Sudan's National Intelligence Security Services (NISS) Chief Salah Gosh began discreetly supporting the protest movement as a hedge to his personal fortunes and as means to create influence in any transition to come. Separately, a moment of truth arrived where Gosh and Mohammed Hamdan Hemedti, the leader of the RSF, a massive paramilitary force used primarily in Darfur, both refused President Bashir's order to forcibly disperse the protesters who had gathered in the capital's largest protest encampment. The refusal was also President Bashir's end; reflecting an internal consensus amongst the security apparatus that his ouster was now unavoidable.

On 6 April 2019, the unrest reached a tipping point following the sit-in in front of the military headquarters. Five days later, on 11 April 2019, the military announced that President Bashir had been overthrown by the newly established Transitional Military Council (TMC), led by Lt-Gen Abdel Fattah Abdelrahman Burhan.

Although Bashir was gone, the revolution was not over. The protesters were deeply concerned the TMC would install a new autocracy; continuing Bashir's system but with a new, sanitised face. Amid rising tensions as the protesters continued holding out for a full transfer to civilian rule, on 3 June a massive security clearance operation of the sit-in was launched by armed forces linked to the TMC. It is widely accepted that the operation was undertaken by the RSF but inquiries are ongoing.[3]

Taking Sudanese and international observers by surprise for its suddenness and brutality, the operation resulted in the deaths of up to 241 protesters. The ensuing outrage lent impetus to discreet diplomatic efforts by the 'Quad' (US/UK and UAE/KSA) which supported the public facing mediation led by Ethiopia's Prime Minister Abiy Ahmed Ali, supported by the African Union's mediator Mohammed Lebatt. Together these efforts crystallised around an agreement to form a joint transitional government with a civilian and a military component. The result was a deal signed between the TMC and the Forces of Freedom and Change, the political coalition created in January 2019 that encompassed nearly all forms of opposition actors: civil society, political parties and armed opposition groups. The agreement, signed in July 2019, mandated the creation of transitional institutions, among them a Sovereign Council comprising both military and civilian components. With the Draft Constitutional Declaration signed in

---

3   Kareem Khadder and Julia Hollingsworth, 'Sudan Death Roll Rises to 100 as Bodies Found in Nile, Say Doctors', in *CNN*, 5 June 2019, https://edition.cnn.com/2019/06/05/africa/sudan-death-toll-intl.

August, power was transferred from the TMC to the Sovereign Council and the other newly created transitional bodies.

2. Sudan's protest movement: Learning from experience

The Sudanese protest movement purposefully resisted structure and central-isation. This decision resulted from lessons drawn through a decade of succes-sive (and unsuccessful) protest movements as well as comparisons with other movements in neighbouring countries, particularly Egypt. Decentralisation allowed it to evade state repression but also to generate geographically wide-spread grassroots participation. The result was an unprecedented degree of mobilisation: a truly mass movement. While this structural decision created a singularly effective protest movement, it came at a cost. The lack of a central structure nullified the protest movement's ability to play a leadership role in the new national situation it had created.

Past unsuccessful protests paved the way for those of 2019. The Change Now and Girifna movements organised protests in September 2013. At that time, the sparks of protest were again lit by cuts to subsidies, this time to wheat and fuel. Like in 2019, the economic travails were a product of Sudan's foreign policy: the messy divorce with South Sudan leading to a loss of oil transit fees for Sudan that necessitated some belt tightening. The protests, organised by student movements using Facebook and other social media, took place at university campuses in Khartoum, Omdurman, El Obeid and other towns.

But organisation and communication weaknesses led to the 2013 protests being rolled up by the Sudanese security services before they could achieve crit-ical mass.[4] Communication technology was penetrated by the security services, allowing protest locations to be found out ahead of time and protest organisers to be tracked down and arrested. Security services headed off gathering spots with advance intelligence and guarded existing gathering points such as Friday Prayer congregations. All of this prevented the emergence of a critical mass of protesters occupying a central location in Khartoum. Finally, the security services were willing to use overwhelming force as soon as the protests bubbled to the surface. This zero-tolerance approach was so brutal that some 200 protesters we killed during one clampdown.[5] By contrast, WhatsApp proved a game changer in the 2019 protests. The secure communications it provided to the protest organisers

---

[4]   Human Rights Watch, *Sudan: Violent Response to Peaceful Protests*, 3 February 2011, https://www.hrw.org/news/2011/02/03/sudan-violent-response-peaceful-protests.

[5]   Mai Hassan and Ahmed Kodouda, 'Sudan's Uprising: The Fall of a Dictator', cit.

enabled a level of coordination and organisation that proved unbreachable and ultimately decisive.

The choice to eschew political organisation, once a new transitional government was formed, left the political leadership to other parties. This, in turn, had an impact on the very character of the Transitional Government. Its civilian component had been legitimised as being representative of the protests, but this was strictly speaking not represented. In fact, as the transition progressed, the protest movement withdrew increasingly from the civilian component of the government while the opposition political parties – the late-comer elite component of the overall protest coalition – came to the forefront. Thus, the values that animated the revolution, demonstration of the democratic will that would lead Sudan towards democracy – and possible future engine for a renewed European commitment in Sudan – began to be less and less represented by the transitional government.

At its high point, the 2019 protest movement embraced a vast scope of actors ranging from local protest organisers through to elite political parties and the armed opposition. But the backbone of the mobilisation was the local interaction between community, student and youth actors. The organising unit was the Revolutionary Committee. These roughly mirrored in function and presence the government's Popular Committee structure: a decentralised extension of the ruling party that reached down to the neighbourhood level. In essence it was a form of (very) local government but with a largely informal mandate. Groups of Revolutionary Committees, which could be located either in neighbourhoods of large cities or comprise an entire rural town, were bound together by Local Coordination Committees. These were the next level in the political and organisational hierarchy, in loose coordination with each other. Overlapping with these but moving up the political (and social/economic) ladder was the Sudan Professional Association (SPA). This trade union-type, upper middle-class body was less geographically representative and rather more urban and elite-centred. Formed originally in 2016 as a product of the increasingly independent non-governmental 'shadow' unions, it was composed of existing smaller unions of doctors, lawyers and journalists. Moving to more formal political parties and armed opposition groups, the Sudan Call, formed in 2014, comprised the Sudan Revolutionary Front (SRF) armed group alliance as well as traditional national political parties, including Ummah, the National Consensus Forces (a coalition of political parties formed to stand against the National Congress Party during the 2010 Sudanese elections) and the Confederation of Sudanese Civil Society, a civil society grouping linked to the Sudanese lawyer Amin Mekki Medani.[6]

Women played an important role throughout these structures with groups and individuals taking key positions in the SPA and eventually in the Forces for Freedom and Change (FFC).[7] Women shared the same general political/economic grievances but also had particular antipathy towards the Bashir government's Public Order Laws and Family Laws.[8] The latter codified an extremely conservative interpretation of Islamic law as it applies to women including permitting marriage at the age of ten, while the former placed burdensome strictures on women's participation in public life. In the protests themselves, women played different roles,[9] many joining the dangerous protests themselves and others helping organise support systems to sustain the protesters: food, water and other provisions.

As the protests gathered steam, an umbrella body was formed out of necessity to bring all of these actors under one tent: the Forces for Freedom and Change. Seeking to demonstrate a united front in the face of historical change, the FFC succeeded in clustering all levels of opposition under its banner. This included the SPA, but with only tacit approval, and the Local Coordination Committees. This notwithstanding, there were tensions due to the (justified) fear of the Local Coordination Committees, and to a lesser degree the SPA, that political hijacking could occur once the movement came under one structure. Experience dictated that the savvier organisational operators, the political parties, could and would find ways to turn the structure to their advantage.

The SPA had planned an economics-focused protest for 25 December 2018. Seeing how protests outside the capital had begun and how these had moved from demanding improvements on the economic situation to calling for Bashir's removal, the SPA decided to go political as well. With a turnout near the 10,000

6   IRIN, 'Sudan: Who's Who in the Opposition', in *The New Humanitarian*, 26 July 2012, https://www.thenewhumanitarian.org/node/252320; Tom Lantos Human Rights web-site: *Dr. Amin Mekki Medani*, https://humanrightscommission.house.gov/node/556.

7   Nagwan Soliman, 'Sudan Spring: Lessons from Sudanese Women Revolutionaries', in *GIWPS Blog*, 11 April 2020, https://giwps.georgetown.edu/?p=10925.

8   Liv Tønnessen, 'Sudanese Women's Revolution for Freedom, Dignity and Justice Continues', in *CMI Sudan Blog*, 2020, https://www.cmi.no/publications/7355.

9   Sydney Young, 'The Women's Revolution: Female Activism in Sudan', in *Harvard International Review*, 25 May 2020, https://hir.harvard.edu/the-womens-revolution-female-activism-in-sudan.

mark, the event represented the largest protest the capital Khartoum had witnessed in decades.

Moving quickly, the SPA linked up with existing political opposition parties and the armed groups based outside Sudan to form the FFC. The SPA was already naturally situated in the middle between the political parties – with which it shared the same urban elite milieu although not a political party itself – and the Local Coordination Committees. Thus it was the SPA which on 1 January 2019 struck an alliance with 21 other organisations in a joint declaration calling for a national transitional government to replace Bashir. The declaration marked the birth of the FFC.

The events after the ouster of President Bashir in April 2019 forced the Local Coordination Committees into new terrain beyond mobilisation and demonstrations. They began to develop a political platform of their own, independent of the SPA and the FFC and often critical of their positions.

Two trends emerged: first, the maximalists who remained faithful to the letter of the SPA's January 2019 declaration and who demanded the surrender of power to a wholly civilian transitional government with no role for the army and the security apparatus; and the compromisers, willing to embrace a tactical arrangement with the TMC.

After the formation of the Transitional Government, protests continued to be used as a political tool by the protest movement: a kind of check on performance and adherence to the 'spirit of the revolution'. But this tool emerged as limited in terms of accountability. It became clear that excessive protest would legitimise a countercoup by the military component. It could be claimed that protests, if they reached a massive scale, constituted a state of anarchy which the military component would be compelled to deal with under the rubric of restoring order and in the interest of the state.

3. The transition at the national level: A divided house

Two national-level dynamics are germane here. First is the tension between the established political/armed opposition and the new protest movements (SPA and Local Coordination Committees), which originated from the fact that, although a Transitional Constitution was formally negotiated in the name of the entire FFC, it was driven largely by the SPA leading to a de facto (if not de jure) exclusion of the armed opposition who were still based abroad. The second dynamic is the division between the civilian and military components in the

Transitional Government, which were tied together in an impossible governing arrangement, with each trying to dominate the other.

It is difficult to overstate how dramatically the protests upended the power dynamic within the opposition. For decades, the Sudanese opposition comprised roughly two elements: mainstream major political parties and armed opposition groups. The former were Khartoum elites whose focus was the political centre of the country. The latter stemmed from the Sudanese peripheries, which had traditionally been the locus of armed uprising against political marginalisation.

For decades, the armed opposition groups had concluded various peace agreements with the government of Sudan: in Darfur, in the Two Areas and even in East Sudan. These agreements tended to be classic wealth- and power-sharing arrangements that would catapult the armed opposition group leaders into central government positions while many aspects of redress to armed conflict were relegated to vague 'implementation' processes left to technical committees and international development agencies. These agreements were invariably partial (not all leaders signed off on them) and were never fully implemented by the government. This led to the conclusion that a more root-and-branch approach was needed. This realisation crystallised around the idea of launching a national dialogue to address the Sudan problem in its entirety. The convergence of analysis between the periphery armed groups and the political opposition over the years led to the conclusion that the two must articulate a common vision of the problem and its solution. This found its expression in the creation of the Sudan Call, an overarching opposition body that included the armed opposition umbrella (the SRF) and the main political opposition forces: the Ummah Party, the Democratic Unionist Party and a smattering of leftists – Ba'ath, Nasserists and most importantly the Communists.

All of these elites had difficulty in claiming massive popular support. In fact, both the international community and the opposition engaged with fantasies. The international community needed an opposition to engage in negotiations with the government, while the opposition itself used exclusive access to the negotiations to create a legitimacy it lacked via popular mandate.

This all changed radically when the protest movement gained momentum in 2019. For the first time in decades, there was clearly a mass movement apparent for all to see. Here were the masses that the elite opposition always claimed to speak for and be able to mobilise. But the protests had mobilised quite independently from the elite opposition. Indeed, when some opposition leaders tried to associate themselves with the protests – for example by joining the sit-ins – they were roundly rejected and shown the door.

The international community was so taken by the promise of the new Sudan the protesters' views seemed to herald, as well as by the overwhelming political power generated for the first time via popular mobilisation, that it abandoned almost completely its old negotiation paradigm revolving around the elite opposition. Sudan was turning a new page and would be guided by new political realities. So as the protests gathered steam, the elite opposition found themselves out of the loop with the protest leaders and out of contact with the international community.

The protests movement, sure of its overwhelming influence and sceptical of the 'professional opposition', made very perfunctory gestures towards overall opposition unity by including the Sudan Call, nominally, within the greater FFC. But it was clear that the locus of decision-making was in Khartoum with the protesters, who were not depending on the Sudan Call for guidance or approval.

When the inevitable split came in June 2019, with the SRF pulling out of the FFC over the failure to agree on a common position in the negotiations with the TMC, its impact hardly registered. The sense was of the dawn of a new era: decades of 'professional' opposition had not brought the change, but rather the new force of the protest movement did.

Turning to the other 'house divided', the Transitional Government combined two opposing camps – the military and civilian components – with little incentive for real cooperation. This bifurcated leadership led to a form of government forum shopping amongst Sudan's partners. States could choose to engage either the military or the civilian component, in what was either a vote of support for that given faction or seeking the most favourable position on a given issue.

The military component felt it was the real power but needed to hide its hand for fear of the protest movement. It was encouraged in this position by its regional backers: Egypt for the Sudanese Armed Forces and the UAE for RSF leader Hemedti. The civilian component began with massive popular goodwill towards its head, new Prime Minister Abdalla Hamdouk. But the unknown and inexperienced executive he led proved hapless. Hamdouk himself enjoyed the backing of the protest movement but once in office he relied more on the FFC, which grew to inhabit the role of ruling party (behind the civilian component). This was incongruous in that the more institutional the FFC grew, the further the protest movement withdrew from it. Thus, as the PM treated the 'political party' more as his real caucus, its democratic bona fides was eroding, placing the real mass movement beyond the FFC's representation.

In the months that followed, as Sudan's economic situation not only failed to improve but deteriorated, goodwill began to evaporate. The protest movement remobilised in one of its biggest gatherings in summer 2020, directing its demands at PM Hamdouk.[10] Where this might have threatened PM Hamdouk's post – an unelected official in theory understood to be representative of the protest movement – the fear of a military-led countercoup tempered the protest movement. Understanding that calls to replace the PM could pave the way for the military to justify taking, the protest movement tempered its actions (though not its passion).

4. Return of the armed opposition: The Juba negotiations

There is a Sudanese political parable comparing the country's politics to a barrel of crabs: as soon as one nears escape the rest will pull it back down. So it was for the elite opposition who received their second chance in the fall of 2019.

Three factors led to the resurrection of their political fortune. First, the new government had set the incredibly ambitious objective of achieving peace with all armed groups. Having set this as the metric of success, the government bound its hands as peace was then for the armed groups to deliver. Second, the military component of the government was caught in a zero-sum competition with its civilian partners. They saw the armed groups as both a prize to demonstrate their bona fides to the greater population and as recruits to strengthen their side. The peace agreement would create an alliance and the armed groups would align with the military; all with a view to positioning for whatever might come after the transition period. Third, the regional powers – Egypt, the UAE/KSA, as well as Sudan's neighbours with the exception of Ethiopia – still judged the armed groups to be the 'real' power and the protest movement as ideologically hostile and politically volatile, and wanted to help deliver the armed groups to the new government as a means of generating political capital. So the regional powers invested negotiation with the armed groups with the same inflationary attention that the international community once had.

Thus, even as the international community discarded the armed opposition, it returned with a surprising splash with the Juba Declaration of September 2019. This marked the beginning of new negotiations between the Transitional Government and the armed opposition hosted and mediated by the Government of South Sudan (GoSS). The Sudanese government negotiation was spearheaded by the RSF's leader, Hemedti, rather than the civilian component's leadership (the PM), and Tut Gatluak, a senior security official from the GoSS, emerged

---

[10]   Theodore Murphy, 'Sudan Peace Agreement: What It Really Means for the Country's Transition', in *ECFR Commentaries*, 2 September 2020, https://ecfr.eu/?p=8934.

as mediator. The Juba Declaration introduced a range of new armed groups in addition to the existing ones that in reality carried no arms but felt negotiations were their only way into power. The scope of the negotiation topics and the geographic range – not only the classic war-affected peripheries of Darfur and the Two Areas but also Eastern, Northern and Central Sudan – was stunning.[11]

Initially the international community, meaning the Western partners and the African Union/United Nations, reacted tepidly to the Juba forum for two reasons: first concerns that the military was taking the lead in negotiations and, second, concerns about the GoSS mediator, whom many avoided engaging as someone implicated in crimes in South Sudan.

While the Juba negotiations suffered from international neglect, the armed opposition parties enthusiastically engaged in the talks. They had discovered that the Transitional Government was so willing to reach an agreement that it discarded previous red-line positions with ease. Suddenly the issues that had proved intractable for years of negotiations were up for discussion, for example restructuring the administration of Darfur into a single region (rather than three states). So, while the absence of international engagement unnerved the armed opposition – particularly as their buy-in would be necessary to finance the implementation phase – they took the position that any agreement reached was at the very minimum a new high water mark they could refer to in future negotiations.

The international community adopted a posture of benign neglect, assuming the negotiations would peter out, but were forced to take notice as the scope of the topics negotiated began to emerge. Rather than harmless regional agreements, fundamental aspects of the Transitional Constitution were being amended: the duration of the transitional period, the composition of the Sovereign Council and of the Legislature. As this realisation dawned, covid-19 broke out in late winter 2020. The result was that while the talks neared conclusion and grappled with the weightiest issues, the international community's attention to Sudan diminished considerably.

In parallel to the advances being made in the Juba negotiations, the civilian component of the Sudanese government faced increasing difficulties in delivering any economic improvement. The political party aligned to the civilian component, the FFC, suffered splits and even the SPA splintered. This led the government to grow more desperate than ever to secure successes. In turn, the

---

[11] JEM, SPLM-n, SLA/M, SLA/M Transitional Council, Beja Congress/Opposition, Popular United Front for Liberation and Justice, Kush Liberation Movement, Unionist Democratic Party/Revolutionary Forces) and Gathering of Sudan Liberation Forces.

negotiating power of the armed groups in Juba grew. While the FFC held out against some of the armed groups' demands – particularly those eating into its share of power in the Legislature – the combination of the military component's investment in recruiting an ally and the civilian component's desire for a demonstrable win outweighed the naysayers.

5. The region and Sudan: Transition in a sharp-elbowed neighbourhood

All of Sudan's key international partners saw the transition as a once in a lifetime opportunity to shape a new Sudan. They differed – fundamentally – in the political orientation they wanted to give it.

The Middle East Strategic Alliance (MESA) between the KSA, Egypt and the UAE, with the UAE in the lead, identified determining the trajectory of Sudan's transition as a core national security interest. As such they invested at a level far beyond the EU in terms of political/financial capital. The EU's inability to influence the MESA led to a drastic reduction in its ability to influence the internal political situation in favour of its stated goal of supporting the objectives of the civilian-led government.

Three key factors informed MESA's assessment of the absolute importance of shaping Sudan's future trajectory. First, Sudan's location in their neighbourhood meant it could be a source of threats. So the first-order objective was to avoid state collapse. Riven by internal fault lines and bankrupt, the potential for a Somalia scenario was conceivable. Second, as Sudan had been hospitable to political Islam under President Bashir, now there was a chance to uproot it. Finally, Bashir had made a practice of playing the MESA off against its rivals: Iran, Turkey and Qatar. Now it was imperative to firmly secure Sudan in the friendly 'Sunni African' orbit of the MESA, and prevent a return to Bashir's opportunism vis-à-vis the Iran/Qatar/Turkey axis. In sum, the ideal outcome was for a Sudan that would be moderately Sunni, stable and pliant, and exclusively MESA aligned. But within this a very important schism existed and within the MESA points of disagreement existed as to specifics.

These played out between especially Egypt and the UAE. Egypt believed that it knew Sudan best and should be the intellectual lead for the MESA's approach. It also had a long-standing relationship with the Sudanese Armed Forces (SAF), the Army, which they felt was similar to the Egyptian Army and a reliable and loyal pillar on which to build. Here the UAE differed. Deeply preoccupied with the threat from political Islam, the Emirati analysis dictated that over the two decades of National Congress Party rule political Islamism had woven its way into all senior levels of government. To accomplish a clean sweep, rather than try to reform thoroughly permeated bureaucracies, it was better to start afresh. This is what led them to invest so heavily in Hemedti, the RSF leader. The UAE saw him as the only friendly, existing vehicle that was sufficiently free from political Islam. The UAE's conclusion then was to build around the RSF as much intelligence and military capacity as possible so that the RSF might even replace the army and the intelligence at some point. With all parts of the Sudan's security apparatus discerning this agenda, concerns were raised in the strongest terms at the UAE's approach, which could lead to the very state implosion it sought to avoid.[12] Politically, the UAE also made the RSF the conduit for the lifesaving cash injections Sudan desperately needed to stay afloat. Rather than channelling these from government to government, they passed through Hemedti who could then use them to build patronage networks and public displays of largesse. The state's weakness at this moment only served to increase Hemedti's relative strength vis-à-vis the rest of the government.

The MESA viewed the protest movement dismissively. Ideologically the two were fundamentally at odds, a difference that could be managed but would never allow the foundation for a deeper relationship to flourish. Ideology aside, the MESA also did not appreciate the protest movement as an enduring political force. Here their view was that hard power in military institutions is the backbone of the state. Popular uprising brings force to bear but then dissipates like a receding wave. So even if pragmatic considerations could have bridged the ideological gap, the MESA was not convinced the civilians had staying power.

The civilian component's only real regional ally was Ethiopia. Led by Prime Minister Abiy, also brought to power by a popular protest movement in 2018, Addis Ababa aligned ideologically with the Sudanese protesters and the civilian government. The Sudanese protest movement, which eschewed international engagement, even among ideologically friendly western partners, felt Ethiopia under PM Abiy was beyond reproach, a full-fledged ally and a role model for what they hoped to soon achieve themselves.

Against this backdrop, in June 2019, the FFC announced its acceptance of Ethiopian Prime Minister Abiy Ahmed's role to lead mediation with the TMC towards a democratic transition in Sudan.[13] The decision was informed by the

---

[12] 'Sudan: Protests in Front of UAE Embassy Opposing Fighting in Yemen', in *Middle East Monitor*, 27 January 2020, https://www.middleeastmonitor.com/?p=382894.

[13] 'Sudan Opposition Says It Accepts Ethiopia PM as Mediator', in *Al Jazeera*, 7 June 2019, https://aje.io/96xsv.

massive support and fascination among the Sudanese protest movement for the wide-ranging political and economic reforms Abiy launched after he took office in April 2018, following the successful removal by similar protest movement of Prime Minister Hailemariam Desalegn in February 2018. In Abiy the protest movement saw an ideological kindred spirit. Brought to power by public demands for democratic reform and social and economic inclusion, Abiy was seen to be their only true partner in the region.[14]

In August 2019, Ethiopia's mediation efforts resulted in an interim power-sharing deal between the main opposition coalition and the ruling military council, paving the way for a transitional government and subsequent democratic elections.[15] These efforts were built from discrete mediation efforts in the Quad Format (US, UK, UAE and KSA) which assured that the powerful Gulf backers of the military component were on board and moved in parallel to the AU mediation. The success of the mediation and the major role played by Abiy further consolidated favourable public opinion in Sudan towards Ethiopia. Key to Ethiopia's mediation role was the unique entrée it had with the protest movement.

6. Civilian-military relations and the risk of new instability

Sudan's protest movement learned lessons from history and comparative movements in the region, which finally allowed them to become an incredibly powerful political force for change. But they are still grappling with what has come thereafter and their role in that. Sudan's transition is proving that affecting regime change is insufficient. Deeper national transformation requires organised politics and capable governance. For good reasons, the protest movement eschewed political parties or government. But the conclusion that protest needs to transform into politics may constitute the new lesson learned – the alternative being that protests merely pave the way for other players to take power. As it stands now, elites are again in power and the biggest change is the inclusion of the periphery into the centre. That many of the armed movements, representatives from Sudan's marginalised peripheries, now hold executive positions, surely marks a change.

The EU and its member states treated the political dynamics within the greater civilian camp as out of bounds for them. They were encouraged in this by

---

[14] 'Abiy Ahmed Sworn in as Ethiopia's Prime Minister', in *Al Jazeera*, 2 April 2018, https://aje.io/cdad7.

[15] 'Sudan Conflict: Army and Civilians Seal Power-Sharing Deal', in *BBC News*, 17 August 2019, https://www.bbc.com/news/world-africa-49379489.

the hands-off posture adopted by many in the protest movement. But this was a major miscalculation by the Europeans. The transition was as much a political competition between civilian and military as a technocratic reform process. In this competition, the civilians' strength lay not in arms but in political representation. As the civilian political caucus splintered, and as the most representative element – the protest movement – distanced itself from the civilian component of government, the civilians grew weaker. Their ability to act cohesively was also deeply damaged, leaving the PM to tackle difficult reforms with no strong political backing, and instead being pulled in opposing directions by the various elements of the wider civilian block: the FFC, the SPA and the protest movement.

The division between the civilian and military components codified in the Transitional Government was a pragmatic, split-the-difference arrangement that prevented further bloodshed. But in terms of delivering effective government for the hugely important tasks of the transition, it has been a disaster. There are in reality two governments – at times even more – pursuing different agendas and offering different entry points for outside interlocutors: a sort of intergovernmental forum shopping. The divide within the military component, with the RSF pitted against the SAF, replicates the conundrum surrounding Hezbollah, the powerful armed group that controls South Lebanon. As in Lebanon, once established, it proves enduring: a time bomb never buried too far below the surface.

The EU and invested member states enthusiastically embraced the promise of a new liberal Sudan. This success story underpinned policy, unlocking various forms of aid and high-level political recognition. But Sudan's civilians needed EU political support even more than financial. Directly following President Bashir's ouster, the MESA created new political realities – such as cementing the RSF – with Europe completely absent from the calculation. Both at this critical moment but also throughout the transition, Europe failed to engage the MESA in a meaningful way: at a level and with consistency that the MESA understood as serious. What emerged instead, was Europe engaging with the civilians and the MESA with the military, when what was needed was a real compact between the two. This dichotomy continues today: the military cannot mount a counter coup aware that the protest movement will mobilise en masse if they do, but no amount of protesting can create a more effective executive government. Sudan's spectre is a slow unravelling as the transition increasingly fails to deliver rather than a dramatic explosion in a counter coup.

References

Mai Hassan and Ahmed Kodouda, 'Sudan's Uprising: The Fall of a Dictator', in *Journal of Democracy*, Vol. 30, No. 4 (October 2019), p. 89–103, https://www.journalofdemocracy.org/?p=5964

Human Rights Watch, *Sudan: Violent Response to Peaceful Protests*, 3 February 2011, https://www.hrw.org/news/2011/02/03/sudan-violent-response-peaceful-protests

IRIN, 'Sudan: Who's Who in the Opposition', in *The New Humanitarian*, 26 July 2012, https://www.thenewhumanitarian.org/node/252320

Kareem Khadder and Julia Hollingsworth, 'Sudan Death Roll Rises to 100 as Bodies Found in Nile, Say Doctors', in *CNN*, 5 June 2019, https://edition.cnn.com/2019/06/05/africa/sudan-death-toll-intl

Theodore Murphy, 'Sudan Peace Agreement: What It Really Means for the Country's Transition', in *ECFR Commentaries*, 2 September 2020, https://ecfr.eu/?p=8934

Nagwan Soliman, 'Sudan Spring: Lessons from Sudanese Women Revolutionaries', in *GIWPS Blog*, 11 April 2020, https://giwps.georgetown.edu/?p=10925

Liv Tønnessen, 'Sudanese Women's Revolution for Freedom, Dignity and Justice Continues', in *CMI Sudan Blog*, 2020, https://www.cmi.no/publications/7355

Sydney Young, 'The Women's Revolution: Female Activism in Sudan', in *Harvard International Review*, 25 May 2020, https://hir.harvard.edu/the-womens-revolution-female-activism-in-sudan

Francesca Caruso

Chapter 7: Morocco: A Decade of Popular Struggles and Monarchy Resistance

In 2011, popular protests took place in Morocco under the umbrella of the 20 February Movement (20FM) – a popular movement with different souls demanding more justice, dignity and democracy. Yet, despite the 20FM succeeded in pushing the monarchy to adopt a new constitution and open up the political space it broke up quickly because of the internal dynamics of the movement as well as the king's ability to neutralise it gradually.

However, despite the fact that the 20FM did not lead to radical economic and political changes, the movement brought about societal changes that have allowed Moroccans to overcome their fear of speaking up about their deep frustration. Indeed, in the last decade the Kingdom has been exposed to intermittent mass protests that have challenged Morocco's supposed 'exceptionalism' as a country where reform was gradually being pursued from the top – a myth originating in the fact that long before the Arab Spring the monarchy had adopted a series of reforms ostensibly moving the country towards democracy.

The reality, however, is that King Mohammed VI has succeeded in retaining power both with its citizens and political parties, including the Islamic Justice and Development Party (PJD) which, while heading the government from 2011 to 2021, failed (and, in some respect, did not even want) to extract itself from the king's sway. Indeed, the September 2021 elections, in which the PJD suffered a crushing defeat, demonstrate that the historic phase inaugurated by the 20FM and of which the Islamist moderate party was the first beneficiary, is over.

Today, a new era (or a step back to the past) is beginning, in which the protagonists of the political scene are *again* political parties very close to the king. Mohammed VI, for his part, is increasingly self-confident, not least thanks to his successful alignment with the axis of Sunni Arab Gulf states, which has been moving against pro-democracy and social protests all over the region.[1]

---

[1]   This Chapter is the result of desk research and several interviews made between November 2020 and August 2021 with Moroccan representatives of protest movements, political parties, civil society, and intellectuals.

1. The first wave of protests: The 20 February Movement

In the last decade, the first wave of popular protests took place on 20 February 2011, when thousands of demonstrators gathered in the streets of the country, with crowds especially large in Casablanca, Tangier, Al Hoceima and Rabat. According to 20FM leaders, the protests attracted 350,000 people on the first day, although the Official Agency spoke of 30,000. From then on, and throughout the whole of 2011, protest actions by the 20FM recurred periodically, usually on Sundays, with greater popular mobilisation as the day approached the 20th of each month.

The context in which the 20FM erupted was characterised by deep political and socio-economic discontent. In 2011, a growing disillusionment with political institutions persisted and corruption rate was very high. The legislative, judiciary and executive powers were concentrated in the hands of the king, in power since 1999, and political activists could not publicly raise issues over the monarchy, Islam and Western Sahara (the three red lines of public discourse in Morocco) without incurring the wrath of the State. In addition, the economic and infra-structural investments implemented in the previous decade had had only little effects on the poverty rate and social inequalities as well as imbalances between regions and urban and rural areas.[2] Poverty was mainly driven by a high rate of unemployment (according to the World Bank, youth unemployment reached 19 per cent[3]), an unaffordable real-estate market and soaring electricity, water and food prices (after the global food security crisis of 2007–2008, price of basic staples such as cooking oil prices increased by 65 per cent).[4] The international financial crisis of 2008 dealt a severe blow to Morocco's economy, in particular to key sectors such as tourism, remittances coming from Europe and exports.[5]

---

[2]   Anouar Boukhars, *Politics in Morocco. Executive Monarchy and Enlightened Authoritarianism*, London/New York, Routledge, 2011.

[3]   World Bank Data: *Unemployment, Youth Total (% of Total Labor Force Ages 15–24) (Modeled ILO Estimate) - Morocco*, https://data.worldbank.org/indicator/SL.UEM.1524. ZS?locations=MA.

[4]   Climate Diplomacy website: *Food Price Shocks in Morocco*, https://climate-diplom acy.org/case-studies/food-price-shocks-morocco. The suffering and frustration of Moroccans, especially in the rural areas, became visible between 2006 and 2008 with the eruption of the 'Coordinations contre la vie chère et la détérioration des services publics' (Coordination against high cost of living and deterioration of public services).

[5]   Florence Beaugé, 'L'économie marocaine commence à pâtir de la récession internatio-nale', in *Le Monde*, 3 December 2008, https://www.lemonde.fr/la-crise-financiere/arti cle/2008/12/03/l-economie-marocaine-commence-a-patir-de-la-recession-internation ale_1126328_1101386.html.

Despite the difficult socio-economic situation, support for King Mohammed VI was widespread. According to a poll in 2009, one out of two respondents thought that the monarchy was ruling 'democratically'.[6] Most surprisingly, most respondents who were economically unsatisfied attributed their troubles to the government and the political parties – considered by many as 'corrupted'. The disdain towards the political parties (around 33 per cent at the time) was quite evident during the 2007 legislative elections, when the rate of participation shrunk to 43 per cent (it had been 67 per cent in 2002). Sixty-three per cent of those who abstained from voting (63 per cent) were young people,[7] who were considered by many studies as totally depoliticised and inactive.[8] Underlying this assessment was the assumption that the youth was disaffected because of the ruthless repression of opposition forces during the long reign of Hassan II, Muhammad VI's father. The experience of political exclusion and marginalisation had created obstacles to participation and brought the youth to be dispersed and atomised.[9]

However, the large participation of young people within the 20FM demonstrated that the narrative of a depoliticised youth was a myth that had generated a collective myopia. Indeed, by hitting the streets of fifty cities across the country for more than six months, the youth demonstrated both its courage and organisational skills. The 20FM was gradually built up on Facebook, when in 2009 a group page named Alternative Movement for Individual Freedoms (MALI) was created. The movement, made up of young secularists who demanded greater individual and collective freedoms, organised a daylight picnic during Ramadan in Rabat, which was then harshly repressed by the authorities[10] and condemned by most of the local newspapers and clerics. Although the event

6   Florence Beaugé, 'Maroc: le sondage interdit', in *Le Monde*, 3 August 2009, https://www.lemonde.fr/afrique/article/2009/08/03/maroc-le-sondage-interdit_1225217_3212.html.

7   Saloua Zerhouni, 'Le marketing politique. Faible impact electoral', in *Economia*, 22 July 2015, http://economia.ma/fr/content/le-marketing-politique-faible-impact-électoral.

8   Saloua Zerhouni, 'Jeunes et participation politique au Maroc', in *Rapports thématiques IRES*, June 2009, https://www.ires.ma/images/PDFs_publications/jeunes_et_participation_politique_au_maroc.pdf.

9   Saloua Zerhouni and Azeddine Akesbi, 'Youth Activism in Morocco: Exclusion, Agency and the Search for Inclusion', in *Power2Youth Papers*, No. 15 (September 2016), https://www.iai.it/en/node/6815.

10 Human Rights Watch, *Morocco: End Police Actions against Persons Accused of Breaking Ramadan Fast*, 19 September 2009, https://www.hrw.org/node/237795.

had minimal participation, it is considered by many leaders of the 20FM as 'a catalyst event' which drove hundreds of young Moroccans to engage in political activism.[11] Subsequently to the MALI's picnic, other small events contributed to strengthening the virtual community, which gradually became more and more tangible. In January 2011, a Facebook group called 'Moroccans converse with the king' – which later changed its name in 'Freedom and democracy now' – directly addressed Mohammed VI to express a demand for change.[12]

Not by accident, the Facebook group was created in conjunction with the fall of Tunisia's long-standing autocratic ruler, Zine El-Abidine Ben Ali. Indeed, the revolts that were taking place in the region were critical in bringing together, for the first time in the history of Morocco, all members of the opposition movements, associations, individuals and parties under the umbrella of a single movement. Issues that until recently had only concerned certain social groups – such as the recognition of the Amazigh language as a national language – became priorities also for others, whereby the 20FM gained a new sense of cohesion and common purpose.[13]

While historical associations such as the Moroccan Association for Human Rights (AMDH) lent movement members their premises in Rabat, left-wing extra-parliamentary forces, Amazigh and Islamist organisation such as *Al-adl wa'l-ihsane* (AWI), joined the movement from the very beginning. AWI, a semi-clandestine organisation that considers the monarchy a 'compulsory authority' and questions the fact that the king bears the title of 'Commander of the Faithful', was accepted within the ranks of the 20FM on the basis of their demands for a more legally, economically and socially egalitarian state.[14]

As the movement gained more and more support, political parties also came in – albeit discontinuously and sometimes ambiguously, as in the case of the historical Socialist Union of Popular Forces (SUPF) and the PJD. In fact, the PJD, which shares some affinities with the Muslim Brotherhood, opted for staying out of the movement. This decision, taken unilaterally by former secretary

[11] Ahmed Benchemsi, 'Feb20's Rise and Fall: a Moroccan Story', in *Le blog de Ahmed Benchemsi*, 17 July 2012, http://ahmedbenchemsi.com/?p=556.
[12] Ibid.
[13] Silvia Colombo et al., 'New Trends in Identity Politics in the Middle-East and North Africa and their Impact on State-society Relations', in *MENARA Working Papers*, No. 14 (October 2018), https://www.iai.it/en/node/9573.
[14] Thierry Desrues, 'Le Mouvement du 20 février et le régime marocain: contestation, révision constitutionnelle et élections', in *L'Année du Maghreb*, Vol. VIII (2012), p. 359–389, https://doi.org/10.4000/anneemaghreb.1537.

general Abdelilah Benkirane pushed a group of young members (called Baraka) to participate in the demonstrations on an individual basis. Contrary to AWI, the PJD had stood for a strategic alliance with the monarchy ostensibly for the sake of peaceful change for decades. Adhering to the 20FM, which was against the *Makhzen* (i.e., the deep State) would have meant admitting to having pursued the wrong strategy for years.[15] However, Benkirane's gamble payed off in November 2011, when the PJD won the legislative elections, taking 107 seats out of 395 and thus the right to lead the government.

As the 20FM eventually gained momentum, its initially generic calls in support of freedom, dignity and social justice became more political, challenging monarchical absolutism (as opposed to the monarchy as such). In 2011, all the mechanisms of authoritarianism were still in place.[16] Art. 19 of the constitution affirmed that the king was the 'Commander of the Faithful': a sacred and inviolable figure who had powers transcending the constitution itself. The king could declare the state of emergency, would preside over the Supreme Council of the Judiciary and appoint the prime minister and cabinet members at will. He also had the power to bypass the executive, legislative and judiciary functions by taking personal executive steps and issuing laws. The parliament could be dissolved by the king: more than being an institution legislating independently, it was a sort of *shura* council, a forum for consultation providing advice to the ruler. The political parties were a tool in the hands of the monarchy under the tutelage of the Ministry of Interior, and the cabinet mainly comprised members of wealthy families well-connected to the monarchy.[17]

Although the 20FM never called for the elimination of the monarchy, the movement knew that without a division of powers real change would not come. For this reason, the movement called for the drafting of a new constitution that would place sovereignty in the people, the abolition of art. 19 and a parliamentary monarchy based on the separation of powers. The movement targeted in particular the judiciary, where corruption was widespread,[18] as one of the causes of a faltering economy that suffered from the lack of the rule of law and impunity of wrongdoers. The 20FM, or at least elements of it, also called for the nationalisation of royal holding companies (at the time accounting for almost 8 per

---

[15]   Interview with Moroccan intellectual, 26 January and 29 July 2021.

[16]   Anouar Boukhars, *Politics in Morocco*, cit., p. 39.

[17]   Ibid., p. 49–52.

[18]   According to Transparency International, in 2011 Morocco ranked 80th out of 180 countries in terms of perceived corruption. See Transparency International website: *2011 Corruption Perceptions Index*, https://www.transparency.org/en/cpi/2011.

cent of national GDP[19]), access to health, education and employment, recognition of Amazigh culture and language, freedom of conscience, equality between men and women, as well as abolition of government control of the audio-visual media.[20]

2. Mohammed VI and the neutralisation of the 20FM

The constitutional reforms of July 2011 pushed by the king and the legislative elections of November 2011 won by the PJD dealt a fatal blow to the movement. But the fragmentation of the 20FM had begun earlier, in March 2011, when frictions between the various components of the movement started to emerge.

The king proceeded to capitalise on that. Addressing the nation on 9 March, Mohammed VI refrained from criticising the demonstrations and expressed his willingness to adopt constitutional reforms (i.e. recognition of Morocco's plurality, the consolidation of the rule of law, allow the Parliament to pass laws on most issues, and a prime minister chosen from the electorate) to consolidate Morocco's democracy and development.[21] However, the king never mentioned the 20FM, did not question the monarchy and did not address corruption, bribery and inequality.

Immediately after the speech, Mohammed VI moved forward with the constitutional reform process, pardoned political prisoners and increased the minimum wage. As a consequence, the 20FM's appeal ebbed. In the eyes of Moroccans, even though the movement had been able to obtain the constitutional reform, the king remained the ultimate guarantee that reforms could be adopted: Mohammed VI thus became both the spokesman and the driver of change.[22] This strategy to neutralise the 20FM was accompanied by the repression of protests – during the Casablanca 20FM protests on 13 March, for instance, dozens of protesters were injured and around 100 arrested[23] – and of single activists.

While Mohammed VI was pursuing its strategy, fractures within the movement widened. Members of traditional parties favoured a more hierarchical structure

---

[19]   Project on Middle East Democracy, *The 'February 20' Movement*, June 2011, https://pomed.org/wp-content/uploads/2011/06/Press_Kit_June2011.pdf.

[20]   Thierry Desrues, 'Le Mouvement du 20 février et le régime marocain. . .', cit.

[21]   Kingdom of Morocco, *Texte intégral du discours adressé par SM le Roi à la Nation*, 9 March 2011, https://www.maroc.ma/fr/node/62.

[22]   Thierry Desrues, 'Le Mouvement du 20 février et le régime marocain. . .', cit.

[23]   AFP, 'Maroc: la police disperse violemment une manifestation à Casablanca', in *Jeune Afrique*, 13 March 2011, https://www.jeuneafrique.com/?p=154312.

within the movement, while young activists preferred a decentralised system. The 20FM's coordination techniques (weekly and local general assemblies, and decisions taken according to consensus rather than majority voting) became a major weakness, as decisions would never go beyond the 'let's demonstrate'.[24]

It was ideological differences, however, that gave the *coup de grace* to the cohesion of the movement. The constitutional reform process during which the king consulted political parties, trade unions and civil society groups, created fractures between those who supported the monarchy as the ultimate driver of constitutional changes and those who wanted a constituent assembly elected by the people. Also, some associations, such as the *Association nationale des diplômés chômeurs du Maroc* (National Association of Unemployed Graduates of Morocco), representing an important part of the Moroccan unemployed,[25] soon fell out of love with the movement because of its failure to combine political with economic demands,[26] although in some places demonstrations also targeted the monopoly of natural resources and an equal distribution of job and rents.

Islamists and secularists within the movement started to clash over gender issues. While the secular forces of the movement chanted 'women and men have the same rights' walking together during the demonstrations, the Islamists chanted 'women and men are the same towards militancy' and walked separately.[27] According to AWI, in March 2011 leftists within the movement contended that AWI had no place in the 20FM because its progressive and democratic demands collided with the principles of the Islamist organisation.[28] While it is likely that this antagonism drove AWI out of the movement – of which they claim to be among the creators – there are other reasons behind AWI's decision to step out of 20FM. According to AWI, an alternative to a monarchical system can be achieved peacefully and in the long term by igniting a pious revolution against

---

[24] Ahmed Benchemsi, 'Feb20's Rise and Fall: a Moroccan Story', cit.

[25] According to the Haut-Commissariat au Plan, the Moroccan institution in charge of data production, in 2011, 20 per cent of unemployed were graduates. Today the rate is 25 per cent. For more details see: the website of the Haut-Commissariat au Plan, *Taux de chômage national selon le diplôme*, https://www.hcp.ma/Taux-de-chomage-natio nal-selon-le-diplome_a267.html.

[26] Cédric Baylocq and Jacopo Granci, ' "20 février". Discours et portraits d'un mouvement de révolte au Maroc', in *L'Année du Maghreb*, Vol. VIII (2012), p. 239–258, https://doi. org/10.4000/anneemaghreb.1483.

[27] Sara Borrillo, *Femminismi e Islam in Marocco. Attiviste laiche, teologhe, predicatrici*, Naples, Edizioni scientifiche italiane, 2017, p. 115.

[28] Phone interview with AWI member, 26 January 2021.

the corrupted and misguided secular state and realise a sort of Islamist revolution in Morocco.[29] In this perspective, siding with 20FM was for AWI instrumental to its fight against corruption and despotism. After the adoption of the
new constitution and the legislative elections, AWI's motives for staying in the
movement faded because 20FM lost its revolutionary potential.[30]

The dynamic between the Islamists – in this case AWI – and the secular forces
of 20FM must also be analysed from the perspective of a rivalry between the
Islamists themselves, that is, between AWI and the PJD.[31] After the elections and
the PJD joining the government, AWI might have been afraid that by continuing
to support and participate in the protests it could have given excuses to the PJD
to marginalise and repress it.

3. The second and third waves of protests

While the 20FM broke up quickly in 2011, it brought some societal changes: for
the first time Moroccans had addressed directly the regime thus overcoming
their fear of speaking up and highlighting the symptoms of a deep frustration.[32]

A second wave of protests, called 'the Rif protests', broke out in 2016. Contrary
to the 20FM, the Rif protests did not start on social media nor did they bring
together different associations and political parties. The mobilisations were
embedded in the local dynamics of the Rif – a region located in the North of
the country – but were then supported at the national level as they focused on
challenges facing Moroccan citizens who did not belong to the elites and lived in
under-developed regions.

The demonstrations started in Al Hoceima in 2016, when a fishmonger,
Mouhcine Fikri, was crashed in a garbage compactor as he tried to retrieve his
swordfish catch from the authorities, which had seized it as the fishing season
was over. However, Fikri's death ignited public resentment, which resulted in
spontaneous demonstrations. What began as a movement calling for an inquiry
into this death turned into one of the longest protest actions in the region since

---

[29]   Anouar Boukhars, *Politics in Morocco*, cit., p. 149–150.
[30]   Phone interview with AWI member, 26 January 2021.
[31]   Phone interview with Moroccan intellectual, January and July 2021.
[32]   Aude Mazoue, 'Maroc: le Mouvement du 20-février "n'a pas été massif mais a entraîné
       des changements de société"', in *France 24*, 20 February 2021, https://www.france24.
       com/fr/afrique/20210220-maroc-le-mouvement-du-20-février-n-a-pas-été-massif-
       mais-a-entraîné-des-changements-de-société.

2011.[33] Composed mainly by young people, supported by their families and a large part of the Al Hoceima's population, the *hirak* turned quickly into a protest movement claiming better economic and social conditions.

The town of Al Hoceima has had tense relations with the monarchy since the 1920s, when the Berber population of the region defeated the Spanish army and declared a short-lived Rif Republic (1923–1926). As well as having serious problems of reconciliation with the state,[34] the region had been ignored for decades by the regime, thus being economically marginalised. In 2015, Mohammed VI launched an important development programme called *Al Hoceima Manarat al Mutawassit* (Al Hoceima Mediterranean Lighthouse). But the Rif protests denounced the several shortcomings of this programme in terms of infrastructure projects, malfunctioning of the hospitals, the absence of universities and, more fundamentally, the lack of real opportunities for young people[35] – in 2014, the unemployment rate in Al Hoceima was 21 per cent, well above the average of the other regional municipalities (12 per cent).[36] This compelled Al Hoceima youth to emigrate to Europe or to opt for informal and illegal activities.

During the protests, demands ranged from public investment and infrastructures (roads and highways to better connect the region to the rest of the country), to the establishment of a cancer treatment centre (cancer rates in the town are high, which is often attributed to Spain's use of mustard gas in 1926 or the Moroccan army's bombing in 1958). The most radical protesters also demanded the return of Abdelkrim's remains, the first president of the Rif Republic, from Cairo and his commemoration as an Amazigh-democratic figure, and not just as an anti-colonial symbol.[37]

As the Riffian revolution became a cultural icon and an emblem of an alternative Morocco also outside this region, with implications for the country's stability,[38] the regime started to repress the movement. For months, police blockades

---

[33] Aida Alami, 'Morocco's Stability is Roiled by Monthslong Protests over Fishmonger's Death', in *The New York Times*, 26 August 2017, https://www.nytimes.com/2017/08/26/world/africa/morocco-berber-rif-nasser-zefzafi.html.

[34] In 1956, Hassan II violently crushed a rebellion in the Rif.

[35] Aida Alami, 'Morocco's Stability is Roiled by Monthslong Protests over Fishmonger's Death', cit.

[36] David Gouery, 'La pauvreté, à l'origine du Hirak?', in *TAFRA Blog*, 5 February 2019, https://tafra.ma/?p=2776.

[37] Hisham Aidi, 'Is Morocco Header Toward Insurrection?', in *The Nation*, 13 July 2017, https://www.thenation.com/?p=253592.

[38] Ibid.

surrounded the city, demonstrations were banned and *hirak* leaders and members jailed. In 2018, 53 people were handed sentences from two to twenty years in prison. This wave of repression has turned the movement claims from having a socio-economic dimension to a human-rights one. But, as a prominent Moroccan intellectual says, 'the regime is comfortable with this: the activists focus on the release of the prisoners, and not anymore on social and economic changes, and when the king pardons the prisoners they all say how good the regime is'.[39] As the Al Hoceima protests were repressed, the regime achieved its main goal. In 2018, the demonstrations ended and local youth started to emigrate again. This regional trend mirrored a national one. According to the Arab Barometer, in 2019 lack of economic opportunities and public services, corruption and an increasing repression of human rights were driving nearly half of Moroccans into considering emigrating.[40]

From the experience of the 20FM and the Rif protests, new forms of mass mobilisations, which can be called a third wave of protests, took place through innovative methods that gave protesters some leeway. In April 2018, a country-wide boycott against three companies, Sidi Ali bottled water, Centrale Danone and Afriquia gas stations, took place. Organised on social media by activists, the boycotts targeted these companies because they all represented the economic *Makhzen*, or the monopoly of the economy in the hands of few. According to a study conducted by *L'Economiste*, within two weeks 90 per cent of Moroccans were aware of the campaign and three quarters of citizens – in particular the youth – participated in the boycott in some way.[41] However, despite the fact that the boycott persisted for several months and Centrale Danone reduced prices, it failed to impact decisions of the other two companies (which did not lower prices of their products) and to launch a social movement, mainly because of a lack of an identifiable leadership.[42]

Despite being very different in their strategies, the 20FM demonstrations, the Rif protests and the mass-boycotts all pointed out the deep governance failures

---

[39]   Phone interview with prominent Moroccan intellectual, December 2020.

[40]   Daniella Raz, *Youth in the Middle East and North Africa*, Arab Barometer, August 2019, https://www.arabbarometer.org/wp-content/uploads/ABV_Youth_Report_Public-Opi nion_Middle-East-North-Africa_2019-1.pdf.

[41]   Nadia Salah, 'Enquête l'Economiste-Sunergia/Boycott: Danone, un cas très special', in *L'Economiste*, No. 5279 (24 May 2018), https://www.leconomiste.com/node/1028758.

[42]   Mohammed Masbah, '"Let it Spoil!": Morocco's Boycott and the Empowerment of "Regular" Citizen', in *Al Jazeera Centre for Studies Reports*, 14 November 2018, https://studies.aljazeera.net/en/reports/2018/11/181114115931285.html.

often linked to corruption, inefficiency and patronage networks.[43] As a matter of fact, all the ingredients – such as the economic crisis, the unsatisfied demands – for a future revolt are currently still there.

4. Internal dynamics and external powers: The ability of Mohammed VI to hold the reins of the Kingdom

Albeit the 20FM inaugurated, in a spectacular way, a period of long-lasting mobilisation, exposing the Kingdom to intermittent mass protests, it did not lead to radical changes. Moreover, the adoption of the new constitution did not represent any meaningful and deep change in the institutional architecture of the state. The adoption of the organic laws as required to implement the constitutional provisions was delayed for years, and for the most part the implementation of the organic laws has happened without the participation of civil society.[44]

Regional dynamics such as the civil wars in Libya and Syria and the rise of the jihadist threat in North Africa were exploited by the monarchy as an excuse to end the political opening shortly thereafter. Indeed, since 2011 Morocco has been witnessing a hardening repression. According to Freedom House, today authorities use a number of financial, legal and harassment mechanisms to punish journalists – especially those who focus on the king, Western Sahara and Islam, the three red lines that citizens must not cross. In 2020, several journalists and intellectuals, such as the historian Maâti Monjib, were detained.[45]

It is likewise important to take into account that retrenchment of civic space in Morocco occurred in a decade in which the PJD penetrated the political system significantly. Indeed, the constitutional reforms of July 2011 opened up the political space and provided political parties with new avenues. As had happened in other Arab countries, the Islamist party was better positioned than the others to garner popular consent. The historian Maâti Monjib had warned against this prospect:

> The worst case scenario [for the protest movement in Morocco] would be for the PJD to come out as victorious, with one of its leaders named head of the government, as such

---

43   Chloe Teevan, 'The EU, Morocco, and the Stability Myth', in *Sada*, 16 June 2019, https://carnegieendowment.org/sada/79514.
44   Silvia Colombo et al., 'New Trends in Identity Politics in the Middle-East and North Africa. . .', cit.
45   Freedom House, 'Morocco', in *Freedom in the World 2021*, https://freedomhouse.org/node/4135. See also Human Rights Watch, 'Morocco/Western Sahara', in *World Report 2021. Events of 2020*, 2021, p. 463–469, https://www.hrw.org/node/377405.

an outcome would restore credibility to the king's reforms and the PJD would be unable to push for any core reforms once within the system.[46]

Indeed, after coming out on top at the December 2011 elections, the Islamist party became the monarchy's best ally through a sort of normalisation process, which had actually started already in the 1990s under the leadership of Benkirane. As the PJD became the titular head of the government, it started to enjoy resources and avoid harsh repression like the one faced by the opposition parties.[47] But the king's blessing of the Islamist party was part of a wider monarchy strategy: the PJD was the best ally for stabilising the country thanks to its grassroots and to its strong organisation.[48]

During the 2011 electoral campaign, the PJD presented its programme for a 'new Morocco', echoing the 20FM grievances. The programme was based on five pillars, among which a democratic state without corruption, a dynamic economy protecting social justice and a country without foreign interferences.[49] But once in government, the PJD failed to deliver: from the fight against corruption and the implementation of a judicial reform, the party essentially gave up, whether because of a lack of political will or due to the strength of the vested interests of its leadership.[50] Its ambiguity was clear during the Rif protests, when the PJD turned its back to the *hirak*. In 2017, after almost one year of demonstrations, the PJD – together with five other ruling political parties – criticised the *hirak* as 'secessionist', thus endorsing the securitisation discourse adopted by the regime, which subsequently led to the repression of the movement.[51]

Two factors explain the attitude of the PJD towards the Rif protests. First, the PJD's electorate is mainly constituted by the urban middle class, which has no radical claims but rather pays taxes and hopes to secure a future for its children.

[46]   Maâti Monjib, 'Will Morocco's Elections Subdue Popular Protests?', in *Sada*, 22 November 2011, https://carnegieendowment.org/sada/46041.

[47]   Mohammed Masbah, 'Morocco: Can the PJD Still Absorb Popular Anger?', in *Bawader*, 30 March 2020, https://www.arab-reform.net/?p=9509.

[48]   Ibid.

[49]   PJD, *Pour un Maroc nouveau. Programme électoral du Parti de la Justice et du Développement. Elections législatives du 25 novembre 2011*, https://jalileloutmani.files. wordpress.com/2011/11/lc3a9gislatives-2011-programme-pjd-fr.pdf.

[50]   Intissar Fakir, 'Morocco's Islamist Party. Redefining Politics Under Pressure', in *Carnegie Papers*, December 2017, https://carnegieendowment.org/publications/75121.

[51]   Smail Hamoudi, *'Securitization' of the Rif Protests and Its Political Ramifications*, Moroccan Institute for Policy Analysis (MIPA), September 2019, https://mipa.instit ute/7003.

Second, the PJD is extremely concerned about the regime's reaction against itself.[52] Thus, whereas the PJD has always said that change should occur from the inside, it is the system that has eventually changed the party.[53]

While PJD may be reasonably accused of opportunism, it should be noted that any party or political force would have difficulties to break away from Mohammed VI, as after all Morocco's institutional structure and political system do not allow the ruling party to be independent from the king and set its own policies. Moroccans showed no understanding though. The result of the legislative elections of September 2021, in which the PJD won only 12 seats compared to the 102 gained by the *Rassemblement National des Indépendants* (RNI), a party very close to the monarchy, was a massive defeat. Still in 2016 the Islamist party had won 125 seats, 18 per cent more than in 2011.

The September 2021 elections have demonstrated that the historical phase triggered by the 20FM in 2011, of which the PJD was the first beneficiary, is over. Today the protagonists of the political scene are political parties very close to the king and against which the 20FM and the boycott movement fought. Indeed, Morocco's new prime minister is RNI's secretary, Aziz Akhannouch, a businessman close to Mohammed VI with the largest private wealth in the country and the owner of Afriquia, one of the three private companies targeted by the boycott movement.

The growing self-confidence of Mohammed VI at the national level has also to do with the success of his foreign policy. Indeed, in the last decade the king has managed to consolidate an alliance with the EU and the United States and strengthen relations with Gulf and African countries,[54] while also deepening ties with China and Russia.

Right after Mohammed VI's public speech of 9 March 2011, for instance, the EU expressed its satisfaction towards Morocco with a tangible increase in annual aid and in the number of bilateral agreements. These actions were in contrast with the decision that the EU had just taken to review its policies towards North African countries in light of the Arab uprisings and apply a 'more for more' approach by which the Southern Mediterranean countries would be rewarded only

---

[52]   Nina Kozlowski, 'Maroc: les islamistes du PJD face à l'usure du pouvoir', in *Jeune Afrique*, 22 January 2021, https://www.jeuneafrique.com/1108508/politique/maroc-le-pjd-face-a-lusure-du-pouvoir.

[53]   Ibid.

[54]   Nizar Messari, 'Moroccan Foreign Policy Under Mohammed VI: Balancing Diversity and Respect', in *IAI Commentaries*, No. 20|78 (October 2020), https://www.iai.it/en/node/12287.

if they progressed along the democratic path. The fact that the EU exempted Morocco from its 'more for more' approach might be explained as follows. First, with insecurity on the rise across the MENA region, the EU decided to be content with Morocco's limited democratic reforms so as to secure a cooperative government in Rabat and avoid creating further instability. Second, such EU member states as France and Spain, Morocco's largest trading partners, were keen to de-emphasise democracy promotion in order to protect their established ties with the monarchy and the political-economic system reliant on it.[55] Even though a large majority of the Moroccan population continues to favour rapid political change and rejects the status-quo,[56] the EU has refrained from linking its ambition to forge its 'strategic, multidimensional and privileged relationship' with Morocco[57] to progress on democracy, human rights and the rule of law.[58] The EU's reluctance to do so may have even become a moot point, however. The Moroccan regime today is less vulnerable to pressure from the EU to improve its human rights record, given the king's success in diversifying Morocco's external relations, including growing ties with China and Russia.

Moreover, the regime has now its own cards to put pressure on the EU by easing migration controls at its borders and let migrants take the road to Europe – especially with member States, such as Spain, who are not aligned with the Moroccan position on the Western Sahara issue. In May 2021, following Spain's decision to host for medical treatment Brahim Ghali, leader of the Polisario front that fights for the independence of Western Sahara, Rabat relaxed its border controls with the Spanish enclave of Ceuta, letting around 8,000 people cross into Europe,[59] before excluding Spain from 'Operation Marhaba' (supposed to manage the return of Moroccans living abroad to Morocco) for the summer of 2021. The incident provoked a severe diplomatic crisis between Rabat and Madrid, prompting the Spanish government to send military reinforcement to the territories, while continuing to host Ghali.

---

55 Silvia Colombo and Benedetta Voltolini, '"Business as Usual" in EU Democracy Promotion Towards Morocco? Assessing the Limits of the EU's Approach towards the Mediterranean after the Arab Uprisings', in *L'Europe en Formation*, No. 371 (2014), p. 41–57, https://doi.org/10.3917/eufor.371.0041.
56 Daniella Raz, *Youth in the Middle East and North Africa*, cit.
57 European Union and Morocco, *Joint Declaration for the Fourteenth Meeting of the Association Council*, 27 June 2019, https://europa.eu/!vJ99Fh.
58 Chloe Teevan, 'The EU, Morocco, and the Stability Myth', cit.
59 'Morocco Wants Investigation Into Polisario Chief's Spain Arrival', in *Al Jazeera*, 22 May 2021, https://aje.io/uxlmy.

What has most helped Rabat to take a harder line with Spain was the December 2020 United States recognition of Moroccan sovereignty over Western Sahara, which ended nearly thirty years of US support for UN-led negotiations based on the promotion of a referendum in the territories to determine whether to grant it autonomy, independence or full integration with Morocco.[60] However, Trump's decision – which came with the US proposal of selling to Rabat 1 billion dollars in weapons – was part of a deal which envisaged a partial diplomatic normalisation between Morocco and Israel, together with the promotion of economic and technological cooperation between the two states. The agreement had far-reaching regional and domestic implications. At the regional level, despite the agreement was harshly criticised by some Arab countries, such as Algeria, it paid off with Morocco's target allies, namely the Gulf states. Indeed, today Rabat is closer to the Arab Gulf allies, especially the United Arab Emirates, which have pursued their own détente policy towards Israel to secure a firmer US commitment to their security and have recognised Morocco's sovereignty over the Western Sahara. That said, Morocco's strategic alliance with some Arab Gulf countries had started earlier and paid off also in economic terms. In 2011, for instance, Gulf countries strongly supported Rabat with 5 billion dollars of financial aid, as well as with military, infrastructure and tourism investments. In exchange of financial support, Morocco endorsed – with some exceptions – critical foreign policy choices of Abu Dhabi and Riyadh such as the war in Yemen or pressure on Iran.

At the internal level, the partial normalisation with Israel is a double-edged sword for the monarchy.[61] On the one side, the king's decision (the Parliament was not consulted) provoked popular criticism with protests in support of the Palestinian cause or against the normalisation, especially in May 2021 in solidarity with Palestinians facing Israeli attacks in Gaza. But on the other side, the king was capable to appease domestic criticism by expressing pro-Palestine support and by presenting this deal as a tool for acting as a mediator between Palestinians and Israelis.[62] Also, with the political parties, the king emerged unhurt while the PJD paid the price of the decision during the last legislatives

[60] Kristen E. Eichensehr et al., 'United States Recognizes Morocco's Sovereignty Over Western Sahara', in *American Journal of International Law*, Vol. 115, No. 2 (April 2021), p. 318–323, https://doi.org/10.1017/ajil.2021.11.

[61] Yasmina Abouzzouhour, 'Partial Normalization: Morocco's Balancing Act', in *Bawader*, 10 August 2021, https://www.arab-reform.net/?p=19484.

[62] Yasmina Abouzzouhour, 'Morocco's Partial Normalization with Israel Comes with Risks and Gains', in *Order from Chaos*, 14 December 2020, https://brook.gs/34e05YW.

elections. Indeed, despite some critical voices within the Islamic party, the king's decision has been supported by the party leadership and this move might be considered as one of the triggering factors that contributed to the PJD defeat. Historically, in the Arab world, people have always considered Islamist parties as a tool to get out of their sense of submission to the West. The fact that the so-called normalisation process happened with the PJD in power has shattered this myth.

However, at the international level, the partial normalisation and the US recognition of Morocco's sovereignty over Western Sahara did not bring major changes. After Trump's move, the United Nations declared that its position remained unchanged, underscoring the need to relaunch diplomacy in accordance with relevant UN Security Council resolutions on the conflict,[63] while the EU remained silent, thus confirming its ambiguous position. Indeed, for many years the EU has been neglecting the Western Sahara issue by focusing, instead, to its bilateral relations with Morocco,[64] especially with trade agreements that have been applied also to the disputed territories. Yet, despite the hesitation of Brussels, recent developments may lead the EU to adopt a different approach. In September 2021, the European Court of Justice (CJEU) declared invalid two of the EU-Morocco trade agreements on agriculture and fishery over Western Sahara – as they were not agreed with the consent of the Sahraoui people. Brussels has immediately reacted by publishing a joint statement with Rabat underlying its willingness to ensure bilateral trade cooperation with the Kingdom. That said, the CJEU decision underscores the need for the EU institutions to respect European laws and, therefore, rebalance its ties with Morocco.[65]

Conclusion

Although the 20FM movement prompted the Moroccan monarchy to enact reforms, such as the adoption of a new constitution, the post-2011 period has not brought about radical changes from an economic, social and political point of view.

---

[63] Michelle Nichols, 'U.N. Security Council to Talk Western Sahara after Trump Policy Switch', in *Reuters*, 17 December 2020, https://reut.rs/3ajkCPG.

[64] Hugh Lovatt, 'Western Sahara, Morocco, and the EU: How Good Law Makes Good Politics', in *ECFR Commentaries*, 30 September 2021, https://ecfr.eu/?p=78120. See also: Malcolm Cavanagh, 'The EU's Confused Western Sahara Position – A Foreign Policy Failure, Or an Opportunity?', in *LSE Department of International Relations Blog*, 4 May 2021, https://wp.me/p2Slxn-Qw.

[65] Ibid.

The new constitution has not modified the institutional architecture of the state in any appreciable measure. Unsurprisingly the Islamist party that won the first legislative elections after the 2011 protests, the PJD, was eventually unable – and unwilling – to govern independently of the monarch. This behaviour and alignment with the monarchy has led the PJD to lose popular support. The regime, while stalling the reform process, has unleashed its repressive machine against citizens and political activists. Finally, King Mohammed VI has managed to hold the reins of power also thanks to the new external alliances he has built up over the years, especially with the United States and the Arab gulf states.

This notwithstanding, Morocco has kept witnessing sporadic and intermittent protests which, although different in composition and strategies, have highlighted the fact that the 20FM has brought lasting societal changes. Today, all the ingredients for a future revolt are still present: lack of economic opportunity, insufficient provision of public goods by the state and restrictions to individual and collective rights. But no one knows if it will ever take place, neither in which form, nor when. This is even more the case in the current historical juncture that was opened with the defeat of the PJD in the elections and the return of political parties close to the king to the centre of the political scene.

References

Yasmina Abouzzouhour, 'Morocco's Partial Normalization with Israel Comes with Risks and Gains', in *Order from Chaos*, 14 December 2020, https://brook.gs/34e05YW

Yasmina Abouzzouhour, 'Partial Normalization: Morocco's Balancing Act', in *Bawader*, 10 August 2021, https://www.arab-reform.net/?p=19484

Hisham Aidi, 'Is Morocco Header Toward Insurrection?', in *The Nation*, 13 July 2017, https://www.thenation.com/?p=253592

Aida Alami, 'Morocco's Stability is Roiled by Monthslong Protests over Fishmonger's Death', in *The New York Times*, 26 August 2017, https://www.nytimes.com/2017/08/26/world/africa/morocco-berber-rif-nasser-zefzafi.html

Cédric Baylocq and Jacopo Granci, '"20 février". Discours et portraits d'un mouvement de révolte au Maroc', in *L'Année du Maghreb*, Vol. VIII (2012), p. 239–258, https://doi.org/10.4000/anneemaghreb.1483

Florence Beaugé, 'L'économie marocaine commence à pâtir de la récession internationale', in *Le Monde*, 3 December 2008, https://www.lemonde.fr/la-crise-financiere/article/2008/12/03/l-economie-marocaine-commence-a-patir-de-la-recession-internationale_1126328_1101386.html

Florence Beaugé, 'Maroc: le sondage interdit', in *Le Monde*, 3 August 2009, https://www.lemonde.fr/afrique/article/2009/08/03/maroc-le-sondage-interdit_1225217_3212.html

Ahmed Benchemsi, 'Feb20's Rise and Fall: a Moroccan Story', in *Le blog de Ahmed Benchemsi*, 17 July 2012, http://ahmedbenchemsi.com/?p=556

Sara Borrillo, *Femminismi e Islam in Marocco. Attiviste laiche, teologhe, predicatrici*, Naples, Edizioni scientifiche italiane, 2017

Anouar Boukhars, *Politics in Morocco. Executive Monarchy and Enlightened Authoritarianism*, London/New York, Routledge, 2011

Malcolm Cavanagh, 'The EU's Confused Western Sahara Position –A Foreign Policy Failure, Or an Opportunity?', in *LSE Department of International Relations Blog*, 4 May 2021, https://wp.me/p2Slxn-Qw

Silvia Colombo and Benedetta Voltolini, ' "Business as Usual" in EU Democracy Promotion Towards Morocco? Assessing the Limits of the EU's Approach towards the Mediterranean after the Arab Uprisings', in *L'Europe en Formation*, No. 371 (2014), p. 41–57, https://doi.org/10.3917/eufor.371.0041

Silvia Colombo et al., 'New Trends in Identity Politics in the Middle-East and North Africa and their Impact on State-society Relations', in *MENARA Working Papers*, No. 14 (October 2018), https://www.iai.it/en/node/9573

Thierry Desrues, 'Le Mouvement du 20 février et le régime marocain: contestation, révision constitutionnelle et élections', in *L'Année du Maghreb*, Vol. VIII (2012), p. 359–389, https://doi.org/10.4000/anneemaghreb.1537

Kristen E. Eichensehr et al., 'United States Recognizes Morocco's Sovereignty Over Western Sahara', in *American Journal of International Law*, Vol. 115, No. 2 (April 2021), p. 318–323, https://doi.org/10.1017/ajil.2021.11

European Union and Morocco, *Joint Declaration for the Fourteenth Meeting of the Association Council*, 27 June 2019, https://europa.eu/!vJ99Fh

Intissar Fakir, 'Morocco's Islamist Party. Redefining Politics Under Pressure', in *Carnegie Papers*, December 2017, https://carnegieendowment.org/publications/75121

David Gouery, 'La pauvreté, à l'origine du Hirak?', in *TAFRA Blog*, 5 February 2019, https://tafra.ma/?p=2776

Smail Hamoudi, *'Securitization' of the Rif Protests and Its Political Ramifications*, Moroccan Institute for Policy Analysis (MIPA), September 2019, https://mipa.institute/7003

Human Rights Watch, *Morocco: End Police Actions against Persons Accused of Breaking Ramadan Fast*, 19 September 2009, https://www.hrw.org/node/237795

Human Rights Watch, 'Morocco/Western Sahara', in *World Report 2021. Events of 2020*, 2021, p. 463–469, https://www.hrw.org/node/377405

Kingdom of Morocco, *Texte intégral du discours adressé par SM le Roi à la Nation*, 9 March 2011, https://www.maroc.ma/fr/node/62

Nina Kozlowski, 'Maroc: les islamistes du PJD face à l'usure du pouvoir', in *Jeune Afrique*, 22 January 2021, https://www.jeuneafrique.com/1108508/politique/maroc-le-pjd-face-a-lusure-du-pouvoir

Hugh Lovatt, 'Western Sahara, Morocco, and the EU: How Good Law Makes Good Politics', in *ECFR Commentaries*, 30 September 2021, https://ecfr.eu/?p=78120

Mohammed Masbah, ' "Let it Spoil!": Morocco's Boycott and the Empowerment of "Regular" Citizen', in *Al Jazeera Centre for Studies Reports*, 14 November 2018, https://studies.aljazeera.net/en/reports/2018/11/181114115931285.html

Mohammed Masbah, 'Morocco: Can the PJD Still Absorb Popular Anger?', in *Bawader*, 30 March 2020, https://www.arab-reform.net/?p=9509

Aude Mazoue, 'Maroc: le Mouvement du 20-février "n'a pas été massif mais a entraîné des changements de société"', in *France 24*, 20 February 2021, https://www.france24.com/fr/afrique/20210220-maroc-le-mouvement-du-20-février-n-a-pas-été-massif-mais-a-entraîné-des-changements-de-société

Nizar Messari, 'Moroccan Foreign Policy Under Mohammed VI: Balancing Diversity and Respect', in *IAI Commentaries*, No. 20|78 (October 2020), https://www.iai.it/en/node/12287

Maâti Monjib, 'Will Morocco's Elections Subdue Popular Protests?', in *Sada*, 22 November 2011, https://carnegieendowment.org/sada/46041

Michelle Nichols, 'U.N. Security Council to Talk Western Sahara after Trump Policy Switch', in *Reuters*, 17 December 2020, https://reut.rs/3ajkCPG

PJD, *Pour un Maroc nouveau. Programme électoral du Parti de la Justice et du Développement. Elections législatives du 25 novembre 2011*, https://jalileloutmani.files.wordpress.com/2011/11/lc3a9gislatives-2011-programme-pjd-fr.pdf

Project on Middle East Democracy, *The 'February 20' Movement*, June 2011, https://pomed.org/wp-content/uploads/2011/06/Press_Kit_June2011.pdf

Daniella Raz, *Youth in the Middle East and North Africa*, Arab Barometer, August 2019, https://www.arabbarometer.org/wp-content/uploads/ABV_Youth_Report_Public-Opinion_Middle-East-North-Africa_2019-1.pdf

Nadia Salah, 'Enquête l'Economiste-Sunergia/Boycott: Danone, un cas très special', in *L'Economiste*, No. 5279 (24 May 2018), https://www.leconomiste.com/node/1028758

Chloe Teevan, 'The EU, Morocco, and the Stability Myth', in *Sada*, 16 June 2019, https://carnegieendowment.org/sada/79514

Saloua Zerhouni, 'Jeunes et participation politique au Maroc', in *Rapports thématiques IRES*, June 2009, https://www.ires.ma/images/PDFs_publications/jeunes_et_participation_politique_au_maroc.pdf

Saloua Zerhouni, 'Le marketing politique. Faible impact electoral', in *Economia*, 22 July 2015, http://economia.ma/fr/content/le-marketing-politique-faible-impact-électoral

Saloua Zerhouni and Azeddine Akesbi, 'Youth Activism in Morocco: Exclusion, Agency and the Search for Inclusion', in *Power2Youth Papers*, No. 15 (September 2016), https://www.iai.it/en/node/6815

Silvia Colombo

Chapter 8: Tunisia's Quest for Democracy: Unfinished Domestic Revolution and Regional Geopolitical Entanglements

Tunisia is at a historical juncture following the moves by President Kaïs Saïed on 25 July 2021 that suspended the Parliament, stripped lawmakers of their immunity and fired Prime Minister Hichem Mechichi. While shocking, these actions have not been totally unexpected. The past decade has seen the completion of the political and institutional democratic transition marked by the elections for the Constitutional Assembly (October 2011), the vote for the new Constitution (January 2014), parliamentary and presidential elections (October and November 2014, respectively), the Carthage Agreement (July 2016) that led to the national unity government led by Youssef Chahed, and the latest presidential and parliamentary elections that ran between 15 September and 13 October 2019.

Tunisia has had to withstand many challenges. On the domestic front, dire socio-economic conditions, augmented by austerity measures adopted by the government, have fuelled the frustration and anger of the population – particularly of the new generations. In parallel, security concerns related to violent extremism and instability spilling over from Libya have risked jeopardising the political and institutional gains starting from 2015. Finally, the virulent spread of covid-19, particularly during the first months of 2021, dramatically unmasked the ruling authorities' inefficient management of the state.

All of this has caused recurrent cycles of popular protests and mobilisations to become a constant feature of Tunisia's recent history. While cycles of protests have tended to show similar features in terms of people's participation, forms of mobilisation as well as the broad response by the ruling authorities, it would be a mistake to consider them as instances of the same pattern. There are indeed profound differences between the 2011 protests that sparked the Tunisian revolution against the despotic regime of Zine El-Abidine Ben Ali, on the one hand, and the protest iterations between 2016 and 2021, on the other. Although they are part of the same process of democratic transition and consolidation, they have contributed to it in different forms and have, on their part, been affected by it differently.

The two most striking differences with the 2011 protests concern, first, the significant place of socio-economic claims and their impact on political and institutional dynamics and, second, the growing role of external players. Understanding such differences is crucial to shed light onto Tunisia's quest for democracy, its potential future trajectory and the stumbling blocks it has been facing.

1. Tunisia's protest movements: A decade-long learning experience

Despite its much-touted supply-side economic reforms, by the end of the 2000s the Ben Ali regime had proven incapable of solving Tunisia's developmental problems. A sustained per capita growth in GDP of about 5 per cent was recorded annually from the mid-1990s to 2008 and the World Bank Doing Business Report unsurprisingly acknowledged the economic success of Tunisia and called it a 'top reformer'.[1] Nevertheless, GDP growth had not trickled down to the bulk of the population, mainly due to the predatory behaviours of a crony capitalist elite centred on the president's extended family and entourage, poor macroeconomic management, a highly centralised and inefficient bureaucracy, excessive state presence in the economy and a large informal sector providing low-skill, low-paid employment for the high number of Tunisian graduate students swelling the ranks of the so-called *diplômés chômeurs* (unemployed graduates). Factors such as unemployment, governance deficits and unfair contracting had indeed inspired the protests that broke out in Gafsa in early 2008.[2] Prior to this, Tunisia had experienced several other protests, for example the January 1978 unrest and the Bread Riots of 1984.[3]

In the 'delicate authoritarian bargain' between the regime and society in Tunisia 'everything seemed to be in place as long as the former succeeded in providing economic and social gains', thus cultivating its legitimacy and political

---

[1] World Bank, *Doing Business 2009. Comparing Regulation in 181 Economies*, Washington, World Bank and Palgrave Macmillan, 2008, p. 79, http://hdl.handle.net/10986/6313.

[2] John Chalcraft, *Popular Politics in the Making of the Modern Middle East*, New York, Cambridge University Press, 2016; Laryssa Chomiak, 'The Making of a Revolution in Tunisia', in *Middle East Law and Governance*, Vol. 3, No. 1–2 (March 2011), p. 72.

[3] David Seddon, 'Riot and Rebellion: Political Responses to Economic Crisis in North Africa, Tunisia, Morocco and Sudan', in Berch Berberoglu (ed.), *Power and Stability in the Middle East*, London, Zed Books, 1989, p. 114–135.

stability in return.[4] However, economic grievances, rising economic inequalities and regional disparities pushed social discontent up at the end of the 2000s.
At that time, the global financial crisis experienced by European countries –
Tunisia's main trading partners – jolted the Tunisian economy.[5] Honwana and
Mnasri estimate that 31 per cent of the youth with an engineering degree, 50
per cent with a technical and master's degree, and 68 per cent with a master's
degree in legal studies were unemployed at the end of the first decade of the 21st
century.[6] The self-immolation of the young street vendor Mohamed Bouazizi in
Sidi Bouzid in December 2010 triggered mass demonstrations, which quickly
turned into a full-scale revolution. Ben Ali made a last-ditch attempt to calm
youth's anger by announcing a package of urgent measures, including the pledge
to create new 300,000 jobs in two years – but to no avail.[7] This was followed by
a fierce reaction: Ben Ali placed snipers on roofs as he saw his fortunes dwindle.
He eventually fled to Saudi Arabia on 14 January 2011, a move that contributed to igniting the fire of revolutions across the Middle East and North Africa
(MENA) region.

The fact that the uprising started in the peripheries was not a surprise. Since
Tunisia gained independence in 1956, a historical concentration of investments
(mainly in tourism and infrastructures) in coastal areas (such as Tunis, Monastir,
Mahdia and Sousse) had resulted in the continuing marginalisation of internal
regions (such as Sidi Bouzid, Kasserine, Medinine and Gafsa), creating an explosive cleavage between the centre and the periphery of the country. The marginalisation of interior regions had only worsened under Ben Ali's regime which, over
two decades, took deliberate decisions that progressively reduced Tunisia's interior regions to reservoirs of cheap labour, agrarian products and raw materials for
the more developed industries and service sectors operating in the coastal areas.[8]

---

4   Mohammad Dawood Sofi, 'Rethinking the Root Causes of the Tunisian Revolution
    and Its Implications', in *Contemporary Arab Affairs*, Vol. 12, No. 3 (September 2019),
    p. 41–64.
5   Lahcen Achy, 'Tunisia's Economic Challenges', in *Carnegie Papers*, December 2011,
    https://carnegieendowment.org/publications/46304.
6   Chamseddine Mnasri, 'Tunisia: The People's Revolution', in *International Socialism*,
    No. 130 (Spring 2011), p. 19–26, http://isj.org.uk/?p=720; Alcinda Honwana, *Youth
    and Revolution in Tunisia*, London/New York, Zed Books, 2013, p. 26.
7   See Bilal Randeree, 'Tunisian Leader Promises New Jobs', in *Al Jazeera*, 10 January 2011,
    https://aje.io/h7sqe.
8   Silvia Colombo and Hamza Meddeb, 'Fostering Inclusiveness: A New Roadmap for EU-
    Tunisia Relations and the Engagement with Civil Society', in Emmanuel Cohen-Hadria

Tribal and family affiliations were at the core of the clientelist resource distribution system meant to maintain fragile stability. However, people excluded from patronage networks started to accumulate rage and frustration. On the eve of the fall of Ben Ali, poverty was estimated at 42 per cent in the Centre-West and at 36 per cent in the North-West, whereas it was at the much lower rate of 11 per cent in Tunis and the Centre-East of the country.[9]

The factors that prompted the January 2011 Tunisian revolution were not confined to the devastating socio-economic situation. On the political front, there were equally important reasons for discontent and frustration. Following Ben Ali's coming to power in 1987, an early phase of political liberalisation opened, during which the new president released hundreds of political prisoners, including Islamists, admitted new political parties and negotiated a National Pact with the country's main opposition forces, abolished state security courts, put a ceiling on the number of presidential terms and relaxed controls over television and radio.[10]

However, soon thereafter, the true face of the president and his regime started to reveal itself when he ordered the systematic repression of any forms of opposition and dissent and curtailed basic rights and liberties. The main victims of these measures were human rights activists, journalists and members of the opposition, particularly the Islamist-leaning ones.[11] These practices contrasted with the image of Tunisia as a liberalising, moderate country, cultivated both by Tunisian authorities and its external partners, international financial institutions, such as the World Bank, and the European Union. This is in line with what Perkins calls *'démocratie à la tunisienne'*, namely Tunisia's ability to keep up appearances by pursuing democratic governance selectively.[12] Citizens were given the opportunity to discuss and endorse the work of their government but not to set its

---

(ed.), 'The EU-Tunisia Priviledged Partnership – What Next?', in *EuroMeSCo Joint Policy Studies*, No. 10 (April 2018), p. 36, https://www.iemed.org/?p=16266.

[9]   Ibid.; Hamza Meddeb, 'Peripheral Vision: How Europe Can Help Preserve Tunisia's Fragile Democracy', in *ECFR Policy Briefs*, January 2017, https://ecfr.eu/?p=3752.

[10] Silvia Colombo, *Political and Institutional Transition in North Africa. Egypt and Tunisia in Comparative Perspective*, London/New York, Routledge, 2018, p. 38.

[11] Kristina Kausch, 'Tunisia: The Life of Others. Project on Freedom of Association in the Middle East and North Africa', in *FRIDE Working Papers*, No. 85 (June 2009), http://web.archive.org/web/20100621183853/http://www.fride.org/descarga/FRIDE_WP85_INGLES_FINAL.pdf.

[12] Kenneth Perkins, *A History of Modern Tunisia*, Cambridge, Cambridge University Press, 2004.

agenda.[13] This appearance of participation was particularly painful for the youth, who represented a great chunk of Tunisia's population and thus the bulk of the marginalised.

The significance of the events of 2010–2011 for Tunisian youth cannot be underestimated, as after all the Tunisian revolution was unanimously hailed as a 'youth revolution'.[14] The mobilisation of Tunisian youth went beyond the purely generational struggle. Youth demands and strategies in 2011 were illustrative of the full array of challenges resulting from the exclusion of the Tunisian population at large from economic, political and socio-cultural arenas and caused by the failure of the post-independence development models.[15]

The intensity with which the Tunisian youth experienced the protests stems from the fact that they had developed a particular consciousness about being 'young'.[16] As Herrera and Bayat have argued with regard to the Mediterranean countries in general, schooling, mass media, iconic urban spaces (such as public parks, squares and shopping malls), as well as new information communication technologies, all played a crucial role in fostering a particular consciousness about being young, facilitating mutual exchanges and peer interaction also across national borders.[17] During the multiple demonstrations of early 2011, the courage of Tunisia's younger generations, who challenged the ruthlessness of the regime, contributed to drawing other people into the protest fray. This was the story, for instance, of some civil society organisations (CSOs), the powerful Trade Unions movement broadly represented by the *Union Générale Tunisienne du Travail* (UGTT), lawyers and opposition political figures, who joined the protest at a later stage.[18] It also pushed the armed

---

[13] Ibid., p. 208.

[14] Vanessa Szakal, 'Regards croisés sur le mal-être de la jeunesse tunisienne', in *Nawaat*, 11 May 2017, https://nawaat.org/2017/05/11/regards-croises-sur-le-mal-etre-de-la-jeunesse-tunisienne.

[15] M. Chloe Mulderig, 'Adulthood Denied: Youth Dissatisfaction and the Arab Spring', in *BU Pardee Issues in Brief*, No. 21 (October 2011), https://www.bu.edu/pardee/?p=10776.

[16] Maria Cristina Paciello and Daniela Pioppi, 'Youth Empowerment as a Collective, Bottom-Up and Long-Term Process', in *IEMed. Mediterranean Yearbook 2014*, p. 68, https://www.iemed.org/?p=29081.

[17] Linda Herrera and Asef Bayat (eds), *Being Young and Muslim. New Cultural Politics in the Global South and North*, Oxford, Oxford University Press, 2010.

[18] To be more precise the base of the syndicate at the regional and provincial levels did join the demonstrations spontaneously from the beginning – as it had done during the

forces to give up their role as guardians of a dying regime and to side with the demonstrators.[19]

In addition to the centrality of youth, the gender dimension is also worth underscoring as a key element both during the revolution and in its aftermath. While institutionally Tunisian women have enjoyed significantly more progressive rights in comparison to the situation of women in other Arab countries since the passing of the *Code de statut personnel* in 1956, gender-based discrimination has reinforced other dimensions of domestic marginalisation (generational factors, regional disparities) as demonstrated by the fact that young women had lower employment rates than young men (13.3 per cent versus 30.3 per cent in 2011) and much lower ones compared to male adults (44.3 per cent).[20]

In light of these features, the Tunisian revolution has been hailed as a 'populist, youthful, and technological [. . .] uprising'.[21] Internet, media and social networking sites were very effective tools in organising the protests, catalysing the revolution that otherwise would have evolved at a much slower pace.[22] According to Masri, social media gave substantive, symbolic and organisational force to the revolution.[23] More importantly, social media acted as the most important tool in transforming a large number of people from mere observers of activism to activists themselves.[24]

Tunisian youth in particular were masters when it came to the use of the latest communication technologies. Tunisia was the first Arab country to provisionally install the Internet in 1991. From the mid-1990s on, the Ben Ali regime

---

2008 Gafsa protests. On the contrary, initial immobilism applied to the cadres of the syndicate who were closer to the Ben Ali regime. See Joel Beinin, *Workers and Thieves. Labor Movements and Popular Uprisings in Tunisia and Egypt*, Stanford, Stanford Briefs, 2015.

[19]   Author's phone interview with Tunisian activist, May 2021.

[20]   Organisation for Economic Co-operation and Development (OECD), *Investing in Youth: Tunisia. Strengthening the Employability of Youth during the Transition to a Green Economy*, Paris, OECD Publishing, 2015, p. 20, https://read.oecd.org/10.1787/978926 4226470-en.

[21]   Kenneth Perkins, *A History of Modern Tunisia*, cit., p. 225.

[22]   Anita Breuer, Todd Landman and Dorothea Farquhar, 'Social Media and Protest Mobilization: Evidence from the Tunisian Revolution', in *Democratization*, Vol. 22, No. 4 (2015), p. 764–792.

[23]   Safwan M. Masri, *Tunisia: An Arab Anomaly*, New York, Columbia University Press, 2017, p. 32.

[24]   Jon B. Alterman, 'The Revolution Will Not Be Tweeted', in *The Washington Quarterly*, Vol. 34, No. 4 (Fall 2011), p. 103–116, https://www.csis.org/node/28318.

invested heavily in promoting the telecommunications sector, endowing Tunisia with one of the most developed telecommunications infrastructures (including the Internet) in the region. Some reports suggest that in 2001, out of a population of 10.5 million, the number of Internet users reached almost 4 million.[25] On the other hand, the regime closely monitored Internet use and frequently resorted to one of the world's most repressive control of communication, at different levels. Censorship included shutting down the Internet service for any amount of time and banning various websites and blogs.

Even before Bouazizi's self-immolation sparked nationwide protests, tech-savvy activists had been at the forefront of confronting the regime. A good example in this regard is that of the 2008 Gafsa protests. As expected, the Tunisian press hardly bothered to cover these incidents, whereas the international media reported on them frequently. The authorities then censored foreign broadcasting. Activists used an alternative yet dynamic platform to transmit the information about the Gafsa incident to a wider audience, primarily through emails and Facebook. Another important Facebook campaign became popular in the country under the name of 'Tunisia in White' (*Tunisie en Blanc*), in which young activists tried to break Internet censorship.[26]

It was in 2011 that social media really became the main tool in the hands of a tech-savvy generation actively engaged in breaking the national media blackout in Tunisia. The widespread use of cell phones, the Internet, Facebook, Twitter, YouTube channels and blogs represented an electronic alternative platform for social and political activism Tunisian authorities found extremely difficult to exercise control on. Digital media also provided an element of emotional mobilisation: beyond enabling filming and sharing the protests, more importantly electronic communication served as a powerful means to expose the authoritarian face of Ben Ali's regime and its propaganda, including by revealing regime abuses and disclosing government corruption to a wider audience within and beyond Tunisia. This role was compounded by that of international media networks, such as Al Jazeera, El Hiwar, Al Arabiya, the BBC and CNN, covering the revolution.

With Ben Ali's flight to Saudi Arabia in January 2011, the main goal of the brave, short-term Tunisian popular mobilisation had been accomplished. However, throughout the following decade protests and demonstrations never

---

[25] Amira Aleya-Sghaier, 'The Tunisian Revolution: The Revolution of Dignity', in *The Journal of the Middle East and Africa*, Vol. 3, No. 1 (2012), p. 37.
[26] Laryssa Chomiak, 'The Making of a Revolution in Tunisia', cit., p. 72–75.

stopped. They actually acquired even more importance in keeping the bar high in terms of people's demands vis-à-vis the unfolding democratic transition and consolidation process. They effectively became part of a learning experience at the grassroots level. Most of them have originated from the southern part of the country, thus reinforcing the idea of two-speed Tunisia in development terms, and have been mainly motivated by the pressing issues of (youth) unemployment and underdevelopment.

In January 2016, a wave of social unrest and violent demonstrations began in Kasserine, after the death of a young man who had contested the results of a hiring procedure, and spread through sixteen other governorates. The protesters complained about unemployment and denounced the corruption plaguing the regional administration.[27] In September 2016, in the mining region of Gafsa and in the Jendouba governorate (close to the Algerian border), demonstrators protested against economic marginalisation and local corruption for several weeks.[28] In March 2017, strikes and demonstrations in Tataouine completely blocked all economic activity in the region. According to reports of the event, 'protesters proclaimed their right to employment and the development of their marginalised region, where many oil companies operate without accepting any social or environmental responsibility for the development of the area'.[29]

Indeed, environmental rights have gradually climbed the ladder of the priorities of popular mobilisation in Tunisia with the setting up of coalitions across CSOs working on overarching issues also in cooperation with external partners.[30] Demonstrators in Tataouine called for concrete measures to foster economic development and people's participation in the legal economy, for example by setting up a free trade zone with neighbouring Libya, and to strip national and international investors, which have access to natural resources, of exploitation

---

[27] Silvia Colombo and Hamza Meddeb, 'Fostering Inclusiveness', cit., p. 42; Vanessa Szakal, 'After Kasserine, Protests Break Out in 16 Governorates', in *Nawaat*, 22 January 2016, https://nawaat.org/portail/2016/01/22/after-kasserine-protests-break-out-in-16-gover norates.

[28] Hamza Meddeb, 'Peripheral Vision', cit.; Maha Yahya, 'Great Expectations in Tunisia', in *Carnegie Papers*, March 2016, https://carnegieendowment.org/publications/63138.

[29] Hamza Meddeb, 'Precarious Resilience: Tunisia's Libyan Predicament', in *MENARA Future Notes*, No. 5 (April 2017), p. 7, https://www.iai.it/en/node/7722.

[30] For more insights on environmental rights in the context of the Tunisian mobilisation, see Eric Goldstein, 'Tunisia's Legacy of Pollution Confronts Democratic Politics', in *Open Democracy*, 23 May 2014, https://www.opendemocracy.net/en/north-africa-west-asia/tunisias-legacy-of-pollution-confronts-democratic-politics.

rights.[31] New protests broke out in January 2018 after the passing of the new economic and financial law and following the announcement of new rounds of austerity measures.[32] A national strike to demand pay increases for public employees in January 2019 brought the country to a halt.[33]

The army and the security apparatuses in general have tended to adopt a harsher response vis-à-vis these more recent protests compared to the 2011 ones due to the general over-securitisation of popular mobilisation and activism by Tunisian authorities influenced by changing regional and international circumstances. This response – which has involved the use of water cannons, police barricades and indiscriminate arrests – has triggered further unrest and has led to violent clashes between officers and protesters.[34]

The high rate of covid-19 infections registered in the country particularly in the first half of 2021, together with the governing authorities' mismanagement of the prevention and vaccination campaigns, led to the multiplication of protests, which took place in spite of the restrictions. It is not by coincidence that President Kaïs Saïed's decisions on 25 July 2021 were taken during the peak of the covid-19 wave with average rates of infections at more than 7,000 daily cases.

All in all, Tunisia's decade-long mobilisation has been characterised by the emergence of new claims framed along previously dormant or hidden collective identities. As argued elsewhere, while before 2011 identity-related issues were generally regarded as taboo – to protect the seemingly homogeneous Arab-Muslim nature of Tunisian identity and the peaceful character of the country – the revolution provided the space and opportunity for a new discourse around the role of minorities to emerge. This discourse has been powerfully framed within the 'right to diversity' language (*droit à la différence*) thanks to the

---

[31] Youssef Cherif, 'The Kamour Movement and Civic Protests in Tunisia', in *Carnegie Articles*, 8 August 2017, https://carnegieendowment.org/publications/72774; Alessandra Bajec, 'Tunisia: In Tataouine, Socio-Economic Marginalization Is a Time Bomb', in *Bawader*, 24 July 2020, https://www.arab-reform.net/?p=11217.

[32] Lilia Blaise, 'Nearly 800 Arrested in Economic Protests in Tunisia', in *The New York Times*, 12 January 2018, https://www.nytimes.com/2018/01/12/world/africa/tunisia-tunis-protests-arrests.html; International Crisis Group, Interview with Michaël Béchir Ayari, *Stemming Tunisia's Authoritarian Drift* (video), 11 January 2018, https://www.crisisgroup.org/node/5916.

[33] 'Tunisia's Powerful UGTT Workers Union Holds Nationwide Strike', in *Al Jazeera*, 17 January 2019, https://aje.io/j5edj.

[34] Yasmina Abouzoohour, 'Caught in Transition: Tunisia's Protests and the Threat of Repression', in *ECFR Commentaries*, 23 February 2021, https://ecfr.eu/?p=68181.

relentless work of Tunisian civil society.[35] For example, sectarian, ethnic and even tribal fault lines have started to emerge at the societal level, thus leading to fissures within society and to political competition.

For example, moderate/pragmatic Islamists, such as supporters of the moderate Islamist Ennahda party, and more radical ones (e.g., those supporting the Salafists) started to compete for visibility and power, drawing political lines of demarcation between secularists and Islamists and within the Islamist camp itself.[36] Another fault line that has been projected onto Tunisian society for the first time is that between Arab and Amazigh, often inspired by the experience of Moroccan ethnic struggles.[37] Finally, regional and local collective identities have been sharpened vis-à-vis the central powers through the manipulation of previously hidden tribal identities (e.g., for example in the Sfax region), leading to a partial reappearance of tribalism as a way to affirm local identities that are not sufficiently taken into account at the national level.[38]

All these new identity-based claims have had an impact on the two biggest and most important groups in the demonstrations, the youth and the women. Like in other Arab countries, the Tunisian youth have quickly divided along ideological, religious and mainly socio-economic fault lines. This was demonstrated already during the January 2011 revolution when the youth in the cities mainly protested for civil rights while the youth in the countryside took to the streets chanting slogans for better economic conditions, equality and social justice.[39] This applies also to women's activism. The Tunisian mobilisation around women's issues after 2011 has been deeply divided particularly between the conservative/Islamist-leaning groups, on the one hand, and the progressive/secular ones, on the other.[40]

---

[35] Silvia Colombo et al., 'New Trends in Identity Politics in the Middle East and North Africa and Their Impact on State-Society Relations', in *MENARA Working Papers*, No. 14 (October 2018), p. 12–13, https://www.iai.it/en/node/9573.

[36] Silvia Colombo and Benedetta Voltolini, 'The EU's Engagement with "Moderate" Political Islam: The Case of Ennahda', in *LSE Middle East Centre Papers*, No. 19 (July 2017), http://eprints.lse.ac.uk/84065.

[37] Silvia Colombo et al., 'New Trends in Identity Politics in the Middle East and North Africa...', cit., p. 14.

[38] Author's interview with a Tunisian intellectual, Tunis, February 2018.

[39] Author's interview with a Tunisian representative of the youth movement, Tunis, February 2018.

[40] Author's interview with a Tunisian representative of the women's movement, Tunis, February 2018.

2. Political and institutional transition in Tunisia: From the streets to the ballots and back?

When Ben Ali fled the country, many young Tunisians found themselves at the forefront of a historic political transition. Youth-led associations flourished (around 11,400 new organisations in the wake of the revolution[41]), all trying to push for the government to adopt an agenda of change centred on youth's problems. Strengthening civil society and youth participation thus became the main objectives of the domestic and global agenda on Tunisia, mainly through the work of charities, grassroots CSOs and international cooperation.[42] However, it soon became clear that satisfying young Tunisians' demands for more opportunities both in the political and in the economic realms was not easy.

At the institutional level, after two years of intense bargaining, in January 2014 Tunisia was presented with a new Constitution. The renewed focus on youth was illustrated by Article 8 stating that: '[y]outh are an active force in building the nation. The state seeks to provide the necessary conditions for developing the capacities of youth and realising their potential, supports them to assume responsibility, and strives to extend and generalise their participation in social, economic, cultural and political development.'[43] Other constitutions of the region do not mention young generations and their role within society so explicitly. However, the policies adopted by successive governments were either in full continuity with the past as they proposed to reinforce supply-side approaches or only able to come up with palliative measures or temporary concessions at best.[44]

The 2012-launched National Strategy for Employment 2013–2017 achieved only meagre results. Since 2011, the main employer for the youth in Tunisia has continued to be the informal sector: the share of young people finding a job in the informal sector increased from 28 per cent in 2010 to 32 per cent in 2015,

[41]   Wafa Ben-Hassine, 'Tunisian Civil Society's Unmistakable Role in Keeping the Peace', in *MENASource*, 19 January 2018, https://www.atlanticcouncil.org/?p=107659.

[42]   International Labour Office, *Transition vers le marché du travail des jeunes femmes et hommes en Tunisie: Résultats de l'enquête auprès des entreprises*, Geneva, International Labour Organisation, 2015, https://www.ilo.org/employment/areas/youth-employment/WCMS_444913/lang--en; European External Action Service (EEAS), *The European Union and Tunisia launch the EU-Tunisia Youth Partnership*, 1 December 2016, https://europa.eu/!9CTjuQ.

[43]   Silvia Colombo and Hamza Meddeb, 'Fostering Inclusiveness', cit., p. 45.

[44]   Pietro Marzo, 'Why Youth Empowerment Can Sustain Tunisia's Democratic Consolidation', in *IAI Working Papers*, No. 16|09 (April 2016), p. 7, https://www.iai.it/en/node/6215.

and reached 54 per cent in 2017.[45] Some of them have also become involved in cross-border smuggling and trafficking with nearby countries such as war-torn Libya and Algeria.[46] In addition, irregular migration, radicalisation and violent extremism have tarnished the image of 'revolutionary heroes' that had been previously attributed to the youth.[47] Indeed young Tunisians have represented the largest group of foreign fighters who have joined the Islamic State to be trained and fight in Syria and Iraq or elsewhere.[48] The International Centre for the Study of Radicalisation and Political Violence has estimated that Tunisia has fuelled ISIS with young Tunisian fighters at a constant pace, reaching a total of three thousand.[49]

Moving from security challenges to domestic politics, from an institutional and procedural point of view Tunisia has ticked all the boxes towards accomplishing democratic transition mainly thanks to the prevailing moderation and consensus-driven attitudes as well as the search for peaceful coexistence and compromise among the different domestic political and social forces.[50] This

---

[45]   Silvia Colombo and Hamza Meddeb, 'Fostering Inclusiveness', cit., p. 44–45; 'Tunisie: L'emploi des jeunes doit être une priorité nationale', in *Directinfo*, 4 October 2017, https://directinfo.webmanagercenter.com/?p=331189.

[46]   Max Gallien, 'Informal Institutions and the Regulation of Smuggling in North Africa', in *Perspectives on Politics*, Vol. 18, No. 2 (June 2020), p. 492–508, https://doi.org/10.1017/S1537592719001026.

[47]   Author's interview with a civil society activist working on youth de-radicalisation, Tunis, February 2018; World Bank, 'Breaking the Barriers to Youth Inclusion', in *World Bank Reports*, No. 89233-TN (2014), p. xiii-xiv, http://hdl.handle.net/10986/20693; Isabel Schäfer, 'Fostering a Youth-Sensitive Approach in the EU's Policies towards the South and East Mediterranean Countries – The Case of Tunisia', in Silvia Colombo (ed.), 'Youth Activism in the South and East Mediterranean Countries since the Arab Uprisings: Challenges and Policy Options', in *EuroMeSCo Joint Policy Studies*, No. 2 (February 2016), p. 66–67, https://www.iemed.org/?p=17077.

[48]   Dario Cristiani, 'The Geography of Discontent: Tunisia's Syrian Fighter Dilemma', in *Terrorism Monitor*, Vol. 12, No. 20 (24 October 2014), https://jamestown.org/?p=14493; Georges Fahmi and Hamza Meddeb, 'Market for Jihad. Radicalization in Tunisia', in *Carnegie Papers*, October 2015, https://carnegieendowment.org/publications/61629.

[49]   Aaron Y. Zelin, 'The Tunisian-Libyan Jihadi Connection', in *ICSR Insights*, 6 July 2015, https://icsr.info/?p=9368.

[50]   Leonardo Morlino, *Changes for Democracy. Actors, Structures, Processes*, Oxford/New York, Oxford University Press, 2012; Amel Boubekeur, 'Islamists, Secularists and Old Regime Elites in Tunisia: Bargained Competition', in *Mediterranean Politics*, Vol. 21, No. 1 (2016), p. 107–127, https://doi.org/10.1080/13629395.2015.1081449; Alfred Stepan, 'Tunisia's Transition and the Twin Tolerations', in *Journal of Democracy*, Vol.

is not to say that the Tunisian political transition to democracy has been devoid of conflicts, some if which have even escalated into criminal actions such as the assassination of prominent secular leader Chokri Belaid on 6 February 2013 and the murder of leftist leader Mohamed Brahmi in late July 2013. The years between 2011 and 2015 were particularly tense. Some have claimed it to be a period of 'national cold war', while others have defined it as the 'golden age' of civil society activism – in an interesting but complementary conflict of perceptions.[51]

In spite of their proliferation after 2011, political parties have remained extremely weak. More than two hundred parties exist today but only around fifty among them can be regarded as viable organisations and only fifteen have made it into the Parliament during the latest round of parliamentary elections.[52] Some of these parties are empty shells unable to channel new ideas into the policy-making process. The reform agenda has stalled and the revolutionary spirit of the protests has been diluted.[53] Successive coalition governments have failed to reform the justice system, which remains only partially independent and characterised by laws dating back to the beginning of the 1900s, and the security sector, which continues to be undemocratic, inefficient and coercive.

What is more troublesome, successive political executives have failed to address socio-economic problems and regional disparities, leading to growing internal mobilisation, which in turn has negatively impacted the legitimacy of both national and local authorities, undermining societal resilience. The economy has been stagnating in the past decade and suffered a heavy blow in 2020 in terms of GDP growth (-8.6 per cent), with unemployment reaching 16.3 per cent and rampant inflation.[54] Expectations for a better economic future have

23, No. 2 (April 2012), p. 89–103, https://www.journalofdemocracy.org/articles/tunisias-transition-and-the-twin-tolerations.

[51]   Author's phone interviews with Tunisian activists, May–June 2021.

[52]   Author's phone interview with a Tunisian CSO representative, October 2020.

[53]   Luigi Narbone, 'The EU-Tunisian Relationship After 2011: Resilience, Contestation and the Return of the Neglected Socio-Economic Question', in *Middle East Directions Research Project Reports*, No. 2020/18 (December 2018), p. 5, https://hdl.handle.net/1814/69264; Sharan Grewal and Shadi Hamid, 'The Dark Side of Consensus in Tunisia: Lessons from 2015–2019', in *Brookings Reports*, January 2020, https://brook.gs/2S3brbd.

[54]   Yasmina Abouzoohour, 'Caught in Transition', cit.

plummeted. In 2019, only a third of Tunisians believed that the situation would improve in the coming years, compared to 78 per cent in 2011.[55]

This has led to the subsuming of some of the claims voiced by the protesters under political and institutional, mainly bureaucratic, processes without real change, to conflicts between the key institutions (the President and the Parliament first and foremost) that fuel governance problems, and lastly to the return of political figures from the days of Ben Ali. During the 2018 municipal elections participation was low and traditional parties (of both Islamist and secular leanings) performed badly compared to independent candidates. Similarly, in the 2019 presidential and parliamentary elections new political figures, espousing populist slogans and agendas, gained traction. It is in this context that traditional political forces have suffered an even heavier blow due to the existing uncertainty linked to the 25 July presidential moves.

The President's decisions to concentrate powers in his hands, suspend parts of the 2014 constitution and create a new, hybrid constitutional order that could pave the way to authoritarian restoration came at a delicate moment. Tunisia was moving towards the initial stage of consolidating its democracy, but it was still far from achieving the goal. According to Linz, in a consolidated democracy 'none of the major political actors, parties, or organized interests, forces, or institutions consider that there is any alternative to democratic processes to gain power, and [. . .] no political institution or group has a claim to veto the action of democratically elected decision makers. [. . .] To put it simply, democracy must be seen as the "only game in town".[56] Clearly this is not the case in Tunisia today. As demonstrated by the 25 July moves and subsequent presidential decrees, the risk of regression to a crisis situation remains around the corner.

All this notwithstanding, Tunisia has managed to remain afloat and has displayed a significant degree of resilience in trailing the complex consolidation path mainly thanks to a vibrant and engaged civil society that has taken upon itself the role of watchdog and custodian of the political processes, from electoral politics to political governance and transparency. The birth of several micro-movements and associations – something that was completely new in light of the previous decades of authoritarianism and repression – has led to a sense

---

55   Arab Barometer, *Arab Barometer V: Tunisia Country Report*, 2019, https://www. arabbarometer.org/wp-content/uploads/ABV_Tunisia_Report_Public-Opinion_2 018-2019.pdf.

56   Juan J. Linz, 'Transitions to Democracy', in *The Washington Quarterly*, Vol. 13, No. 3 (Summer 1990), p. 158.

of empowerment. In spite of all the existing challenges, Tunisian civil society has acted as the real engine of change and as a barrier to the vagaries of the politicians and the formal political actors.

It has mainly been thanks to the civil society's continuous mobilisation following 2011 that some progress has been made in making the Tunisian state more democratic, accountable and responsive.[57] For example, on gender issues, the concept of 'equality' has made its way into the final text of the Constitution with Article 20 stating that: 'all the citizens have the same rights and the same duties. They are equal in front of the law without any discrimination.' In addition, Article 45 defines the role of the state as the guarantor of women's protection.[58] Furthermore, it was thanks to the mobilisation of more than a hundred women's associations that a new law introducing the concepts of 'violence against women', of 'moral and sexual violence', and of 'economic exploitation' was finally adopted in July 2017 after having stalled in the legislative process for more than twenty years.[59] Similarly, it was thanks to the growing societal salience acquired by regional and local collective, identity-based claims that the issue of the inequalities between the centre and the peripheries entered the public debate forcefully, to the extent that the 'Code des collectivités locales', namely the organic law regulating regional and local governance was adopted by the Parliament only ten days before the Tunisian municipal elections held on 6 May 2018.[60]

3. Regional turmoil and the need to protect Tunisia's democratisation process: The role of the EU

If the years between 2011 and 2015 were characterised by intense domestic political conflicts as a result of institutional disagreements and popular struggles over civic and political rights, since 2015 socio-economic issues have taken precedence amongst the factors around which popular activism has coalesced. This has been compounded by external interferences, which have made Tunisia's path towards democracy increasingly fragile.

---

[57]   Silvia Colombo, *Political and Institutional Transition in North Africa*, cit.
[58]   Silvia Colombo and Hamza Meddeb, 'Fostering Inclusiveness', cit., p. 46.
[59]   Ibid., p. 34–56.
[60]   The previous local elections in Tunisia had been held in 2010. See Silvia Colombo et al., 'New Trends in Identity Politics in the Middle East and North Africa. . .', cit., p. 23.

The democratisation literature insists on the importance of considering external factors particularly during the democratic consolidation phase.[61] In this sense, Tunisia's experience represents a textbook case. At the regional level, external variables range from the impact of the Libyan conflict on Tunisia's material insecurity, particularly in the South,[62] to the increasingly visible actions taken by some Arab Gulf countries. At the international level, such variables concern the evolution of Europe-Tunisia relations, both at the EU level and at member states level, and the role of other external players such as the United States and the international financial institutions (for example the International Monetary Fund, with which Tunisia negotiated a 2.9 billion US dollars bailout in April 2016) in supporting or endangering Tunisian democratisation. The negative influence exerted by the neighbouring Libyan conflict and by Gulf-driven propaganda and political/economic pressures on Tunisia's democratisation has not been offset by a positive engagement by the EU and other external players.

Tunisia was the first country to sign an Association Agreement with Europe in the framework of the Euro-Mediterranean Partnership in the mid-1990s. At the time of the 2011 revolution and during the initial phase of the democratic transition, the EU was among the most forthcoming supporters of Tunisia's desire to break with the past. In the framework of its own soul-searching exercise, the EU realised that it had underestimated the needs and power of the society. The spectrum of initiatives and funds channelled through civil society in Tunisia therefore increased. They were systematised with the launch of the *Programme d'Appui à la Société Civile* (amongst others), which mobilised 7 million euro in support of more than seventy civil society-focused projects between 2012 and 2016. The EU also co-funded the creation of the *Jamaity.org* platform in 2014, bringing together more than 1,600 Tunisian CSOs that had been active during the 2011 revolution.[63]

In spite of this positive record, the EU's engagement with civil society in Tunisia remains fraught with problems. First, the EU's support to CSOs has been

---

[61]   See, for example, Laurence Whitehead (ed.), *The International Dimensions of Democratization. Europe and the Americas*, Oxford, Oxford University Press, 1996; Amichai Magen and Leonardo Morlino (eds), *International Actors, Democratization and the Rule of Law. Anchoring Democracy?*, New York/London, Routledge, 2009.

[62]   Robbie Gramer and Humza Jilani, 'Libya an Obstacle on Tunisia's Path to Stability', in *Foreign Policy*, 6 August 2018, https://foreignpolicy.com/2018/08/06/libya-an-obsta cle-on-tunisias-path-to-stability.

[63]   Silvia Colombo and Hamza Meddeb, 'Fostering Inclusiveness', cit., p. 39. For more information, see the official website: https://jamaity.org.

fragmented along different policy lines (such as development cooperation, the promotion of human rights and democracy) and funding instruments, each of which has its own logic and little coordination. Second, the agenda that informs the EU's support for civil society has largely been driven by the EU itself or at best has been worked out in cooperation with the government authorities, with no significant involvement of the CSOs in the planning and designing of activities. Third, the EU tends to promote civil society based on its own liberal-democratic model, which has meant that some CSOs have had access to funds, training and engagement opportunities because they are more in line with Western rhetoric and procedures, while others have been overlooked irrespective of their links to and ability to foster political and social change.[64]

An attempt to overcome these flaws was made with the so-called Tripartite Dialogue. This flagship initiative, 80 per cent of which was funded by the EU, was implemented by EuroMed Rights between 2013 and 2019 with the aim to create a space for dialogue and consultation between CSOs, government authorities and the EU on issues such as migration, social and economic rights, justice and gender equality. Its ultimate goal was to set up a regular, consultative and decision-oriented mechanism to involve Tunisian CSOs in the decision-making process and increase transparency and accountability.[65]

The end of the Tripartite Dialogue is illustrative of the broader trend of EU-Tunisia relations.[66] After the initial support to the Tunisian revolution and the protest movement, since 2015 EU-Tunisia relations have undergone a process of over-securitisation, parallel to the process that has gone on at the domestic level with the adoption of the much-debated counter-terrorism law in that year.[67] While rhetorically insisting on the need to foster resilience at the state *and* the societal level in the framework of the Global Strategy for the European Union's Foreign and Security Policy, the EU has in practice pursued an agenda of transition without transformation, which is what most people in Tunisia complain

---

[64] Author's interview with the director of a prominent Tunisian CSO, Tunis, January 2018.

[65] Silvia Colombo and Hamza Meddeb, 'Fostering Inclusiveness', cit., p. 40; Author's interview with an advocacy officer at EuroMed Rights working on the Tripartite Dialogue, Tunis, February 2018.

[66] Author's phone interviews with Tunisian activists, May-June 2021.

[67] Youssef Cherif and Kristina Kausch, 'Reluctant Pioneers. Towards and New Framework for EU-Tunisia Relations', in Emmanuel Cohen-Hadria (ed.), 'The EU-Tunisia Priviledged Partnership – What Next?', in *EuroMeSCo Joint Policy Studies*, No. 10 (April 2018), p. 12–32, https://www.iemed.org/?p=16266.

about.[68] This agenda has been characterised by a focus on anti-terrorism, anti-radicalisation and control of irregular migration, on the one hand, and on the *mise à niveau* of the Tunisian economy as a means to facilitate trade cooperation and lay the groundwork for the negotiation of a deeply imbalanced Deep and Comprehensive Free Trade Agreement (DCFTA), which has not yet seen the light – according to EU policy makers – due to the limited absorption capacity of Tunisia.[69] Social aspects standing at the core of Tunisia's struggles for inclusive and democratic development have been disregarded.[70]

Other external players have exploited the gap left by the EU to meddle in Tunisian domestic affairs. Changing patterns of conflict in the broader MENA region, influenced by growing geo-political and geo-economic competition, have posed severe challenges to Tunisia's internal stability, democratic consolidation and pro-European course. Not only has this course been severely tested by the impact of the Libyan conflict, which has caused among other things an increase in the military budget from 0.57 billion US dollars (1.3 per cent of GDP) in 2010 to 1 billion (2.56 per cent of GDP) in 2019,[71] but other regional players, *in primis* Turkey and some of the Arab Gulf states, have all stepped up their political, economic and ideological outreach to Tunisia in ways that have been extremely damaging.

Tunisia has suffered from the polarisation and intra-Sunni rivalry between the Arab Gulf states linked to the Qatar boycott in place between 2017 and early 2021.[72] On the one hand, Qatar positioned itself as Tunisia's most important and reliable Gulf-based economic partner by offering a stimulus package worth 1 billion US dollars in loans as well as employment opportunities for up to 20,000

---

[68]   Silvia Colombo, '"Principled Pragmatism" Reset: For a Recalibration of the EU's Diplomatic Engagement with the MENA Region', in *IAI Papers*, No. 21|39 (September 2021), https://www.iai.it/en/node/13972.

[69]   For a more critical assessment of the DCFTA and the Tunisian point of view, see Elyes Ghanmi and Guillaume Van der Loo, 'What Kind of Future for the EU-Tunisia DCFTA?', in Emmanuel Cohen-Hadria (ed.), 'The EU-Tunisia Priviledged Partnership – What Next?', in *EuroMeSCo Joint Policy Studies*, No. 10 (April 2018), p. 58–83, https://www.iemed.org/?p=16266.

[70]   Tarek Megerisi, 'Back from the Brink: A Better Way for Europe to Support Tunisia's Democratic Transition', in *ECFR Policy Briefs*, June 2021, https://ecfr.eu/?p=74706.

[71]   See MacroTrends website: *Tunisia Military Spending/Defense Budget 1960–2021*, https://www.macrotrends.net/countries/TUN/tunisia/military-spending-defense-budget.

[72]   Youssef Cherif, 'The Gulf Crisis Threatens Tunisia's Stability', in *MENASource*, 8 November 2017, https://www.atlanticcouncil.org/?p=106822.

Tunisian university graduates in 2012. In doing so, Qatar capitalised on its long-lasting relation to Ennahda. A similar role has been played by Turkey, which has acquired growing centrality in Tunisian affairs mainly thanks to its intervention in the Libyan conflict.[73]

On the other hand, the United Arab Emirates (UAE) has increased its outreach towards and clout over political opponents of Ennahda and other Tunisian Islamist movements. This anti-Islamist focus is in line with the counter-revolutionary, status-quo oriented policies the UAE has adopted in the broader MENA region since 2011. In the Tunisian case, it has poisoned the political landscape and contributed to raising the tone of confrontation between key domestic political and institutional figures. The tensions between President Kaïs Saïed and the Speaker of the Parliament, and Ennahda leader, Rachid Ghannouchi, are part of this picture.[74] While they largely stem from endogenous political dynamics and the competition for power between two very different political leaders, the UAE's pressures and interferences have been instrumental in turning this personalities-based conflict into a fully-fledged institutional and political crisis with evident pro/anti-Islamist overtones following 25 July 2021.

Conclusion

In 2011 Tunisia presented a paradox. Many were surprised at how it was possible that a politically stable, educationally progressive and economically prosperous country could explode into country-wide protests that caused the downfall of one of the strongest police states in the MENA region.[75] Although the 2011 revolution was sudden and rapid, its genesis had begun much earlier, with its roots in an acute social, political and economic crisis.

The demands of the Tunisian demonstrators in the initial phase of the revolution were simple and similar to those that would eventually be heard in other countries – from Egypt to Syria and from Yemen to Libya. They called for political freedoms, decent economic opportunities and self-dignity.[76] Significantly,

---

[73] Sarra Hlaoui, 'Pour Ghannouchi, la priorité est au Qatar et à la Turquie', in *Business News*, 28 April 2020, https://www.businessnews.com.tn/pour-ghannoui-la-priorite-est-au-qatar-et-a-la-turquie,519,97956,3.

[74] Frida Dahmani, 'Tunisie : guerre froide entre Kaïs Saïed et Rached Ghannouchi', in *Jeune Afrique*, 2 July 2020, https://www.jeuneafrique.com/mag/1007068.

[75] Safwan M. Masri, *Tunisia: An Arab Anomaly*, cit.

[76] Peter J. Schraeder and Hamadi Redissi, 'Ben Ali's Fall', in *Journal of Democracy*, Vol. 22, No. 3 (July 2011), p. 5–19.

Tunisia kicked off the unfolding of the 'politics of resistance' and the end of the 'politics of fear'.[77] But this was just the beginning of a decade-long mobilisation process that has continued until today.

Delving into the demands and claims of the demonstrators from 2011 onwards, it is possible to observe a change of focus from civic and political rights (legitimacy, accountability, participation, freedom of expression, representation, effectiveness, gender-based demands) to socio-economic rights with a focus on sustainability (fair employment, environmental rights, end to corruption and to abusive contracts and practices embodied by resource exploitation). This shift signals the transition from the democratic transition phase to the democratic consolidation one and underscores the sense of urgency felt by the Tunisian people at large to undertake veritable socio-economic reforms to consolidate the political-institutional gains. Having a constitution that nominally protects fundamental socio-economic rights is not enough, if these rights cannot be acted upon by the population. Furthermore, regional and international dynamics penetrating into Tunisia's politics and society have proven poisonous for the country's democratic consolidation and have led to a change of discourse at the people's level: from 'Tunisia opening up to the world' to 'Tunisia protecting itself from the world'.[78]

In conclusion, Tunisia's long, complex and still open-ended experience with popular mobilisation allows us to appreciate two aspects. The first concerns the reason why Tunisia has been, and still is, important in the context of broader popular mobilisation dynamics in the MENA region. First, Tunisia is the place where it all started in December 2010 and as such it has dramatically influenced revolutionary, political and institutional experiences elsewhere in the MENA while at the same time significantly diverging from them particularly in the short-term period (2011–2014).[79] Second, the Tunisian revolution has manifested the power of collective, rather than individual, eruptions of popular frustration and anger, their active creative potential and their political implications amidst institutional opportunities and obstacles. Third, it is the only country that has achieved substantial progress in terms of democratic transition; at the same time, it is the country with the longest record of protests in the MENA, which has become a constitutive part of its political life and a sign of societal dynamism and of political

[77] Charles Tripp, *The Power and the People. Paths of Resistance in the Middle East*, New York, Cambridge University Press, 2013, p. 4.
[78] Author's phone interview with a Tunisian intellectual, May 2021.
[79] Silvia Colombo, *Political and Institutional Transition in North Africa*, cit.

dialectic. Last but not least, it has seen growing domestic tensions and instability deriving from regional insecurity spill-overs, pressures and interferences, which have not spared other countries in the region as well.

The second aspect is what Tunisia has taught us throughout this decade from the policy perspective. Among the key factors here, it is possible to recall the difference between democratic transition and democratic consolidation – the latter being a much longer and complex process; the importance of addressing socio-economic issues early on during the democratic transition phase in order to prevent them from endangering democratic consolidation; and the need to shield Tunisia from external pressures and interferences and to strengthen bilateral and multilateral relations with those players that are ready to engage with Tunisian society on the basis of an agenda centred on veritable democracy, inclusive rights and social justice. It remains to be seen whether the EU will be up to the challenge.

References

Yasmina Abouzoohour, 'Caught in Transition: Tunisia's Protests and the Threat of Repression', in *ECFR Commentaries*, 23 February 2021, https://ecfr.eu/?p=68181

Lahcen Achy, 'Tunisia's Economic Challenges', in *Carnegie Papers*, December 2011, https://carnegieendowment.org/publications/46304

Amira Aleya-Sghaier, 'The Tunisian Revolution: The Revolution of Dignity', in *The Journal of the Middle East and Africa*, Vol. 3, No. 1 (2012), p. 18–45

Jon B. Alterman, 'The Revolution Will Not Be Tweeted', in *The Washington Quarterly*, Vol. 34, No. 4 (Fall 2011), p. 103–116, https://www.csis.org/node/28318

Arab Barometer, *Arab Barometer V: Tunisia Country Report*, 2019, https://www.arabbarometer.org/wp-content/uploads/ABV_Tunisia_Report_Public-Opinion_2018-2019.pdf

Alessandra Bajec, 'Tunisia: In Tataouine, Socio-Economic Marginalization Is a Time Bomb', in *Bawader*, 24 July 2020, https://www.arab-reform.net/?p=11217

Joel Beinin, *Workers and Thieves. Labor Movements and Popular Uprisings in Tunisia and Egypt*, Stanford, Stanford Briefs, 2015

Wafa Ben-Hassine, 'Tunisian Civil Society's Unmistakable Role in Keeping the Peace', in *MENASource*, 19 January 2018, https://www.atlanticcouncil.org/?p=107659

Lilia Blaise, 'Nearly 800 Arrested in Economic Protests in Tunisia', in *The New York Times*, 12 January 2018, https://www.nytimes.com/2018/01/12/world/africa/tunisia-tunis-protests-arrests.html

Amel Boubekeur, 'Islamists, Secularists and Old Regime Elites in Tunisia: Bargained Competition', in *Mediterranean Politics*, Vol. 21, No. 1 (2016), p. 107–127, https://doi.org/10.1080/13629395.2015.1081449

Anita Breuer, Todd Landman and Dorothea Farquhar, 'Social Media and Protest Mobilization: Evidence from the Tunisian Revolution', in *Democratization*, Vol. 22, No. 4 (2015), p. 764–792

John Chalcraft, *Popular Politics in the Making of the Modern Middle East*, New York, Cambridge University Press, 2016

Youssef Cherif, 'The Gulf Crisis Threatens Tunisia's Stability', in *MENASource*, 8 November 2017, https://www.atlanticcouncil.org/?p=106822

Youssef Cherif, 'The Kamour Movement and Civic Protests in Tunisia', in *Carnegie Articles*, 8 August 2017, https://carnegieendowment.org/publications/72774

Youssef Cherif and Kristina Kausch, 'Reluctant Pioneers. Towards and New Framework for EU-Tunisia Relations', in Emmanuel Cohen-Hadria (ed.), 'The EU-Tunisia Priviledged Partnership –What Next?', in *EuroMeSCo Joint Policy Studies*, No. 10 (April 2018), p. 12–32, https://www.iemed.org/?p=16266

Laryssa Chomiak, 'The Making of a Revolution in Tunisia', in *Middle East Law and Governance*, Vol. 3, No. 1–2 (March 2011), p. 68–83

Silvia Colombo, *Political and Institutional Transition in North Africa. Egypt and Tunisia in Comparative Perspective*, London/New York, Routledge, 2018

Silvia Colombo, ' "Principled Pragmatism" Reset: For a Recalibration of the EU's Diplomatic Engagement with the MENA Region', in *IAI Papers*, No. 21|39 (September 2021), https://www.iai.it/en/node/13972

Silvia Colombo and Hamza Meddeb, 'Fostering Inclusiveness: A New Roadmap for EU-Tunisia Relations and the Engagement with Civil Society', in Emmanuel Cohen-Hadria (ed.), 'The EU-Tunisia Priviledged Partnership –What Next?', in *EuroMeSCo Joint Policy Studies*, No. 10 (April 2018), p. 34–56, https://www.iemed.org/?p=16266

Silvia Colombo and Benedetta Voltolini, 'The EU's Engagement with "Moderate" Political Islam: The Case of Ennahda', in *LSE Middle East Centre Papers*, No. 19 (July 2017), http://eprints.lse.ac.uk/84065

Silvia Colombo et al., 'New Trends in Identity Politics in the Middle East and North Africa and Their Impact on State-Society Relations', in *MENARA Working Papers*, No. 14 (October 2018), https://www.iai.it/en/node/9573

Dario Cristiani, 'The Geography of Discontent: Tunisia's Syrian Fighter Dilemma', in *Terrorism Monitor*, Vol. 12, No. 20 (24 October 2014), https://jamestown.org/?p=14493

Frida Dahmani, 'Tunisie : guerre froide entre Kaïs Saïed et Rached Ghannouchi', in *Jeune Afrique*, 2 July 2020, https://www.jeuneafrique.com/mag/1007068

European External Action Service (EEAS), *The European Union and Tunisia launch the EU-Tunisia Youth Partnership*, 1 December 2016, https://europa.eu/!9CTjuQ

Georges Fahmi and Hamza Meddeb, 'Market for Jihad. Radicalization in Tunisia', in *Carnegie Papers*, October 2015, https://carnegieendowment.org/publications/61629

Max Gallien, 'Informal Institutions and the Regulation of Smuggling in North Africa', in *Perspectives on Politics*, Vol. 18, No. 2 (June 2020), p. 492–508, https://doi.org/10.1017/S1537592719001026

Elyes Ghanmi and Guillaume Van der Loo, 'What Kind of Future for the EU-Tunisia DCFTA?', in Emmanuel Cohen-Hadria (ed.), 'The EU-Tunisia Priviledged Partnership –What Next?', in *EuroMeSCo Joint Policy Studies*, No. 10 (April 2018), p. 58–83, https://www.iemed.org/?p=16266

Eric Goldstein, 'Tunisia's Legacy of Pollution Confronts Democratic Politics', in *Open Democracy*, 23 May 2014, https://www.opendemocracy.net/en/north-africa-west-asia/tunisias-legacy-of-pollution-confronts-democratic-politics

Robbie Gramer and Humza Jilani, 'Libya an Obstacle on Tunisia's Path to Stability', in *Foreign Policy*, 6 August 2018, https://foreignpolicy.com/2018/08/06/libya-an-obstacle-on-tunisias-path-to-stability

Sharan Grewal and Shadi Hamid, 'The Dark Side of Consensus in Tunisia: Lessons from 2015–2019', in *Brookings Reports*, January 2020, https://brook.gs/2S3brbd

Linda Herrera and Asef Bayat (eds), *Being Young and Muslim. New Cultural Politics in the Global South and North*, Oxford, Oxford University Press, 2010

Sarra Hlaoui, 'Pour Ghannouchi, la priorité est au Qatar et à la Turquie', in *Business News*, 28 April 2020, https://www.businessnews.com.tn/pour-ghannoui-la-priorite-est-au-qatar-et-a-la-turquie,519,97956,3

Alcinda Honwana, *Youth and Revolution in Tunisia*, London/New York, Zed Books, 2013

International Crisis Group, Interview with Michaël Béchir Ayari, *Stemming Tunisia's Authoritarian Drift* (video), 11 January 2018, https://www.crisisgroup.org/node/5916

International Labour Office, *Transition vers le marché du travail des jeunes femmes et hommes en Tunisie: Résultats de l'enquête auprès des entreprises*, Geneva, International Labour Organisation, 2015, https://www.ilo.org/employment/areas/youth-employment/WCMS_444913/lang--en

Kristina Kausch, 'Tunisia: The Life of Others. Project on Freedom of Association in the Middle East and North Africa', in *FRIDE Working Papers*, No. 85 (June 2009), http://web.archive.org/web/20100621183853/http://www.fride.org/descarga/FRIDE_WP85_INGLES_FINAL.pdf

Juan J. Linz, 'Transitions to Democracy', in *The Washington Quarterly*, Vol. 13, No. 3 (Summer 1990), p. 143–164

Amichai Magen and Leonardo Morlino (eds), *International Actors, Democratization and the Rule of Law. Anchoring Democracy?*, New York/London, Routledge, 2009

Pietro Marzo, 'Why Youth Empowerment Can Sustain Tunisia's Democratic Consolidation', in *IAI Working Papers*, No. 16|09 (April 2016), https://www.iai.it/en/node/6215

Safwan M. Masri, *Tunisia: An Arab Anomaly*, New York, Columbia University Press, 2017

Hamza Meddeb, 'Peripheral Vision: How Europe Can Help Preserve Tunisia's Fragile Democracy', in *ECFR Policy Briefs*, January 2017, https://ecfr.eu/?p=3752

Hamza Meddeb, 'Precarious Resilience: Tunisia's Libyan Predicament', in *MENARA Future Notes*, No. 5 (April 2017), https://www.iai.it/en/node/7722

Tarek Megerisi, 'Back from the Brink: A Better Way for Europe to Support Tunisia's Democratic Transition', in *ECFR Policy Briefs*, June 2021, https://ecfr.eu/?p=74706

Chamseddine Mnasri, 'Tunisia: The People's Revolution', in *International Socialism*, No. 130 (Spring 2011), p. 19–26, http://isj.org.uk/?p=720

Leonardo Morlino, *Changes for Democracy. Actors, Structures, Processes*, Oxford/New York, Oxford University Press, 2012

M. Chloe Mulderig, 'Adulthood Denied: Youth Dissatisfaction and the Arab Spring', in *BU Pardee Issues in Brief*, No. 21 (October 2011), https://www.bu.edu/pardee/?p=10776

Luigi Narbone, 'The EU-Tunisian Relationship After 2011: Resilience, Contestation and the Return of the Neglected Socio-Economic Question', in *Middle East Directions Research Project Reports*, No. 2020/18 (December 2018), https://hdl.handle.net/1814/69264

Organisation for Economic Co-operation and Development (OECD), *Investing in Youth: Tunisia. Strengthening the Employability of Youth during the*

Transition to a Green Economy, Paris, OECD Publishing, 2015, https://read.oecd.org/10.1787/9789264226470-en

Maria Cristina Paciello and Daniela Pioppi, 'Youth Empowerment as a Collective, Bottom-Up and Long-Term Process', in *IEMed. Mediterranean Yearbook 2014*, p. 67–71, https://www.iemed.org/?p=29081

Kenneth Perkins, *A History of Modern Tunisia*, Cambridge, Cambridge University Press, 2004

Bilal Randeree, 'Tunisian Leader Promises New Jobs', in *Al Jazeera*, 10 January 2011, https://aje.io/h7sqe

Isabel Schäfer, 'Fostering a Youth-Sensitive Approach in the EU's Policies towards the South and East Mediterranean Countries –The Case of Tunisia', in Silvia Colombo (ed.), 'Youth Activism in the South and East Mediterranean Countries since the Arab Uprisings: Challenges and Policy Options', in *EuroMeSCo Joint Policy Studies*, No. 2 (February 2016), p. 61–74, https://www.iemed.org/?p=17077

Peter J. Schraeder and Hamadi Redissi, 'Ben Ali's Fall', in *Journal of Democracy*, Vol. 22, No. 3 (July 2011), p. 5–19

David Seddon, 'Riot and Rebellion: Political Responses to Economic Crisis in North Africa, Tunisia, Morocco and Sudan', in Berch Berberoglu (ed.), *Power and Stability in the Middle East*, London, Zed Books, 1989, p. 114–135

Mohammad Dawood Sofi, 'Rethinking the Root Causes of the Tunisian Revolution and Its Implications', in *Contemporary Arab Affairs*, Vol. 12, No. 3 (September 2019), p. 41–64

Alfred Stepan, 'Tunisia's Transition and the Twin Tolerations', in *Journal of Democracy*, Vol. 23, No. 2 (April 2012), p. 89–103, https://www.journalofdemocracy.org/articles/tunisias-transition-and-the-twin-tolerations

Vanessa Szakal, 'After Kasserine, Protests Break Out in 16 Governorates', in *Nawaat*, 22 January 2016, https://nawaat.org/portail/2016/01/22/after-kasserine-protests-break-out-in-16-governorates

Vanessa Szakal, 'Regards croisés sur le mal-être de la jeunesse tunisienne', in *Nawaat*, 11 May 2017, https://nawaat.org/2017/05/11/regards-croises-sur-le-mal-etre-de-la-jeunesse-tunisienne

Charles Tripp, *The Power and the People. Paths of Resistance in the Middle East*, New York, Cambridge University Press, 2013

Laurence Whitehead (ed.), *The International Dimensions of Democratization. Europe and the Americas*, Oxford, Oxford University Press, 1996

World Bank, 'Breaking the Barriers to Youth Inclusion', in *World Bank Reports*, No. 89233-TN (2014), http://hdl.handle.net/10986/20693

World Bank, *Doing Business 2009. Comparing Regulation in 181 Economies*, Washington, World Bank and Palgrave Macmillan, 2008, http://hdl.handle.net/10986/6313

Maha Yahya, 'Great Expectations in Tunisia', in *Carnegie Papers*, March 2016, https://carnegieendowment.org/publications/63138

Aaron Y. Zelin, 'The Tunisian-Libyan Jihadi Connection', in *ICSR Insights*, 6 July 2015, https://icsr.info/?p=9368

Arturo Varvelli, Mattia Giampaolo and Lorena Stella Martini

Chapter 9: A Decade Later: Revising European Approaches towards the MENA Region

Ten years after the beginning of the uprisings that have been shaking the MENA region, the worrying socio-economic and political conditions that back in 2010 should have warned local governments as well as international observers, especially in neighbouring Europe, have nothing but worsened, as has been demonstrated by the emergence of new surges and waves of discontent in several countries. Indeed, despite cosmetic reforms and attempts to spur economic growth, the political and socio-economic grievances that originally fuelled the uprisings ten years ago still represent a main source of dissatisfaction and unrest in countries such as Tunisia, Egypt and to a lesser extent Morocco, while very similar claims have motivated masses to take to the streets in Algeria, Iraq, Lebanon and Sudan.

Ten years after the so-called Arab uprisings another appraisal needs to be made: Europe still has not effectively revised its approach to promoting democracy and development in the Mediterranean region. The 2011 revolutions opened the debate to rethink the European Neighbourhood Policy (ENP) with the aim of advocating for a democratic and stable region at the southern borders of the European Union.[1] However, the EU has found it increasingly difficult to take up a coherent strategy, faithful to its founding values. This was demonstrated by the Libyan conflict, where the EU witnessed a deep division among its member states (notably France and Italy), or by the debate on human rights and support for authoritarian rule sparked, among other events, by the murder of Italian researcher Giulio Regeni by the Egyptian security forces.

The EU member states have shown a tendency to privilege short-term policies and an approach based on securitisation, and to repeat their past mistakes instead of learning from them. In particular, the will to curb migration and promote security without addressing the roots of these issues, as well as the blind trust in the neo-liberal economic reform scheme have come once again to the surface, generating an increasingly deep gap between 'what the people want'

---

[1] Andrea Teti et al., *Democratisation against Democracy. How EU Foreign Policy Fails the Middle East*, Cham, Palgrave Macmillan, 2020, p. 103.

and the EU project in the area,[2] while putting European legitimacy in the region at risk.

In light of these considerations, this chapter provides a critical review of EU policies towards the Mediterranean, followed by a concise focus on the socio-economic grievances that are still plaguing the Middle East and North Africa (MENA) countries today, with an eye to the evolutions that occurred throughout the last decade. Drawing from this analysis, some concrete recommendations for a renewed European approach towards the MENA region will be laid out.

1. The EU and the Mediterranean: Neither development nor democracy

The EU's approach to the MENA has been characterised by a short-term approach, mostly focused on security and, at the economic level, on neo-liberal reforms. Despite its rhetoric on democratisation and human rights, in order to protect its own interests the EU has shown a tendency to bet on the authoritarian rulers of the region. When the uprisings exploded in the region in 2011, Europe appeared surprised and unable to react to changes on the political scene.

Despite the evident need to revise the instruments of Euro-Mediterranean relations according to evolution on the ground, the EU seems to find it difficult to outline an approach combining the pursuit of its major interests, staying true to its founding values and the promotion of a long-term, sustainable strategy for the MENA region, one which could enhance development in the area at the economic, social and political level. This is further demonstrated by the socio-economic grievances that still haunt most countries in the region.

1.1 The EU' approach to the Mediterranean before 2011: Between security and economic reforms

The European Mediterranean policies have always pursued, notably after the Barcelona Process, a political and an economic goal.[3] On the political side, Europe has attempted to transfer its fundamental values, such as the respect for human rights, democracy and political freedoms, in its relations with the MENA countries. Economically speaking, Europe, in the last three decades, has tried to promote the inclusion of regional countries within the global market,

---

2   Ibid., p. 122.
3   Ibid., p. 27.

maintaining, at least on paper, the focus on improving economic development while at the same time protecting workers' rights.

To operationalise this approach and empower EU action in the Mediterranean, in 1995 the Barcelona Process (Euro-Mediterranean Partnership) was launched; it was then followed by the current 'two pillars' of EU action in the Mediterranean: in 2004 the European Neighbourhood Policy (ENP) and, in 2008, the Union for the Mediterranean (UfM).[4]

The ENP was intended to strengthen the Barcelona Process through bilateral cooperation in order to respond to regional social and economic challenges, while demanding partners to commit to supposedly shared values of democracy, human rights and the respect of the rule of law.[5] In 2008, this initiative was complemented by the launch of the UfM with the aim of implementing policies at the inter-governmental level in terms of economy, environment, education and energy. An important element to underline is the multilateral character, at least on paper, of the UfM, whose objective is the creation of a regional coordinated action in order to promote social, economic, security and educational cooperation by involving different countries of the region, among them Mauritania, Morocco, Algeria, Tunisia, Libya, Egypt, Jordan, Palestine, Israel, Lebanon, Syria, Turkey and Albania.[6]

In this framework, market liberalisation was the core factor to develop both economic and political conditions and to '[expand] democratic culture from the economic realm into politics generally.'[7]

This, as outlined below, became the central pillar of the EU's engagement with the countries in the region following the uprisings in 2011 through instrument of the Deep and Comprehensive Free Trade Agreements (DCFTAs). These agreements are aimed at promoting access to the European market of the MENA economies in some key economic sectors such as agriculture, industrial standards, dispute settlement and services.[8]

---

[4] Andrea Teti (ed.), *The EU's Partnership with the Southern Mediterranean: Challenges to Cohesion and Democracy*, Brussels, Greens/EFA in the European Parliament, March 2019, https://www.researchgate.net/publication/332550457.

[5] Andrea Teti et al., *Democratisation against Democracy*, cit., p. 75.

[6] European Commission, *Barcelona Process: Union for the Mediterranean* (COM/2008/0319), 20 May 2008, https://eur-lex.europa.eu/legal-content/EN/TXT/?uri=CELEX:52008DC0319.

[7] Andrea Teti et al., *Democratisation against Democracy*, cit., p. 28.

[8] European Commission, *Overview of FTA and other Trade Negotiations*, updated October 2021, p. 5–6, http://trade.ec.europa.eu/doclib/html/118238.htm.

However, the effects of this approach ended up being more negative than positive: despite the favourable impacts at the macroeconomic level (notably from the beginning of 2000 until 2007), outcomes at the microeconomic level deeply worsened. Indeed, macroeconomic indicators demonstrate that since 2000 countries such as Egypt, Tunisia and Morocco have reported a good economic growth; between 2005 and 2009, the region's GDP grew by 5.1 per cent, while export rates increased in countries such as Tunisia (7.6 per cent), Egypt (14.5 per cent) and Morocco (also 14.5 per cent).[9]

In the same period, the entire region also proved to be extremely attractive for foreign direct investments (FDIs): in 2005, MENA FDI inflows relative to GDP surpassed the average for other emerging and developing economies. Indeed, between 2005 and 2007, FDIs directed to Egypt accounted for an average of 7 per cent of GDP, while in Tunisia the ratio was close to 6 per cent.[10] These positive macroeconomic trends and indicators were employed to justify the success of the neo-liberal policies implemented by international financial institutions and by agreements established by the EU. However, a glance at living conditions in those same countries in the corresponding period shows how reality was far from the above-mentioned figures. Food prices increased between 2007 and 2009, and inflation doubled; youth unemployment rate in Tunisia and Morocco reached 30 per cent and 32 per cent respectively,[11] while 60 per cent of the unemployed Egyptians were youth.[12] Alongside the global financial crisis in 2008, FDI flows from the EU towards the region experienced a decline. In Egypt, FDIs decreased by 29.3 per cent, in Tunisia by 39.5 per cent and in Morocco by 20.1 per cent.[13]

---

[9]   André Sapir and Georg Zachmann, 'A European Mediterranean Economic Area to Kick-Start Economic Development', in Sven Biscop, Rosa Balfour and Michael Emerson (eds), 'An Arab Springboard for EU Foreign Policy?', in *Egmont Papers*, No. 54 (January 2012), p. 37–47, https://www.ceps.eu/?p=7389; Adam Hanieh, *Lineages of Revolt. Issues of Contemporary Capitalism in the Middle East*, Chicago, Haymarket Books, 2013, p. 147.

[10] Organisation for Economic Co-operation and Development (OECD), *FDI in Fragile and Conflict-Affected Economies in the Middle East and North Africa: Trends and Policies*, Paris, OECD, December 2018, http://www.oecd.org/mena/competitiveness/ERTF-Jeddah-2018-Background-note-FDI.pdf. For figures on Tunisia see: World Bank Data, *Foreign Direct Investment, Net Inflows (% of GDP) - Tunisia*, https://data.worldbank.org/indicator/BX.KLT.DINV.WD.GD.ZS?locations=TN.

[11] Adam Hanieh, *Lineages of Revolt*, cit., p. 146–147.

[12] Ibid.

[13] Ibid.

At the same time, starting from the 2000s, the austerity measures adopted by governments, following loans provided by the International Monetary Fund, resulted in the increased deterioration of the material conditions of both the poor and middle classes. Cuts in public sector and subsidies, as an effect of the IMF loans adopted by governments in the MENA region, led to social tensions in Tunisia, Morocco and Egypt. The austerity measures adopted by the governments followed the crisis of public debt and the huge state expenditure on services. Despite the liberalisation era, starting from the 1990s, most Arab countries failed to create a virtuous private sector which would help to foster jobs and good governance. The waves of strikes and protests that took place in Tunisia and Egypt between 2006 and 2009 demonstrated the effects of these policies on the ground. The spread of mobilisations was met by increasingly rigid reactions by local governments. Therefore, the more governments supported the pattern of development responsible for popular discontent, the more repressive the regimes became.

If on one side, this pushed some actors in Europe such as the European Parliament to focus their attention on the worrying civil and human rights records characterising many countries on the Southern shore of the Mediterranean, as well as on the urgency for a more effective democratisation, on the other, it was paradoxical to remark that the very existence of these regimes and their stability was not even questioned by EU member states, which counted on cooperating with them, particularly in terms of security and migration. Moreover, European countries attempted to reinforce their position and interests also due the increasing competition with China over the MENA market.[14]

1.2 The Arab revolutions: From surprise to the need for change

As protests spread all over the region, starting from Tunisia and Egypt, none of the EU member states could have imagined such a rapid change and domino effect. Dictators such as Ben Ali in Tunisia, Mubarak in Egypt and Gaddafi in Libya, who were considered by the EU stable partners to deal with, were pushed to abandon their pluri-decade power after great waves of popular protests.[15] Unsurprisingly, some member states unsuccessfully attempted to offer their last support to the moribund regimes in order not to lose their relationships with

---

[14]   Camille Lons et al., 'China's Great Game in the Middle East', in *ECFR Policy Briefs*, October 2019, https://ecfr.eu/?p=2760.

[15]   In Libya, the downfall of Gheddafi came after the international intervention under NATO.

them. For instance, France offered security aid to Ben Ali's regime to contain the protests through the then Foreign Minister Michèle Alliot-Marie.[16]

In spite of the initiatives of some single member states, the European Parliament and Commission supported the popular protests, even if somewhat timidly. Catherine Ashton, then High Representative of the European Union for Foreign Affairs and Security Policy and Vice-President of the Commission, and Štefan Füle, then Commissioner for the European Neighbourhood Policy, made a statement expressing solidarity to the protesters in Tunisia and 'their democratic aspiration'.[17] Indeed, as acknowledged by Commissioner Füle:

> We must show humility about the past. Europe was not vocal enough in defending human rights and local democratic forces in the region. Too many of us fell prey to the assumption that authoritarian regimes were a guarantee of stability in the region. This was not even Realpolitik. It was, at best, short-termism –and the kind of short-termism that makes the long term ever more difficult to build.[18]

In this framework, the uprisings could have given the EU the possibility to develop a different approach and a different strategy for its ENP. On the contrary, the EU's responses to the Arab uprisings highlighted: a) the lack of a long-term strategy; b) the necessity for the EU to perform as a neutral actor and speak with one voice; and c) the need to develop an alternative economic strategy.

Indeed, despite a quite promising beginning, the different trajectories of the uprisings and the dynamics of political transition in the region highlighted the European difficulty in dealing with the new political actors and challenges on the ground. Indeed, the humanitarian crisis in Syria and the deterioration of the Libyan state provoked huge flows of migrants to European shores, which raised the EU governments' concerns for the management of migration and the stability of European countries. In addition, the emergence of new political actors in the region, notably Islamist groups, and the spread and increasing influence of non-state actors in Syria, Libya and Yemen created a deep polarisation among

---

[16]   Steven Heydemann, 'Embracing the Change, Accepting the Challenge? Western Response to the Arab Spring', in Riccardo Alcaro and Miguel Haubrich-Seco (eds), *Re-thinking Western Policies in Light of the Arab Uprisings*, Rome, Nuova Cultura, 2012, p. 21–29 at p. 22, https://www.iai.it/en/node/1385.

[17]   European Union, *Joint Statement by EU High Representative Catherine Ashton and Commissioner Štefan Füle on the Events on Tunisia*, 14 January 2011, https://www.consilium.europa.eu/uedocs/cms_data/docs/pressdata/EN/foraff/118865.pdf.

[18]   Štefan Füle, *Speech on the Recent Events in North Africa*, Brussels, 28 February 2011, https://ec.europa.eu/commission/presscorner/detail/en/SPEECH_11_130.

regional powers, especially in the Gulf, thus making it even more difficult for Europe to assert its role in the region.

At the same time, the trail of terrorist attacks in France, Germany and Belgium, and the wave of migration following the outbreak of the so-called Arab Spring, has favoured the advance of right-wing populism characterised by a strong anti-migratory and Islamophobic sentiment in many European countries. The concatenation of these factors ended up pushing some European countries to position themselves, in terms of alliances, within the political polarisation of the region and to support, more or less explicitly, those countries such as the United Arab Emirates that made anti-Islamism and authoritarianism their flag.

These complex evolutions led Europe to adopt short-term strategies which, while aiming at fostering European direct interests such as energy resources, security, the fight against terrorism and migration management, also had a relevant impact on the regional political transitions – such as, for example, European quasi-passive acceptance of the Egyptian military coup in 2013 and the murder of the Italian researcher, Giulio Regeni. Hence, in this complex scenario, after a timid initial overture towards democratic change, the EU and its member states turned their moves towards a combination of emergency approach and securitised strategy. This was somehow facilitated by the legacy of the historical relationship of the EU with the states in the region. Indeed, the fact that, throughout the previous two decades, the EU had tended to bet on the regimes and their state apparatus prevented the Union from developing a broader understanding of the whole range of actors that emerged in the aftermath of the uprisings.

Among those actors are also the myriad independent trade unions, professional organisations, human rights groups and all those souls who animated the squares in 2010–11 and then again in 2019 Despite their relevance on the ground, the EU preferred to perpetuate a top-down approach which neglected civil society – except for its most liberal and depoliticised representatives – and ended up supporting the status quo and prioritising security over reform.[19]

In addition, the lack of a uniform European voice has mainly been due to the role of single member states within the crisis arena. The best example of such dynamics is provided by the Libyan civil war, where the spread of instability and

---

[19]   Yannis A. Stivachtis, 'The EU and the Middle East: The European Neighborhood Policy (ENP)', in Yannis A. Stivachtis, *Conflict and Diplomacy in the Middle East. External Actors and Regional Rivalries*, Bristol, E-International Relations, 2018, p. 110–127, https://www.e-ir.info/?p=76373.

the fall of state institutions fuelled the division among member states with a historical role in the North African country, such as Italy and France. Indeed, the rivalry between Italy and France in Libya prevented the EU from talking with one voice in terms of conflict resolution and in terms of political challenges.[20]

The civil war in Libya showed two faces of the EU in terms of foreign policy. On one side, the initiatives of single member states put at risk the EU neutral role in the MENA region. In this framework, the choice of France to openly back the United Arab Emirates' moves in countering initiatives by Turkey and Qatar, as well as French support to Khalifa Haftar since his rise in Libya in 2014, demonstrated how the interests of single states can be predominant over those of the Union. On the same level, Italy, notably in terms of migration and energy resources, took on initiatives in Libya that ended up jeopardising the *de facto* neutral role of the EU and the objectives of the European External Action Service (EEAS). These dynamics show how the legacy of the bilateral nature of the ENP affected the EU action in the region: besides its economic effects, bilateralism also influenced the political field. Furthermore, the uprisings could have been a stress-test for the new-born EEAS, established within the framework of the Lisbon Treaty, which nevertheless failed due to the lack of agreement among member states on key policy issues.[21]

Finally, at the economic level, the aftermath of the uprisings would have also been the occasion to rethink the economic strategy in the region. However, despite the reform of the ENP in 2011, things remained largely unchanged. Within the framework of the ENP, the 'more for more' approach was designed to give a package of support – more financial assistance, increasing access to the EU's internal market, enhanced mobility – to incentivise reforms to approximate EU standards towards a 'deep democracy'.[22] The final goal of this approach was to increase financial aid to the Southern Mediterranean countries through the European Neighbourhood Instrument (ENI) and the promotion of programmes such as SPRING (Support for Partnership, Reform and Inclusive Growth). The programme aimed at encouraging countries on the Southern shore to take on

---

[20]   Nathalie Tocci and Jean-Pierre Cassarino, 'Rethinking the EU's Mediterranean Policies Post-9/11', in *IAI Working Papers*, No. 11|06 (March 2011), p. 9, https://www.iai.it/en/node/3302.

[21]   Gergana Noutcheva, 'Institutional Governance of European Neighbourhood Policy in the Wake of the Arab Spring', in *Journal of European Integration*, Vol. 37, No. 1 (2015), p. 19–36.

[22]   Andrea Teti et al., *Democratisation against Democracy*, cit., p. 154.

reforms at both the economic and the political level,[23] thereby also gradually meeting demands for higher human rights and democracy standards.

However, the 'more for more' approach did not pay back. Indeed, the revised ENP was not able, in the short term, to provide concrete results in terms of reform. European priorities were not able to have a direct impact on social, political and economic reforms. The efforts of the EU in the MENA have crashed against the political instability of the region and, as Bicchi put it, 'the EU political input has thus been "lost in transition".[24]

In 2015 the ENP was reviewed again, yet reality was different from the goals that this reform claimed on paper. With the aim of 'seek[ing] to promote prosperity on its borders',[25] the EU attempted to develop a strategy which could help its neighbourhoods to curb their structural problems such as inequality, poverty, the informal economy and deficiencies in democracy, pluralism and respect for the rule of law.[26] At the core of the reform was the economic development of the Southern partners, notably in sustaining the modernisation of the economy, fostering innovation, creating jobs, boosting skills and promoting economic, social and territorial cohesion. An important change in the reviewed ENP is the EU's focus on the cooperation with civil society organisations (CSOs). With the scope of promoting a more inclusive democratic path, the involvement of civil society has been put at the core of the EU political strategy with its Southern neighbours.[27]

Despite these good intentions, the reform of 2015 resulted in a more pragmatic approach, bending more towards strictly European interests rather than towards those of the Southern Mediterranean countries. Indeed, the priority on the ground was not the promotion of human rights, but the focus on development, investment governance and structural reforms with the aim of protecting EU interests and continuing to place blind trust in autocracies in the region.[28] Once

---

23   Ibid., p. 155.
24   Federica Bicchi, '"Lost in Transition:" EU Foreign Policy and the European Neighbourhood Policy Post-Arab Spring', in *L'Europe en Formation*, No. 371 (2014), p. 26–40 at p. 39, https://doi.org/10.3917/eufor.371.0026.
25   European Commission and High Representative of the Union, *Towards a New European Neighbourhood Policy* (JOINT/2015/6), 4 March 2015, p. 5, https://eur-lex.europa.eu/legal-content/en/TXT/?uri=CELEX:52015JC0006.
26   Ibid.
27   European Commission and High Representative of the Union, *Review of the European Neighbourhood Policy* (JOIN/2015/50), 18 November 2015, https://eur-lex.europa.eu/legal-content/EN/TXT/?uri=CELEX:52015JC0050.
28   Andrea Teti et al., *Democratisation against Democracy*, cit., p. 118.

again, the short-term protection of EU key interests in the region jeopardised the emergence of a new path, especially considering the migration waves that landed on European coasts in 2015 and 2016 and that the EU was unprepared to manage, or the terrorist attacks that struck Europe in the same period.

In this framework, the securitisation approach made a quite explicit come-back: the strong men in the region became once again the 'Arab Presidents for life',[29] representing the only political partner to deal with at the expense of working on a long-term policy contributing to the development of a more stable region. This was exemplified with the return of autocracy in Egypt, whose President al-Sisi, given the country's geostrategic position, became one of the main partners of some member states (above all Italy and France) in terms of trade, security and migration.

1.3 Persisting grievances in the region and the need for youth- and women-centred agendas

A clear-cut indicator that the combination – and often overlap – of local and European responses to the uprisings in the MENA region has not managed to tackle the real drivers behind the protests and to address the real needs of the populations is represented by the grievances that exist till today in many countries in the region. One of the main drivers leading to new displays of dis-content is the rampant socio-economic inequality that opposes increasingly poor populations to corrupt elites clinging to power through different logics of patronage – based either on sectarian, family-related or ethnic lines.[30]

Interestingly enough, the presently widening inequality actually also comes as a result of economic policies that, mainly as a response to the 2011 turmoil in the region, focused on growth in macroeconomic terms – in other words, on the rise of the GDP – without benefiting the majority of the population, redis-tributing the dividends or contributing to actual human development; this par-adoxically – or not – led to an actual increase in income poverty in the MENA region from 2010 to 2019.[31] The economic crisis linked to the covid-19 pandemic

---

[29]	Roger Owen, *The Rise and Fall of Arab Presidents for Life*, Cambridge, Harvard University Press, 2012.

[30]	Lydia Assouad, 'Inequality and Its Discontents in the Middle East', in *Carnegie Articles*, March 2020, https://carnegieendowment.org/publications/81266.

[31]	Intissar Fakir and Sandy Alkoutamy, 'COVID-19: A Harbinger of Greater Inequality', in Valeria Talbot (ed.), *Navigating the Pandemic. The Challenge of Stability and Prosperity in the Mediterranean*, Milan, ISPI, December 2020, p. 50–53, https://www.ispionline.it/en/node/28422.

is making this situation even worse, further rubbing salt in the wounds of the weakest social strata and categories, with women sadly on the forefront.

Speaking of economic grievances, surveys carried out by Arab Barometer highlight that only 25 per cent of citizens interviewed in Algeria, Jordan, Libya, Lebanon, Morocco, Tunisia and Iraq deemed the economic situation in their country to be either good or very good in Spring 2021; in Tunisia, only 6 per cent of people declared themselves satisfied with the economy.[32] When asked the same question back in 2010–2011,[33] 34 per cent of interviewees provided a positive answer – and 27 per cent of Tunisians.

Given the high rate of youth unemployment in the region (according to the latest available data from the World Bank, it reached 25.7 per cent in 2019[34]) and the extremely young age of the regional population (nearly half under 24 years old[35]), the creation of new employment opportunities is essential both to fuel real economic development and to ensure stability, and it is indeed currently perceived as among the priorities for the improvement of national economies. In fact, rising unemployment was a driving force behind protests back in 2011, namely in countries such as Morocco and Tunisia, as it is today in Iraq. Nevertheless, governments are not perceived to be doing a good job at creating employment opportunities: in 2019, results were close to zero in Iraq, Lebanon and Algeria; in Morocco, youth's distrust towards governmental engagement in this concern was double compared to that of those over 30.[36] On the other side

---

[32] The sixth survey wave of Arab Barometer was conducted between July 2020 and April 2021 in Algeria, Jordan, Libya, Lebanon, Morocco, Tunisia and Iraq. In the following paragraphs we mention data retrieved from: Abdul-Wahab Kayyali, *Arab Public Opinion on Domestic Conditions. Findings from the Sixth Wave of Arab Barometer*, Arab Barometer, 22 June 2021, https://www.arabbarometer.org/?p=9804.

[33] We make reference here to the second survey wave of Arab Barometer, conducted in 2010–2011 in Algeria, Egypt, Iraq, Jordan, Lebanon, Libya, Palestine, Sudan, Tunisia and Yemen.

[34] World Bank Data, *Unemployment, Youth Total (% of Total Labor Force Ages 15–24) (Modeled ILO Estimate) - Middle East & North Africa*, https://data.worldbank.org/indicator/SL.UEM.1524.ZS?locations=ZQ.

[35] Veera Mendonca et al., *MENA Generation 2030. Investing in Children and Youth Today to Secure a Prosperous Region Tomorrow*, Amman, United Nations Children's Fund (UNICEF) MENA, April 2019, https://www.unicef.org/mena/reports/mena-generation-2030.

[36] The fifth survey wave of Arab Barometer was conducted between 2018 and 2019 in Algeria, Egypt, Iraq, Jordan, Kuwait, Lebanon, Libya, Morocco, Palestine, Sudan, Tunisia and Yemen. To consult data, please refer to the Arab Barometer website: *Arab Barometer Wave V, 2018–2019*, https://www.arabbarometer.org/?p=798. In the

of the coin, those who do have a job frequently denounce the lack of decent working conditions and the meagre salaries – with a record low registered in Lebanon, where in March 2021 the minimum wage dropped to about \$67 a month because of the plummeting of the Lebanese lira.

This dire background at the Southern borders of Europe pushes many in the region to assert that they would consider migrating elsewhere, with Europe as the first destination – a trend that has represented one of Brussels' main concerns towards the region in the last decade. This will to leave one's own country is understandingly more common among the younger generations: as much as 46 per cent of the youth in the region expressed this wish in 2018–2019, as opposed to 38 per cent in 2010–2011.[37] These data suggest that a strong and solid focus on the youth should not be lost when drafting policies in the MENA region – both from within and from outside. Indeed, the last decade has clearly led to the emergence of youth as a paramount actor in the region, one that cannot be ignored either on the economic or on the political side, and that has the potential to be a driver of change for the region, if allowed to. In this framework, the New Agenda for the Mediterranean, proposed by the European Commission in February 2021 to renew bilateral, regional and transregional patterns of cooperation with the Southern Neighbourhood, focuses on youth empowerment and on the creation of socio-economic opportunity for the youth, also with a view to curbing irregular migration towards Europe.[38] Yet, it remains to be seen whether the agenda will actually contribute to effectively targeting the root causes of migration, which are deeply entrenched in the political and economic management of these countries.

A similar observation regards women: protests in 2011 and beyond have not only seen women as active agents in the public space, they have also underlined the need to consider their perspectives and address their gender-specific grievances in order to attain a thorough political and economic progress able

---

following paragraphs we mention data included in the following two presentations based on this international survey: Michael Robbins, *What Arab Publics Think. Findings from the Fifth Wave of Arab Barometer*, Arab Barometer, 28 January 2020, https://www.arabbarometer.org/?p=6109; Amaney Jamal, Michael Robbins and Salma Al-Shami, *Youth in MENA. Findings from the Fifth Wave of the Arab Barometer*, Arab Barometer, 12 August 2020, https://www.arabbarometer.org/?p=7676.

[37] Source: Arab Barometer Second and Fifth Waves.

[38] Lorena Stella Martini, 'Una nuova Agenda per il Mediterraneo per stare al passo con le sfide del Vicinato meridionale', in *Euractiv*, 31 March 2021, https://euractiv.it/?p=24790.

to benefit the overall national and regional context. Indeed, the diverse uprising movements throughout the region seem to have connected the dots between the dynamics of women's oppression and the need for the emancipation of the broader society;[39] in this sense, it is becoming more and more evident that taking real steps towards the achievement of gender equality would largely contribute to general economic and human development.

2. Revising European approaches towards the MENA region

This short overview of the EU's policies towards its Southern Neighbourhood and of grievances still vocally coming from MENA countries hints at the need to better tailor European approaches towards the region to the real needs of the populations as a first, necessary step to enhance long-term stability in the region and thus foster European interests in a sustainable way for all the parties involved.

In this framework, it has clearly emerged from our analysis that the EU should commit to and cultivate flexible patterns of cooperation whose existence and functionality go beyond the survival of the incumbent regimes. In this endeavour, the non-exclusive selection of interlocutors is essential: while necessary, dialogue with power elites should be accompanied by a deeper and more comprehensive engagement with representatives and members of civil society. A deeper dialogue and cooperative pattern with civil society would also be important to partially bridge the deep information gap, mainly caused by the lack of updated, transparent, official and publicly available data, which often prevents foreign actors from understanding local evolutions in the MENA region.[40]

However, beyond the effective necessity to enhance the EU's will and capacity in this domain, relations with civil society are often extremely hard to establish in national contexts where governmental authorities tend to exert a stifling control on their citizens. This is why, investing in a long-term, sustainable policy of social, political and economic transformation and support towards the countries of the region might be key to provide interlocutors (other than the elites in power) with more space to breathe, start change from within and engage in a really constructive, mutual dialogue with Europe.

---

39   Hussein Solomon, 'Women in the Middle East North African Region Pushing Back against Patriarchy', in *Mail & Guardian*, 14 March 2020, https://mg.co.za/?p=349162.
40   Silvia Colombo, Eduard Soler i Lecha and Marc Otte, 'A Half-Empty Glass: Limits and Dilemmas of the EU's Relations to the MENA Countries', in *MENARA Working Papers*, No. 32 (March 2019), p. 22, https://www.iai.it/en/node/10141.

Another paramount step whose importance has emerged from our analysis is the necessity to build a more unitary approach that could be recognised as truly 'European', going beyond those unilateral initiatives that have often proved unproductive both for the EU member states involved and for the Union as a whole. What is more, the lack of a coherent EU foreign policy towards the MENA region has favoured the emergence of other regional and international actors that have proven to be way more influential than Europe from the point of view of hard as well as soft power,[41] such as China and Russia. In this context, the American role, or rather non-role, in the region has been crucial: starting with Trump, the United States has expressed over and over again its willingness not to meddle in 'Middle Eastern affairs'. This further calls on Europe to take a more unified and strategic approach to the area and to outline a stronger and more efficient foreign policy strategy. As a matter of fact, the failure to be a vocal actor towards a region that constitutes one of the cornerstones of the European external dimension collides with the calls for a 'more geopolitical Europe'[42] and for the projection of European 'strategic sovereignty'. To this end, leaving aside solely rhetorical proclamations, it would be important for EU countries to find an overall common direction for the region that takes into account the actual interests of all parties involved, without flattening the complexity of the different positions at stake.

While European unity remains the key behind a general reviewed approach for the region, when tackling single issues and crises or country cases, the EU could also draw on smaller coalitions of European states with more interest and expertise in the dossier at stake, which could take the lead with the aim of securing European common interests and values.[43] Given their Mediterranean

---

[41] Julien Barnes-Dacey and Anthony Dworkin, 'Promoting European Strategic Sovereignty in the Southern Neighbourhood', in *ECFR Policy Briefs*, November 2020, https://ecfr.eu/?p=63484.

[42] When presenting her Commission members and structure, then President-elect Ursula von der Leyen declared: 'My Commission will be a geopolitical Commission committed to sustainable policies. And I want the European Union to be the guardian of multilateralism. Because we know that we are stronger by doing together what we cannot do alone.' (See: European Commission, *The von der Leyen Commission: For a Union that Strives for More*, 10 September 2019, https://ec.europa.eu/commission/pres scorner/detail/en/IP_19_5542). Calls for a more geopolitically oriented Europe have been characterising her work since the very start of her mandate.

[43] Julien Barnes-Dacey and Anthony Dworkin, 'Promoting European Strategic Sovereignty in the Southern Neighbourhood', cit.

engagement, countries like Germany, France, Italy and Spain would likely emerge on the forefront of this endeavour. Considering the more proactive character of Italian foreign policy under the leadership of Mario Draghi,[44] and given Italian deep interests in the Mediterranean, Italy might have the right profile to assume a leading position for European action in the MENA region – especially on some dossiers which interest Rome the most, such as the Libyan conflict or migration – while also mediating between French protagonism – which seems to have recently waned, at least in Libya – and the German hybrid attitude – between cautiousness and reluctant leadership, as demonstrated by its role in the Berlin process.

As a matter of fact, without an all-round, shared and cooperative vision, any new agenda for the region risks lacking its very bases and jeopardising European efforts, while continuing to expose Europe to blackmail from regional actors – here, migration is the best example. What Europe could do instead would be to make better use of its own political and especially economic leverage to reacquire a stronger position and try to steer the region towards mutually favourable outcomes. In this framework, Europe could take advantage of its expertise in increasingly relevant domains where it is already investing its energies, such as greener and digital development, to support the region on the bumpy road towards sustainable socio-economic development (especially after the pandemic crisis) and stability, which have increasingly emerged as two sides of the same coin. This could contribute to increasingly aligned perspectives, priorities and values, and thus work in favour of the promotion of EU interests towards the region in the longer term.

2.1 A green and digital future for the EU and for the MENA region

The future that the EU is outlining, accelerated by the need to jump-start European socio-economic recovery after the pandemic, is increasingly green and digital. Far from solely concerning the EU, this also involves European relations with its partners, as well as the way newly acquired European expertise and perspectives might help to reshape cooperative patterns with EU partners in the MENA region, thereby igniting new possibilities for all-round growth and increasing European leverage in the area.

In particular, the European Green Deal and its goal of achieving carbon neutrality by 2050 will likely have a strong impact on European engagement with

---

[44] Teresa Coratella and Arturo Varvelli, 'Rome's Moment: Draghi, Multilateralism, and Italy's New Strategy', in *ECFR Policy Briefs*, May 2021, https://ecfr.eu/?p=72487.

the MENA region, considering that relations with many countries in the area are shaped by energy import-export patterns. On the one hand, reducing consumption of fossil fuels to the point of eliminating it might represent an opportunity to constrain the leverage that some countries – especially Gulf countries – exercise on European member states, which often collides with EU core values and principles. On the other, countries such as Libya, Algeria, Egypt and Iraq, where the percentage of fossil fuel exports to the EU over the total is considerable,[45] are likely to suffer from a gradual decrease in European fossil fuel imports – which might be especially difficult to handle for countries that are highly dependent on oil and enduring political turmoil, such as Iraq or Libya. Indeed, as a matter of fact, reducing greenhouse gas emissions by 55 per cent by 2030 as planned by Brussels entails decreasing the volume of fossil fuel imports by more than 25 per cent compared to 2015 levels.[46]

This situation might call for Europe to take some steps to mitigate the effects of its energy transition. To begin with, the EU should share all the relevant information concerning the timing and different phases of decarbonisation with export countries and their industries, while also providing consultancy on the issue if requested.

Furthermore, the EU should increase its efforts to assist its partners in the MENA region in diversifying their economies, both through investments and through the transfer of skills, with the aim of curbing the negative impact of energy transition on regional economies, which is likely to pile onto the economic consequences of the pandemic. This push towards diversification could also apply to economies that highly rely on sectors other than fossil fuels (such as tourism or the overall service sector in countries like Tunisia), where the economy is more likely to suffer from severe shocks in case of crises such as the covid-19 pandemic.

Finally, and more specifically, the EU should encourage and assist MENA countries to invest in renewable energies and in green hydrogen, whose production will be essential for the EU itself.[47] Indeed, on its way to decarbonisation, Europe will need to import a share of renewable energies to use at home,

---

[45] We go from 20.1 per cent for Iraq to 63.69 per cent for Libya. Mark Leonard et al., 'The Geopolitics of the European Green Deal', in *ECFR Policy Briefs*, February 2021, p. 7, https://ecfr.eu/?p=66950.

[46] European Commission, *State of the Union: Questions & Answers on the 2030 Climate Target Plan*, 17 September 2020, https://ec.europa.eu/commission/presscorner/detail/en/qanda_20_1598.

[47] Mark Leonard et al., 'The Geopolitics of the European Green Deal', cit., p. 8.

thus creating a new industrial value chain that – if ethically and consciously implemented – could possibly benefit both sides of the Mediterranean. This also includes some countries – such as Morocco and Tunisia,[48] which indeed already have some action plans for a more renewable future – which are not fossil fuel exporters in the first place. This path has been already explored by Morocco, which has recently engaged in a Green Partnership with the EU.[49]

By engaging in cooperation with the EU and further investing in these domains, MENA countries would lay the basis for a sustainable, long-term development pattern, which could improve local socio-economic conditions, starting from youth unemployment, and pave the way for more stable outlooks (while also contributing to the global fight against climate change). Furthermore, as anticipated above, building new cooperation patterns in domains where Europe is increasingly acquiring expertise is key to increasing European leverage and reputation.

Another key word for the future of Europe is 'digitalisation', as nicely outlined by Next Generation EU. In this framework, the digital transition should also be a driver for EU cooperation towards the MENA region, where under certain conditions it could play a significant role in the post-pandemic recovery of countries in the area. Indeed, the covid-19 crisis has had a heavy impact on regional economies, leading to an increase in poverty and inequality which calls for innovative solutions and structural changes.[50] A comprehensive digital transformation could contribute to addressing perennial issues by offering new opportunities, starting from youth and women's empowerment, while also improving public services and reforming the education sector. At the same time, digitalisation is a double-edged sword that might even increase inequality, namely along the rural-urban axis, while exposing digital entrepreneurs from the region to a fierce global competition they might not be ready to endure.[51]

---

[48] Amine Bennis, 'Power Surge: How the European Green Deal Can Succeed in Morocco and Tunisia', in *ECFR Policy Briefs*, January 2021, https://ecfr.eu/?p=66735.

[49] European Commission, *The EU and Morocco Form a Green Partnership on Energy, Climate and the Environment ahead of COP 26*, 28 June 2021, https://europa.eu/!f9ycN7.

[50] Manuel Langendorf and Alexander Farley, 'Digital Transformation and COVID-19 in MENA: Turning Challenge into Opportunity', in *Wilson Center Viewpoints*, 10 May 2021, https://www.wilsoncenter.org/article/digital-transformation-and-covid-19-mena-turning-challenge-opportunity.

[51] Nader Kabbani, 'How Will Digitalisation Affect Youth Employment in MENA?', in *ISPI Commentaries*, 6 May 2021, https://www.ispionline.it/en/node/30264; see also

Hence, it is in Europe's best interests to combine EU initiatives and efforts aimed at boosting socio-economic development in the region with the savvy promotion of digital transformation. The overall aim should be making new socio-economic opportunities accessible to the widest possible strata of population, with a focus on youth, women and disadvantaged categories; this would be a driver of inclusive growth, while also tackling socio-economic root causes of migration. Moreover, increasing digital connectivity between Europe and the region as well as within the region itself is an important step to enhance integration – which, as we will further see below, is something the Maghreb area desperately needs.

In parallel, should the EU manage to assert its relevance in the digital domain aside strong competitors such as China and the United States, its reputation as a regulatory power could also prove very useful to promote an Internet governance model alternative to the Chinese one, shaped around the adoption of policy frameworks and regulations that prevent the authoritarian exploitation of digital technologies.[52]

2.2 Towards an integrated Maghreb

If Europe wants to promote and reinforce its strategic sovereignty,[53] it should be able to combine its ambition as a geopolitical actor and competitor with the support of its core values – namely human rights, freedom and democracy. This calls for a careful evaluation of which countries may be serious and stable interlocutors for the EU in the Southern Mediterranean region; in this regard, several factors hint at some North African countries, namely Morocco, Algeria and Tunisia.

The centrality of North Africa in the geopolitical and geostrategic equilibrium of the Mediterranean basin is crucial for European interests. The geographical proximity and the importance the region has acquired in terms of security and migration should stimulate a new path aiming at promoting integration in this

---

Manuel Langendorf and Alexander Farley, 'Digital Transformation and COVID-19 in MENA', cit.

[52] Manuel Langendorf, 'Digital Stability: How Technology Can Empower Future Generations in the Middle East', in *ECFR Policy Briefs*, March 2020, https://ecfr.eu/?p=2780.

[53] Mark Leonard and Jeremy Shapiro, 'Strategic Sovereignty: How Europe Can Regain the Capacity to Act', in *ECFR Policy Briefs*, June 2019, https://ecfr.eu/?p=4416.

area. Indeed, excluding oil and gas exports, Maghreb is today the least integrated region in the world.[54]

First, a more integrated Maghreb would contribute to avoiding reproducing the same socioeconomic conditions that have been provoking turmoil during the last decade, promoting instead a more inclusive pattern of economic growth, job creation and good governance.[55] In addition, a more integrated Maghreb could also represent fertile soil for developing a longer-term cooperation with the EU, in different domains: security and migration, but also economy. The Maghreb – and particularly the three above mentioned countries Morocco, Algeria and Tunisia – is already one of the main partners of the EU; however, the relationship has so far been characterised by structural asymmetry, for example in terms of trade between the two shores of the Mediterranean.[56]

Indeed, despite the development of stronger bilateral partnerships during the past decades, economic cooperation between the EU and the Maghreb area is still limited, with great margins for improvement. If on one side Tunisian and Moroccan exports towards the EU grew by 5 per cent each in 2019, Algeria is still a junior partner of the European Union, with a 7 per cent decrease in export towards the EU between 2017 and 2019.[57] Furthermore, while commercial exchanges with the EU represented more than 50 per cent of Maghreb countries' total trade in 2020, these countries only account for 1 per cent or less of the EU's total trade.[58] In addition, despite the timid steps made by some countries of the region towards democracy, their poor economic performance – as is happening in Tunisia – risks regressing good democratic practices and endangering the respect of basic human rights.

---

[54] Omer Karasapan, 'MENA's Economic Integration in an Era of Fragmentation', in *Future Development*, 7 May 2019, https://brook.gs/2H5XWC7.

[55] Mustapha Rouis and Steven R. Tabor, 'Regional Economic Integration in the Middle East and North Africa. Beyond Trade Reform', in *Directions in Development*, 2013, http://hdl.handle.net/10986/12220.

[56] Ana Uzelac, 'Incoherent at Heart. The EU's Economic and Migration Policies towards North Africa', in *Oxfam Briefing Papers*, November 2020, http://dx.doi.org/10.21201/2020.6805.

[57] Francis Ghilès, 'Enhancing Economic Cooperation between EU and Maghreb Countries: Algeria, Morocco and Tunisia', in *Notes Internacionals*, No. 249 (April 2021), https://www.cidob.org/en/publications/publication_series/notes_internacionals/249.

[58] European Commission DG Trade, *Top Trading Partners 2020*, 12 April 2021, https://trade.ec.europa.eu/doclib/html/122530.htm.

For this reason, the EU should promote an alternative approach towards the Maghreb, starting from a new sustainable economic growth by strengthening trade competitiveness and supporting investments in the countries, while at the same time sustaining democratic reforms and the respect of human rights. To achieve these primary goals, Europe should reinforce investments in the area to stimulate the development of a productive private sector that, according to the data, lags well behind the predominant role of public sectors within the GDP.[59] In this context, Europe should invest in the manufacturing sector which still represents the least developed sector in the region.[60]

The political instability and the high rate of corruption within the governments of Tunisia, Algeria and Morocco over the last decade, and before, has been an obstacle to fruitful investments to enhance the productivity of the private sector. In this context, it is important for the EU to support CSOs: not only those linked with NGOs, but especially trade unions and professional organisations. As demonstrated during the uprisings, these bodies are a depository of good human capital to develop and reinforce the democratic path.

This is particularly important when looking at the Tunisian political crisis, after the 'institutional coup' implemented by President Kaïs Saïed. The EU, given its great support to the Tunisian political transition, should put at the core of its action the support of the democratic path and economic aid in order to reinvigorate both its political and the economic engagement. At the political level, it is important to have an inclusive approach to all the political actors in the country and avoid the development of dangerous political polarisation. At the economic level, the EU should support a fairer development in terms of investments with the aim to reduce the regional disparities that characterised the country.

After all, despite diverse internal problems, Tunis, Algiers and to a lesser extent Rabat have all attempted to make changes to their political systems; this should push Europe to support these countries along their pathways of reform as well as in geopolitical terms, endorsing their role in maintaining peace in the region. Indeed, recent geopolitical challenges, such as the Libyan crisis, have demonstrated that these countries might have the right political capital to contribute to reviewing the European approach towards the region even in crisis management and resolution. These three countries are not engaged directly in the political

---

[59]   Lilia Hachem Naas, 'Strengthening Private Sector Engagement in Job Creation in North Africa: Challenges and Responses', in *Great Insights*, Vol. 7, No. 4 (Autumn 2018), p. 6–9, https://ecdpm.org/?p=33862.

[60]   Ibid.

and ideological polarisation in the region (which characterised for example the Libyan conflict) and they have developed a good capacity to play a mediation role in conflicts.[61] In this sense, the EU-supported Maghreb integration process would reinforce both stability and cooperation in terms of economic interests and provide the region with additional weight in terms of geopolitical competition – especially given the stable presence of new regional actors in North Africa (Turkey and Qatar in Tunisia, China in Algeria, and Russia and China in Morocco).

However, despite this developing capacity for mediation, tensions between Algeria and Morocco over Western Sahara are still characterising the relations between the two countries,[62] with the concrete risk of jeopardising their role as mediators of conflicts in the region and on key issues such as security in the Sahel and migration, and of limiting the effectiveness of European efforts towards a more integrated Maghreb. For this reason, the EU should work to increasingly assume a mediation role in the disputes between Rabat and Algiers over the Western Sahara, maintaining a neutral position despite the major involvement of some EU member states, such as France or Spain, in the conflict.

This latter aspect should especially push the EU to adopt a more proactive role in the crisis, and to define a unitarian position in order to avoid a scenario where the interests of single members states jeopardise the overall European stance, as has already happened in Libya between Italy and France.[63] To do this, more institutional capacity on the European side would be needed, from the potential creation of a dedicated desk in the European External Action Service, to the appointment of a Special Representative to deal with the crisis,[64] as the EU does in order to 'promote the EU's policies and interests in troubled regions and countries and play an active role in efforts to consolidate peace, stability and the rule of law'.[65] To do so, Europe should adopt a strategy combining financial support

---

[61] Yasmina Abouzzohour, 'Libya's Tangier Talks: Why Is Morocco Getting Involved?', in *MIPA Articles*, 3 December 2020, https://mipa.institute/8290.

[62] Michaël Tanchum, 'The Post-COVID-19 Trajectory for Algeria, Morocco and the Western Sahara', in *IAI Commentaries*, No. 21|03 (January 2021), https://www.iai.it/en/node/12643.

[63] Arturo Varvelli, 'L'Italia ha bisogno di una nuova politica per la Libia', in *Europa Atlantica-Osservatorio strategico*, 5 June 2020, https://wp.me/pabS04-wN.

[64] Hugh Lovatt and Jacob Mundy, 'Free to Choose A New Plan for Peace in Western Sahara', in *ECFR Policy Briefs*, May 2021, https://ecfr.eu/?p=72863.

[65] European External Action Service (EEAS), *EU Special Representatives*, 31 May 2021, https://europa.eu/!Rr79BX

with closer political and economic relations with the EU itself, while at the same time monitoring the flows of EU funds for Moroccan entities and activities in the territory of Western Sahara.[66]

Conclusion

The surprise effect the 2011 uprisings had on the EU and its policies in the MENA region has been telling. Despite several lessons that could have been drawn from the so-called 'Arab Springs', the increasing geopolitical competition among some regional countries and the pragmatic and interest-driven approaches of some EU member states on crucial issues, such as security, migration and economic cooperation, contributed to fostering a political landscape largely similar to the past. At an economic level, the relentless promotion of neo-liberal reforms in a region where micro-economic data have shown the negative effect of this approach has proven to be a recipe for unrest. This has, however, not led to a rethink of such policies. At the political level, the authoritarian comeback in Egypt, the democratic crisis in Tunisia and the lack of popular legitimacy of the new Algerian government are all signals of widespread discontent and of the perennial state of instability haunting the European Neighbourhood. As a matter of fact, Europe has demonstrated an incapacity to confront old and new challenges.

As argued in this chapter, it is high time for the EU to rethink its approach towards the MENA region, drawing on the mostly unheeded lessons coming from old and new waves of unrest, as well as from new challenges generated by the pandemic crisis. The latter has indeed further underlined the need for a new model of development on both the Northern and Southern shores of the Mediterranean. The EU should act with one voice and try to find a balance not only between how the different capitals conceive the MENA region, but also between European interests, on the one hand, and the needs, wishes and perceptions of populations in the region, on the other. To do so, it is important to also take into consideration the myriad of actors and social subjectivities that have emerged during the uprisings as potential and active drivers for change, reform and democracy. The trap of new and old autocracies in which they have no voice whatsoever in the decision-making process is something that is neither in the EU's interest for a stable Southern Neighbourhood nor in line with European founding values.

---

[66]   Hugh Lovatt and Jacob Mundy, 'Free to Choose', cit.

References

Yasmina Abouzzohour, 'Libya's Tangier Talks: Why Is Morocco Getting Involved?', in *MIPA Articles*, 3 December 2020, https://mipa.institute/8290

Lydia Assouad, 'Inequality and Its Discontents in the Middle East', in *Carnegie Articles*, March 2020, https://carnegieendowment.org/publications/81266

Julien Barnes-Dacey and Anthony Dworkin, 'Promoting European Strategic Sovereignty in the Southern Neighbourhood', in *ECFR Policy Briefs*, November 2020, https://ecfr.eu/?p=63484

Amine Bennis, 'Power Surge: How the European Green Deal Can Succeed in Morocco and Tunisia', in *ECFR Policy Briefs*, January 2021, https://ecfr.eu/?p=66735

Federica Bicchi, '"Lost in Transition:" EU Foreign Policy and the European Neighbourhood Policy Post-Arab Spring', in *L'Europe en Formation*, No. 371 (2014), p. 26–40, https://doi.org/10.3917/eufor.371.0026

Silvia Colombo, Eduard Soler i Lecha and Marc Otte, 'A Half-Empty Glass: Limits and Dilemmas of the EU's Relations to the MENA Countries', in *MENARA Working Papers*, No. 32 (March 2019), https://www.iai.it/en/node/10141

Teresa Coratella and Arturo Varvelli, 'Rome's Moment: Draghi, Multilateralism, and Italy's New Strategy', in *ECFR Policy Briefs*, May 2021, https://ecfr.eu/?p=72487

European Commission, *Barcelona Process: Union for the Mediterranean* (COM/2008/0319), 20 May 2008, https://eur-lex.europa.eu/legal-content/EN/TXT/?uri=CELEX:52008DC0319

European Commission, *The EU and Morocco Form a Green Partnership on Energy, Climate and the Environment ahead of COP 26*, 28 June 2021, https://europa.eu/!f9ycN7

European Commission, *Overview of FTA and other Trade Negotiations*, updated October 2021, http://trade.ec.europa.eu/doclib/html/118238.htm

European Commission, *State of the Union: Questions & Answers on the 2030 Climate Target Plan*, 17 September 2020, https://ec.europa.eu/commission/presscorner/detail/en/qanda_20_1598

European Commission, *The von der Leyen Commission: For a Union that Strives for More*, 10 September 2019, https://ec.europa.eu/commission/presscorner/detail/en/IP_19_5542

European Commission DG Trade, *Top Trading Partners 2020*, 12 April 2021, https://trade.ec.europa.eu/doclib/html/122530.htm

European Commission and High Representative of the Union, *Review of the European Neighbourhood Policy* (JOIN/2015/50), 18 November 2015, https://eur-lex.europa.eu/legal-content/EN/TXT/?uri=CELEX:52015JC0050

European Commission and High Representative of the Union, *Towards a New European Neighbourhood Policy* (JOINT/2015/6), 4 March 2015, https://eur-lex.europa.eu/legal-content/en/TXT/?uri=CELEX:52015JC0006

European Union, *Joint Statement by EU High Representative Catherine Ashton and Commissioner Štefan Füle on the Events on Tunisia*, 14 January 2011, https://www.consilium.europa.eu/uedocs/cms_data/docs/pressdata/EN/foraff/118865.pdf

Intissar Fakir and Sandy Alkoutamy, 'COVID-19: A Harbinger of Greater Inequality', in Valeria Talbot (ed.), *Navigating the Pandemic. The Challenge of Stability and Prosperity in the Mediterranean*, Milan, ISPI, December 2020, p. 50–53, https://www.ispionline.it/en/node/28422

Štefan Füle, *Speech on the Recent Events in North Africa*, Brussels, 28 February 2011, https://ec.europa.eu/commission/presscorner/detail/en/SPEECH_11_130

Francis Ghilès, 'Enhancing Economic Cooperation between EU and Maghreb Countries: Algeria, Morocco and Tunisia', in *Notes Internacionals*, No. 249 (April 2021), https://www.cidob.org/en/publications/publication_series/notes_internacionals/249

Lilia Hachem Naas, 'Strengthening Private Sector Engagement in Job Creation in North Africa: Challenges and Responses', in *Great Insights*, Vol. 7, No. 4 (Autumn 2018), p. 6–9, https://ecdpm.org/?p=33862

Adam Hanieh, *Lineages of Revolt. Issues of Contemporary Capitalism in the Middle East*, Chicago, Haymarket Books, 2013

Steven Heydemann, 'Embracing the Change, Accepting the Challenge? Western Response to the Arab Spring', in Riccardo Alcaro and Miguel Haubrich-Seco (eds), *Re-thinking Western Policies in Light of the Arab Uprisings*, Rome, Nuova Cultura, 2012, p. 21–29 at p. 22, https://www.iai.it/en/node/1385

Amaney Jamal, Michael Robbins and Salma Al-Shami, *Youth in MENA. Findings from the Fifth Wave of the Arab Barometer*, Arab Barometer, 12 August 2020, https://www.arabbarometer.org/?p=7676

Nader Kabbani, 'How Will Digitalisation Affect Youth Employment in MENA?', in *ISPI Commentaries*, 6 May 2021, https://www.ispionline.it/en/node/30264

Omer Karasapan, 'MENA's Economic Integration in an Era of Fragmentation', in *Future Development*, 7 May 2019, https://brook.gs/2H5XWC7

Abdul-Wahab Kayyali, *Arab Public Opinion on Domestic Conditions. Findings from the Sixth Wave of Arab Barometer*, Arab Barometer, 22 June 2021, https://www.arabbarometer.org/?p=9804

Manuel Langendorf, 'Digital Stability: How Technology Can Empower Future Generations in the Middle East', in *ECFR Policy Briefs*, March 2020, https://ecfr.eu/?p=2780

Manuel Langendorf and Alexander Farley, 'Digital Transformation and COVID-19 in MENA: Turning Challenge into Opportunity', in *Wilson Center Viewpoints*, 10 May 2021, https://www.wilsoncenter.org/article/digital-transformation-and-covid-19-mena-turning-challenge-opportunity

Mark Leonard et al., 'The Geopolitics of the European Green Deal', in *ECFR Policy Briefs*, February 2021, https://ecfr.eu/?p=66950

Mark Leonard and Jeremy Shapiro, 'Strategic Sovereignty: How Europe Can Regain the Capacity to Act', in *ECFR Policy Briefs*, June 2019, https://ecfr.eu/?p=4416

Camille Lons et al., 'China's Great Game in the Middle East', in *ECFR Policy Briefs*, October 2019, https://ecfr.eu/?p=2760

Hugh Lovatt and Jacob Mundy, 'Free to Choose: A New Plan for Peace in Western Sahara', in *ECFR Policy Briefs*, May 2021, https://ecfr.eu/?p=72863

Lorena Stella Martini, 'Una nuova Agenda per il Mediterraneo per stare al passo con le sfide del Vicinato meridionale', in *Euractiv*, 31 March 2021, https://euractiv.it/?p=24790

Veera Mendonca et al., *MENA Generation 2030. Investing in Children and Youth Today to Secure a Prosperous Region Tomorrow*, Amman, United Nations Children's Fund (UNICEF) MENA, April 2019, https://www.unicef.org/mena/reports/mena-generation-2030

Gergana Noutcheva, 'Institutional Governance of European Neighbourhood Policy in the Wake of the Arab Spring', in *Journal of European Integration*, Vol. 37, No. 1 (2015), p. 19–36

Organisation for Economic Co-operation and Development (OECD), *FDI in Fragile and Conflict-Affected Economies in the Middle East and North Africa: Trends and Policies*, Paris, OECD, December 2018, http://www.oecd.org/mena/competitiveness/ERTF-Jeddah-2018-Background-note-FDI.pdf

Roger Owen, *The Rise and Fall of Arab Presidents for Life*, Cambridge, Harvard University Press, 2012

Michael Robbins, *What Arab Publics Think. Findings from the Fifth Wave of Arab Barometer*, Arab Barometer, 28 January 2020, https://www.arabbarometer.org/?p=6109

Mustapha Rouis and Steven R. Tabor, 'Regional Economic Integration in the Middle East and North Africa. Beyond Trade Reform', in *Directions in Development*, 2013, http://hdl.handle.net/10986/12220

André Sapir and Georg Zachmann, 'A European Mediterranean Economic Area to Kick-Start Economic Development', in Sven Biscop, Rosa Balfour and Michael Emerson (eds), 'An Arab Springboard for EU Foreign Policy?', in *Egmont Papers*, No. 54 (January 2012), p. 37–47, https://www.ceps.eu/?p=7389

Hussein Solomon, 'Women in the Middle East North African Region Pushing Back against Patriarchy', in *Mail & Guardian*, 14 March 2020, https://mg.co.za/?p=349162

Yannis A. Stivachtis, 'The EU and the Middle East: The European Neighborhood Policy (ENP)', in Yannis A. Stivachtis, *Conflict and Diplomacy in the Middle East. External Actors and Regional Rivalries*, Bristol, E-International Relations, 2018, p. 110–127, https://www.e-ir.info/?p=76373

Michaël Tanchum, 'The Post-COVID-19 Trajectory for Algeria, Morocco and the Western Sahara', in *IAI Commentaries*, No. 21|03 (January 2021), https://www.iai.it/en/node/12643

Andrea Teti (ed.), *The EU's Partnership with the Southern Mediterranean: Challenges to Cohesion and Democracy*, Brussels, Greens/EFA in the European Parliament, March 2019, https://www.researchgate.net/publication/332550457

Andrea Teti et al., *Democratisation against Democracy. How EU Foreign Policy Fails the Middle East*, Cham, Palgrave Macmillan, 2020

Nathalie Tocci and Jean-Pierre Cassarino, 'Rethinking the EU's Mediterranean Policies Post-9/11', in *IAI Working Papers*, No. 11|06 (March 2011), https://www.iai.it/en/node/3302

Ana Uzelac, 'Incoherent at Heart. The EU's Economic and Migration Policies towards North Africa', in *Oxfam Briefing Papers*, November 2020, http://dx.doi.org/10.21201/2020.6805

Arturo Varvelli, 'L'Italia ha bisogno di una nuova politica per la Libia', in *Europa Atlantica-Osservatorio strategico*, 5 June 2020, https://wp.me/pabS04-wN

Andrea Dessì

Chapter 10: Popular Mobilisation and Authoritarian Reconstitution in the Middle East and North Africa: Ten Years of Arab Uprisings

The Arab uprisings, which began in Tunisia and quickly spread across much of the Middle East and North Africa (MENA), have had – and are still having – a transformative impact on the geopolitical map of the region, as well as on the socio-political consciousness, fears and aspirations of citizens and ruling elites alike. Since late December 2010, millions have poured into the streets, braving the repressive apparatuses of authoritarian regimes to demand political reform, increased socio-economic rights and accountability. From Tunisia, protests quickly spread to Egypt, Bahrein, Libya, Syria and Yemen, with more limited demonstrations taking place in Morocco, Jordan, Algeria, Iraq and even Saudi Arabia and Israel during 2011. More recently, renewed protest waves have taken place in localities that had seemingly been spared from the initial uprisings. Since late 2018, citizens in Iraq, Lebanon, Sudan and Algeria – and in more limited forms in Iran, Morocco, Tunisia and Palestine – have taken to the streets to demand far reaching institutional and political reform, directing their grievances at the abysmal state of basic services, the endemic corruption of ruling elites and the ethno-confessional cronyism widely blamed for the persistent erosion of living standards, socio-economic rights and human security.

The scenes of mass popular mobilisation, revolt and revolution that dominated the past decade – and hold certain similarities with wider instances of bottom-up protests in other regions of the world[1] – surprised global audiences,

---

[1]   Aside from the MENA, other examples of global grass-roots mobilisation, most notably the international Occupy movement, materialised during 2011. Between 2018–2019, multiple other examples of popular mobilisations have taken place across Latin and Central America, the US, Asia, Europe and the broader MENA region. See Cara Buckley and Rachel Donadio, 'Buoyed by Wall St. Protests, Rallies Sweep the Globe', in *The New York Times*, 15 October 2011, https://www.nytimes.com/2011/10/16/world/occupy-wall-street-protests-worldwide.html; Carnegie Endowment for International Peace, *Global Protest Tracker*, last updated 7 October 2021, https://carnegieendowment.org/publications/interactive/protest-tracker; Samuel J. Brannen, Christian S. Haig

foreign powers and intelligence communities alike. Many had grown compla-
cent with an unsustainable status quo, falling prey to flawed characterisations of
a supposed political apathy in the region, an incompatibility between democracy
and Islam or a binary choice between authoritarian-imposed stability on the one
hand and insecurity and chaos on the other. Such approaches overlooked the
MENA region's rich history of contentious politics and challenges to authority,
both foreign and domestic, leading extra-regional states, as well as the MENA's
authoritarian regimes themselves, to be caught off guard by the uprisings. Yet,
the extent of popular frustration and lack of opportunities was such that protests
gradually spread to a broad cross-section of society, reaching a critical mass that
could effectively challenge the authoritarian apparatus of the state, demanding
the downfall of the regime and an end to the corruption and cronyism that
characterised – and still characterises – much of the ruling elites of the MENA.

While recognised as a critical juncture for the region, the uprisings that began
in late December 2010 did not happen in a vacuum. The protests were not simply
a sudden explosion of popular anger, facilitated by broader international trends
such as the advent of new technologies, globalisation or disruptions in global
supply chains that increased the cost of basic foodstuffs just prior to the advent
of the protests. Rather, the uprisings are part and parcel of a broader continuum
of social mobilisations, localised protests and challenges to authority that are
traceable back well before 2010–2011, brewing in the margins of society and the
peripheries of centralised state control as a result of a gradual erosion of social
contracts and state governance systems since at least the 1980s. Collectively,
these processes are reflective of an evolving socio-political consciousness across
MENA societies and a constant struggle between a variety of forces pushing
for change, reform or disruption contraposed against others that are inherently
invested in protecting and promoting the status quo.

Like any social event of mass proportions, the uprisings have been influenced
by broader global trends, including those hinted to above and relating to globalisation, new technologies and supply chains or the 2008 financial crisis. Such
developments should be understood as contributing variables for the outbreak
of protests, not their underlining drivers. Indeed, any search for causality must

---

and Katherine Schmidt, 'The Age of Mass Protests. Understanding an Escalating
Global Trend', in *CSIS Reports*, March 2020, https://www.csis.org/node/55678; John
Harris, 'Global Protests: Is 2011 a Year That Will Change the World?', in *The Guardian*,
15 November 2011, https://www.theguardian.com/p/33cjm.

begin *within the region* and the individual national contexts in which protests and revolutions actually took place.

A political economy approach focused on fraying social contracts, mounting socio-economic exclusion and the erosion of basic services is fundamental for such assessments.[2] These need to account for the individual experiences of state formation and re-formation, the history of prior revolts and revolutions and broader trends of geopolitical competition between status quo oriented powers and those seeking to promote revolutionary change or disruption. In short, assessing the evolution of contentious politics and bottom-up pressures for change and reform that erupted in late 2010 cannot discount previous instances of revolt and revolutions, creating a continuum across time and space and seeking to flesh out trends, similarities and/or the cross-fertilisation of ideas, tactics and grievances from one context to the next.

A reflection on the way protest movements in individual country contexts have internalised the experiences of other – previous or contemporary – episodes of revolt or revolution will help to underscore how these events have influenced the evolving socio-political consciousness of MENA societies and their relationship with the state. While status quo forces are clearly on the ascendance, the considerable worsening of socio-economic, political and security indicators across the region since 2011 – as well as the continued activism and poplar mobilisations in a number of localities – point to the risks of any return to complacency with authoritarian-imposed stability, underscoring how future protests and revolts are not only likely but also expected to be more violent, chaotic and disruptive than in the past.[3] Being mindful of the perils of generalisation and the fundamental role of historical contingency to explain the protest trajectories in each context, the broadly shared nature of socio-economic and political grievances across the MENA may provide avenues for cooperation and coordination among opposition groups and protest movements, including among diasporas. This dynamic may provide new means to increase the resilience of those forces pushing for change and reform in the post-2011 MENA, which require more genuine support from the outside, most notably by EU member states and institutions.

---

[2]   See, for instance, Andrea Teti, Pamela Abbott and Francesco Cavatorta, *The Arab Uprisings in Egypt, Jordan and Tunisia. Social, Political and Economic Transformations*, Cham, Palgrave Macmillian, 2018; Andrea Dessì, 'Crisis and Breakdown: How Can the EU Foster Resilience in the Middle East and North Africa?', in *IAI Working Papers*, No. 17|37 (December 2017), https://www.iai.it/en/node/8678.

[3]   Marwan Bishara, 'Beware of the Looming Chaos in the Middle East', in *Al Jazeera*, 3 August 2020, https://aje.io/qgw3q.

1. Geopolitical trends and the post-2011 MENA

MENA states and societies continue to suffer from multiple overlapping challenges.[4] These include internal fragilities tied to fraying social contracts, declining economic indicators and rampant authoritarianism, and the external dimension, where trends of zero-sum geopolitical rivalry, mixed with legacies of foreign interventionism, continue to define the contours of a highly combustible regional ecosystem.[5] Looking back at the past decade, the interplay between domestic fragilities and external inter-state rivalry has been put on clear display, but little of concrete has been done to mitigate its implications.[6] The revolutionary fervour that erupted in late 2010 and continued to spread throughout 2011 represented a clear indictment of decades of failed Arab developmental policies and regime subservience to elite and foreign interests rather than the needs and aspirations of their citizens. If the initial phase of the uprisings in 2011–2012 represented a first inflection point for the region, refocusing attention on internal inequalities, authoritarian repression and corruption, the ensuing period, particularly in the wake of the 2013 military coup in Egypt, was instead characterised by a vengeful return of inter-state geopolitical rivalry and proxy conflict, bringing considerable destruction and suffering to the region.

During this second inflection point, revolutionary and counter-revolutionary forces battled across the MENA in an effort to contain and redirect the winds of change unleashed by the uprisings. As a result, battle lines expanded outwards from concern over domestic fragilities and the political transitions in uprising states to offensive proxy conflicts in the killing fields of Syria and Iraq, the conflict in Yemen and finally to Libya. This occurred notwithstanding the emergence

---

[4]   Small parts of this section are re-elaborated from a previous publication. See, Roberto Aliboni, Francesca Caruso and Andrea Dessì, 'The Middle East and North Africa in 2021: Brewing Crises and Geopolitical Re-Alignments', in Salvatore Capasso and Giovanni Canitano (eds), *Mediterranean Economies 2021*, Bologna, Il Mulino, 2021(forthcoming).

[5]   See Rami G. Khouri, 'How Poverty and Inequality Are Devastating the Middle East', in *Carnegie Topic Articles*, 12 September 2019, https://www.carnegie.org/topics/topic-articles/arab-region-transitions/why-mass-poverty-so-dangerous-middle-east; also see, Rami G. Khouri, 'Poverty, Inequality and the Structural Threat to the Arab World', in *POMEPS Studies*, No. 34 (March 2019), p. 28–32, https://pomeps.org/?p=10700.

[6]   See, for instance, Silvia Colombo and Andrea Dessì (eds), *Fostering a New Security Architecture in the Middle East*, Brussels, Foundation for European Progressive Studies (FEPS) and Rome, Istituto Affari Internazionali (IAI), November 2020, https://www.iai.it/en/node/12507.

of the self-proclaimed Islamic State in Iraq and Syria (ISIS) in 2014 and the shared threat it posed to all states and societies in the Middle East and beyond. The emergence of ISIS, like other Salafi-jihadist actors, stems from a variety of historical and ideological drivers, but in more general terms can be explained as another manifestation of the failures of Arab governance and the inability to provide opportunities and feelings of belonging to citizens.[7]

Instead of fostering joint action or cooperation, the rise of ISIS, like the 2015 Iran nuclear deal and the 2013 coup in Egypt, further enhanced the prevalence of inter-regional proxy conflict and competition. The Iran nuclear deal in particular became the target of a concerted campaign by Israel, Saudi Arabia and the United Arab Emirates (UAE) to undermine the deal, judging it detrimental to their interests. These generally revolve around support for the pre-Arab uprisings status quo and massive US financial and military assistance. Significantly, this was the same grouping of states that had united into a semi-formal alliance of counter-revolutionary forces to oppose Turkey and Qatar's support for Muslim Brotherhood-linked parties in a number of Arab uprising countries since 2011. Unsurprisingly, the Israeli, Saudi and Emirati governments all welcomed the election of Donald J. Trump as US president as a means to roll back the Iran nuclear deal and return US policy towards its traditional support for (or subservience to) the interests of its regional and status quo-oriented allies in the Middle East.[8]

The four years of the Trump Administration would therefore represent the triumph of counter-revolutionary and status quo supporting actors in the Middle East. While socio-economic indicators and political repression continued to worsen within most states of the region, such trends were overshadowed by heightened geopolitical and military tensions with Iran and the opening up of new geopolitical fault-lines, from the 2017 blockade of Qatar promoted by its fellow Gulf Cooperation Council (GCC) members Saudi Arabia and the UAE to the escalating conflict in Yemen and deepening intra-Arab and Turkish rivalries over Syria, Qatar, Palestine, Libya and the Horn of Africa. Trump Administration policies emboldened those status quo and counter-revolutionary forces, who

---

[7]   See for instance, Fawaz A. Gerges, *ISIS: A History*, Princeton, Princeton University Press, 2016; Lorenzo Kamel, 'Cutting ISIS's Lifelines', in *Project Syndicate*, 4 January 2017, https://prosyn.org/ct59DVb.

[8]   See for instance, Andrea Dessì and Vassilis Ntousas (eds), *Europe and Iran in a Fast-Changing Middle East*, Brussels, Foundation for European Progressive Studies (FEPS) and Rome, Istituto Affari Internazionali (IAI), June 2019, https://www.iai.it/en/node/10554.

consequently expanded their campaign to roll back and contain political Islam and any other force invested in seeking to upend the status quo in the MENA, including Iran and its so-called 'Axis of Resistance'.

Yet, these states would soon realise that President Trump, like his immediate predecessor Barack Obama, was not ready to commit to new military engagements in the region and rather sought to orchestrate a means for Washington's regional allies to shoulder increased military and strategic burdens in order for the US to refocus attention towards Asia. The absence of a strong US response to the military incident in the Persian Gulf in September 2019, with coordinated attacks on Saudi Arabia's oil infrastructure likely launched from Iran, was enough for certain Arab states in the Persian Gulf to move towards tentative forms of diplomatic de-escalation with Tehran. There were other reasons for such trends, however. The outbreak of renewed protests since late 2018 in Algeria, Lebanon, Sudan and Iraq – and in less prominent forms in Morocco, Iran, Tunisia and Palestine – would lead to fears of a new wave of uprisings, particularly in light of the accelerated erosion of socio-economic indicators across multiple states in the MENA since 2010.

These occurrences would combine to herald a third inflection point for the region, after those of the 2011 uprisings and the 2013 Egyptian military coup, leading to a hesitant – but likely fleeting – diminishing of inter-state competition and proxy war across the MENA beginning in late 2019.[9] This interval emerged against the backdrop of mounting domestic threats to regime survival, the uncertainties surrounding US policy in the wake of Trump's electoral defeat and a seeming victory of those counter-revolutionary forces intent or returning the region to the pre-uprisings status quo. Such trends were further accentuated by the outbreak of the covid-19 pandemic in early 2020, which heightened socio-economic stress across multiple states in the region. Add to this the impact of the oil price crash in March 2020, as well as the impending energy transitions that will further add burdens to many hydrocarbon-dependent MENA economies, and it appears that ruling elites consciously chose to refocus attention on internal fragilities rather than continuing to fund risky foreign entanglements that divert resources from the domestic realm.

---

[9] See Nathalie Tocci et. al, 'From Tectonic Shifts to Winds of Change in North Africa and the Middle East: Europe's Role', in *IAI Papers*, No. 21|12 (March 2021), https://www.iai.it/en/node/13022; Roberto Aliboni, Francesca Caruso and Andrea Dessì, 'The Middle East and North Africa in 2021, cit.; Fawaz A. Gerges, 'Morning in the Middle East?', in *Project Syndicate*, 4 August 2021, https://prosyn.org/ez8IcSj.

This third inflection point would be characterised by growing conflict fatigue after years of offensive proxy conflicts in Syria, Yemen and Libya, leading counter-revolutionary states to employ other political and economic means to promote the pre-2011 status quo. This does not mean that the region is structurally more stable or secure, however. Rather, it is reflective of a growing confidence on the side of those counter-revolutionary and status quo oriented forces who had returned to the ascendance since the 2013 military coup in Egypt.[10] Supported by the UAE and Saudi Arabia, as well as segments of the Egyptian population, the 2013 coup overthrew the first democratically elected president linked to the Muslim Brotherhood. Further examples of these counter-revolutionary efforts were on display in Libya – where the UAE, Saudi Arabia and post-military coup Egypt intervened to battle a variety of Muslim Brotherhood-linked groups – as well as in the 2017 blockade of Qatar. More recently, the anti-Muslim Brotherhood coalition has also gradually begun to re-engage the regime of Bashar al Assad in Syria in an effort to weaken what remains of the Islamist opposition (segments of which they had initially supported) as well as Turkey's and Iran's positioning in the country.[11] By late 2019 a conviction about the waning appeal of political Islam and the Muslim Brotherhood across the region would contribute to tentative trends of de-escalation with Turkey, Qatar and even (and to a lesser extent) Iran,[12] consequently crystalising the beginnings of this third inflection point for the region.

As the protest movements that had emerged in 2018–19 receded with the advent of covid-19 in 2020, the self-confidence of the counter-revolutionary forces increased, especially given that the UAE and Saudi Arabia were well positioned to exploit the protests to serve their own ends. This was clearly the case in Tunisia, where the UAE supported the election of President Kaïs Saïed in 2019 as a counterweight to the mildly Islamist Ennahda party as well his July 2021 coup

[10] See F. Gregory Gause III, 'Beyond Sectarianism: The New Middle East Cold War', in *Brookings Doha Center Analysis Papers*, No. 11 (July 2014), http://brook.gs/2bl1yS3.

[11] See, for instance, Sima Aldardari, 'Strategic Interests Drive Gulf Policy Towards Syria', in *AGSIW Blog*, 29 December 2020, https://agsiw.org/strategic-interests-drive-gulf-pol icy-toward-syria; 'Saudi Arabia's Intelligence Chief Meets with Syrian Counterpart in Damascus', in *Al-Monitor*, 5 May 2021, https://www.al-monitor.com/node/42512.

[12] See, among others, Ali Bakir, 'Turkey and the UAE: Making Amends and Talking Business in Post-Trump Era', in *Middle East Eye*, 2 September 2021, https://www.middle easteye.net/node/224456; Ali Bakir, 'Turkey-Egypt Relations: What's Behind Their New Diplomatic Push?', in *Middle East Eye*, 12 March 2021, https://www.middleeasteye.net/node/203396.

against the parliament and prime minister;[13] and in Sudan, where the post-revolutionary transition led by the army has been significantly influenced by Abu Dhabi and Riyadh.[14] Similar trends were at play in Lebanon, Iraq and Algeria as well. In these contexts, protest movements have been less influenced from the outside – with citizens taking to the streets through grassroots, decentralised and leaderless mobilisations – but from the standpoint of the UAE and Saudi Arabia (as well as Israel) the weakening of these countries is considered conducive to broader geopolitical goals. Such interests ranged from efforts to limit Iranian influence in Iraq and Lebanon or, when it comes to Algeria, to an erosion of that country's ability to counterbalance the growing influence of the UAE and Saudi Arabia across North Africa, most notably in Tunisia and Libya, as well as in Morocco, a key ally of the Arab monarchies of the Persian Gulf and traditional rival of Algeria.

A further element that would crystalise this third inflection point for the MENA came with the signing of the normalisation deals between Israel and a number of Arab states between late 2019 and 2020. These deals would formalise the alliance of counter-revolutionary and status quo-oriented forces in the MENA, enhancing the self-confidence of those actors seeking to contain both traditional rivals (Iran) and the more recent, post-2011 opponents Turkey and Qatar. The normalisation deals that involved Israel, Bahrein, the UAE, Morocco and Sudan would therefore crown the ascendance of counter-revolutionary forces, a move that would also serve to constrain the new US Administration of Joe Biden (and the European Union) from overhauling key tenants of President Trump's approach towards Palestine and the broader region. This allowed status quo forces to dampen offensive proxy conflicts in Libya and Syria – as well as Yemen – while forcing an increasingly isolated Turkey to reconsider certain elements of its previous support for the Muslim Brotherhood, hesitantly leading

---

[13] See, for instance, 'UAE Says It Supports Tunisian President's Decisions', in *Reuters*, 7 August 2021, https://www.reuters.com/article/tunisia-politicis-emirates-idAFL8 N2PE0PD; Claire Parker, 'Influential Voices in Egypt, Saudi Arabia and UAE Celebrate Tunisia Turmoil As Blow to Political Islam', in *The Washington Post*, 27 July 2021, https://wapo.st/3i8BlbT.

[14] See, for instance, Jean-Baptiste Gallopin, 'The Great Game of the UAE and Saudi Arabia in Sudan', in *POMEPS Memos*, June 2020, https://pomeps.org/?p=12119; Desiée Custers, 'Sudan's Transitional Process in the Face of Regional Rivalries', in *LSE Middle East Center Blog*, 20 November 2020, https://wp.me/p3Khxv-2Ja.

Ankara to explore avenues for a resumption of low-level dialogue with Egypt, the UAE and Saudi Arabia.[15]

Further proof of this growing willingness to recalibrate their policies came in early January 2021, as Riyadh and Abu Dhabi moved to normalise relations with Qatar, ending the 2017 blockade and intra-GCC dispute. Clearly motivated by an effort to improve their standing with the incoming Biden Administration and limit elements of their previous foreign policy and military overstretch since 2013, this move also symbolised the growing ascendancy of counter-revolutionary forces a decade after the initial eruption of the uprisings.

2. Tracing historical continuums in the MENA

This evolving contraposition between the conservative, status quo and Western-backed states in the MENA, and those actors seeking to promote change, revolution or disruption to the prevailing order is nothing new. Like the 2011–2020 waves of uprisings, which have been contextualised as part of a broader continuum of cyclical efforts to engender reform but which have ultimately tended to result in forms of authoritarian reconstitution, the evolving ideological and geopolitical rivalry between status quo forces and those that sought to embrace and encourage the trends unleashed by the 2011 uprisings is similarly reflective of deeper, historical rivalries in the region. In this sense, to understand the uprisings and the subsequent social mobilisation, one has to also appreciate the history of prior revolutionary efforts in the MENA and the extent to which these experiences have influenced and/or been internalised into the socio-political consciousness of MENA societies, opposition movements and ruling elites alike.

Previous examples of revolts and revolutions continue to live on in the individual and collective memories of MENA societies, helping to break taboos, influence and inspire future modalities of protest and resistance. These range from the successful revolts against Ottoman rule and the European colonial powers, especially Algeria's struggle for independence from France in 1954–62, to more recent examples of elite-led military coups in post-independence Arab states (most notably in Egypt, Iraq and Syria). Since the 1980s, the region has witnessed multiple examples of bottom-up mobilisations, which similarly influenced the social consciousness, tactics and politics of the 2011–2020 uprisings. From the 1979 revolution in Iran, which began as a merchant-driven

---

[15]   See, for instance, Pinar Tremblay, 'Erdogan's Rapprochement with Egypt Comes at Expense of Brotherhood', in *Al-Monitor*, 1 July 2021, https://www.al-monitor.com/node/43499.

and broadly secular revolt against the Western-backed Pahlavi dynasty before being appropriated by religious scholars who transformed Iran into the present Islamic Republic; to the 1988 October Riots in Algeria, which led to the first multi-party elections won by the Islamic Salvation Front (FIS) in 1990, followed by the 1992 military coup and an ensuing decade of civil war between the army and Islamist militias,[16] certain reoccurring trends are indeed identifiable when it comes to the history popular revolts and regime-driven responses in the MENA.

These historical events in Iran and Algeria are also representative of older struggles between political Islam on the one hand and the broadly secular but status-quo oriented and Western-aligned regimes on the other, a dynamic that emerged in the wake of the waning appeal of Arab nationalism in the 1970s.[17] This, in turn, was in many ways an *evolution* of a previous clash that traces its roots further back into history, during the so-called Arab Cold War which pitted secular Arab nationalism and Nasserism against the conservative, Western-backed and status-quo oriented Arab Monarchies during the 1950s–1960s.[18]

During this period, Arab nationalism had emerged as the primary anti-status quo force within the region, as Nasserism was opposed to both the Western-backed conservative states *and* the emerging forces of political Islam.[19] As the promise and appeal of Arab nationalism began to wane in the 1970s, the revolutionary mantle would pass on to political Islam and the Muslim Brotherhood, which gradually emerged as the most organised force promoting change, although it was able to find tactical forms of accommodation with the ruling regimes. This contraposition between status quo powers and those forces seeking to promote change via Arab nationalism (and pan-Arabism) first and Islamism (and pan-Islamism) later, is a re-occurring trend throughout the modern history of the region, one that has returned to the forefront of MENA politics since the 2011 Arab uprisings.

Aside from the Islamic revolution in Iran and the Algerian civil war, other turning points with important implications for the socio-political consciousness, tactics and aspirations of MENA states and societies include the Lebanese

---

[16]   See Andrea Dessì, 'Algeria at the Crossroads, Between Continuity and Change', in *IAI Papers*, No. 11|28 (September 2011), https://www.iai.it/en/node/3379.

[17]   Fawaz A. Gerges, *Making the Arab World. Nasser, Qutb, and the Clash That Shaped the Middle East*, Princeton, Princeton University Press, 2018.

[18]   See Malcom Kerr, *The Arab Cold War, 1958–1967. A Study of Ideology in Politics*, London/New York/Toronto, Oxford University Press, 1965.

[19]   William Stivers, *America's Confrontation with Revolutionary Change in the Middle East, 1948–83*, New York, St. Martin's Press, 1986.

civil war (1975–1990); the Soviet invasion of Afghanistan in 1979; the Muslim Brotherhood rebellion in Syria in the early 1980s; the first and second Palestinian Intifadas (1987 and 2000); the Shia and Kurdish rebellions in Iraq during the Iran-Iraq war in the 1980s and first Gulf War in the early 1990s; the Islamist insurgency in Egypt in the early 1990s; the US-led invasions of Afghanistan and Iraq in the early 2000s; the 2005 Cedar Revolution in Lebanon; the wave of political and worker-driven revolts that rocked Egypt following the 2005 presidential elections; and the 2006 victory of Hamas in the Palestinian legislative elections. All of these occurrences are examples of this perennial tension between those actors seeking revolutionary change or disruption and others that are instead invested in the prevailing status quo.

Collectively, these events point to the fallacy of a supposed political apathy across MENA societies and should rather serve as a warning against any return to complacency with a structurally precarious and ultimately unsustainable status quo dominated by authoritarian stability and socio-economic exclusion. A further trend that emerges from the above cursory overview is that of an incremental increase and gradual normalisation of violence and repression, a trend that has been accentuated by the repeated experiences of foreign military interventions, from Afghanistan, to Iraq and beyond. This trend involves both formal state apparatuses and a variety of non-state actors and jihadist groups such as ISIS, which have battled across the region, leading to widespread suffering and the wholescale destruction of entire states and communities. Such violence – in the post-2011 period like in preceding times – has become a tool in the service of the status quo powers seeking to deflate the promises of reform and revolution and constrain the ability of extra-regional actors in the West to revisit central tenants of their alliance frameworks, thereby ensuring continued Western support for counter-revolutionary forces well into contemporary times.

These above trends of ideological competition between what may be termed the forces of revolutionary change (Arab nationalism first, political Islam later) and the status quo-oriented actors closely aligned with external Western powers on the other (Arab monarchies, Israel) would re-emerge again in the context of the 2010–2020 Arab uprisings. Initially, it would be the status quo powers that were put on the defensive. After the overthrow of longstanding regimes, political Islam would rise its head, emerging as the most organised and powerful opposition force in many national contexts, most notably in post-2011 Tunisia, Egypt, Syria and, to a lesser extent, Libya.

These events would in some ways recall the previous experiences of the 1979 revolution in Iran and the Algerian elections and ensuring civil war, developments that re-ignited fears among the Western-aligned Arab monarchies, as well as

Israel, leading to a new chapter in the struggle between political Islam and the status quo powers of the MENA. It would be in this context that Saudi Arabia, the UAE and Israel would align into a semi-formal alliance of counter-revolutionary forces in the MENA, driven by the objective of undermining these nascent forms of Islamist governance in an effort to roll-back the winds of change and promote their own regime survival.

3. Authoritarian resurgence and the promise of future uprisings

While few can debate the renewed ascendency of status quo and counter-revolutionary actors in the contemporary MENA, one would be naïve to ignore the continued risks of internal revolts and revolutions, today and in the near future. The underlining socio-economic drivers for the 2010s uprisings have by no means been resolved. These grievances and internal challenges to stability can only be expected to increase in the short to medium future as a result of the impending energy transitions, covid-19, the climate emergency and the continued lack of legitimacy of ruling elites. The increased use of political repression and the closing down of avenues for citizens and societies to peacefully express their grievances and aspirations for reform, risks further waves of radicalisation, in a highly combustible regional ecosystem where any single spark may well re-ignite waves of mass protests and mobilisations.

Regional meddling and outright violence and destruction have no doubt influenced the fears of other MENA societies, which do not want to replicate the tragic experiences of their brethren in Syria, Yemen, Libya or Egypt. However, it is also true that the scars left by previous experiences of protest and authoritarian reconstitution are fading and are no longer acting as powerful constraints for renewed citizen-based activism or calls for revolution. This is also facilitated by the advent of new technologies and broader trends of demographic growth, given that new generations are less influenced by the memories of previous revolts and the state-sponsored repression that followed.

Setting aside the protests in Sudan, which as mentioned above were hijacked by counter-revolutionary states to deflate much of its true revolutionary potential, the more recent protest movements in Iraq, Lebanon and Algeria – as well as Tunisia and Palestine – are less constrained by the memories of the past and are rather coalescing around new objectives. Protest movements in these states have widened the scope of their demands from the targeting of dictators and their immediate families or business elites witnessed in the initial phase of the 2011 uprisings to a more refined targeting of the broader systems of control and elite cronyism. This expanded focus is reflective of a growing socio-political consciousness and the cross-fertilisation of ideas and tactics between one context to the next.

While the targets and grievances of these more recent protests demonstrate a certain internalisation of previous experiences, it is also true that certain lessons – notably the need to translate protest movements into organised political forces able to promote institutional reform beyond street protests and mobilisations – have been lacking. This absence of organisation and leadership, a key dimension of the decentralised and horizontal nature of the MENA uprisings in 2011 as well as in 2018,[20] continues to be highlighted as a key weakness of these civic and citizen-based movements.

That said, this emerging socio-political consciousness will not be easily contained or repressed, not least given the absence of significant efforts to improve the living standards or socio-political rights of citizens. These new generations will not sit idly by as their corrupt and ideologically bankrupted leaders continue to mismanage the state, stripping national resources or employing forms of co-optation and repression to scare off new protest waves, not least given their access to new technologies and growing awareness about the realities of other states as well as the imbalances of an international system that has failed to provide social goods and improvements to MENA societies. While regimes and status quo actors will continue to push back, banding together and seeking to deploy old tactics of divide and rule, it is unclear that such methods will succeed and if so for how long.

These realities serve as the ultimate reminder that the promise of authoritarian imposed stability has always represented a mirage, at best delaying but never preventing new eruptions of protest and mobilisation. Such explosions are only a matter of time and in the absence of fundamental socio-economic and political reforms as well as an end to intra-regional proxy conflicts and foreign meddling, each successive revolt is likely to be more violent and disruptive than the past. Like any other region of the world, stability can only be ensured via legitimate institutions and an equitable sharing of social goods, elements that require more transparent and accountable state-society relations as well as a movement away from the prevalence of zero-sum intra-regional competition and rivalry among MENA states and their extra-regional backers. Stability, therefore, cannot be imposed and sustained via top-down co-optation or repression, and neither can

---

20   Asef Bayat, *Revolution Without Revolutionaries. Making Sense of the Arab Spring*, Stanford, Stanford University Press, 2017.

it be imposed from the outside, via foreign interventionism, sanctions or diktats. The MENA's historical continuum will therefore continue.

References

Sima Aldardari, 'Strategic Interests Drive Gulf Policy Towards Syria', in *AGSIW Blog*, 29 December 2020, https://agsiw.org/strategic-interests-drive-gulf-policy-toward-syria

Roberto Aliboni, Francesca Caruso and Andrea Dessì, 'The Middle East and North Africa in 2021: Brewing Crises and Geopolitical Re-Alignments', in Salvatore Capasso and Giovanni Canitano (eds), *Mediterranean Economies 2021*, Bologna, Il Mulino, 2021(forthcoming)

Ali Bakir, 'Turkey and the UAE: Making Amends and Talking Business in Post-Trump Era', in *Middle East Eye*, 2 September 2021, https://www.middleeasteye.net/node/224456

Ali Bakir, 'Turkey-Egypt Relations: What's Behind Their New Diplomatic Push?', in *Middle East Eye*, 12 March 2021, https://www.middleeasteye.net/node/203396

Asef Bayat, *Revolution Without Revolutionaries. Making Sense of the Arab Spring*, Stanford, Stanford University Press, 2017

Marwan Bishara, 'Beware of the Looming Chaos in the Middle East', in *Al Jazeera*, 3 August 2020, https://aje.io/qgw3q

Samuel J. Brannen, Christian S. Haig and Katherine Schmidt, 'The Age of Mass Protests. Understanding an Escalating Global Trend', in *CSIS Reports*, March 2020, https://www.csis.org/node/55678

Cara Buckley and Rachel Donadio, 'Buoyed by Wall St. Protests, Rallies Sweep the Globe', in *The New York Times*, 15 October 2011, https://www.nytimes.com/2011/10/16/world/occupy-wall-street-protests-worldwide.html

Silvia Colombo and Andrea Dessì (eds), *Fostering a New Security Architecture in the Middle East*, Brussels, Foundation for European Progressive Studies (FEPS) and Rome, Istituto Affari Internazionali (IAI), November 2020, https://www.iai.it/en/node/12507

Desiée Custers, 'Sudan's Transitional Process in the Face of Regional Rivalries', in *LSE Middle East Center Blog*, 20 November 2020, https://wp.me/p3Khxv-2Ja

Andrea Dessì, 'Algeria at the Crossroads, Between Continuity and Change', in *IAI Papers*, No. 11|28 (September 2011), https://www.iai.it/en/node/3379

Andrea Dessì, 'Crisis and Breakdown: How Can the EU Foster Resilience in the Middle East and North Africa?', in *IAI Working Papers*, No. 17|37 (December 2017), https://www.iai.it/en/node/8678

Andrea Dessì and Vassilis Ntousas (eds), *Europe and Iran in a Fast-Changing Middle East*, Brussels, Foundation for European Progressive Studies (FEPS) and Rome, Istituto Affari Internazionali (IAI), June 2019, https://www.iai.it/en/node/10554

Jean-Baptiste Gallopin, 'The Great Game of the UAE and Saudi Arabia in Sudan', in *POMEPS Memos*, June 2020, https://pomeps.org/?p=12119

F. Gregory Gause III, 'Beyond Sectarianism: The New Middle East Cold War', in *Brookings Doha Center Analysis Papers*, No. 11 (July 2014), http://brook.gs/2bl1yS3

Fawaz A. Gerges, *ISIS: A History*, Princeton, Princeton University Press, 2016

Fawaz A. Gerges, *Making the Arab World. Nasser, Qutb, and the Clash That Shaped the Middle East*, Princeton, Princeton University Press, 2018

Fawaz A. Gerges, 'Morning in the Middle East?', in *Project Syndicate*, 4 August 2021, https://prosyn.org/ez8IcSj

John Harris, 'Global Protests: Is 2011 a Year That Will Change the World?', in *The Guardian*, 15 November 2011, https://www.theguardian.com/p/33cjm

Lorenzo Kamel, 'Cutting ISIS's Lifelines', in *Project Syndicate*, 4 January 2017, https://prosyn.org/ct59DVb

Malcom Kerr, *The Arab Cold War, 1958–1967 A Study of Ideology in Politics*, London/New York/Toronto, Oxford University Press, 1965

Rami G. Khouri, 'How Poverty and Inequality Are Devastating the Middle East', in *Carnegie Topic Articles*, 12 September 2019, https://www.carnegie.org/topics/topic-articles/arab-region-transitions/why-mass-poverty-so-dangerous-middle-east

Rami G. Khouri, 'Poverty, Inequality and the Structural Threat to the Arab World', in *POMEPS Studies*, No. 34 (March 2019), p. 28–32, https://pomeps.org/?p=10700

Claire Parker, 'Influential Voices in Egypt, Saudi Arabia and UAE Celebrate Tunisia Turmoil As Blow to Political Islam', in *The Washington Post*, 27 July 2021, https://wapo.st/3i8BlbT

William Stivers, *America's Confrontation with Revolutionary Change in the Middle East, 1948–83*, New York, St. Martin's Press, 1986

Andrea Teti, Pamela Abbott and Francesco Cavatorta, *The Arab Uprisings in Egypt, Jordan and Tunisia. Social, Political and Economic Transformations*, Cham, Palgrave Macmillian, 2018

Nathalie Tocci et. al, 'From Tectonic Shifts to Winds of Change in North Africa and the Middle East: Europe's Role', in *IAI Papers*, No. 21|12 (March 2021), https://www.iai.it/en/node/13022

Pinar Tremblay, 'Erdogan's Rapprochement with Egypt Comes at Expense of Brotherhood', in *Al-Monitor*, 1 July 2021, https://www.al-monitor.com/node/43499

Contributors

Francesca Caruso is a Researcher within IAI's Mediterranean, Middle East and Africa Programme and Policy Officer of the Mediterranean Women Mediators Network (MWMN). Her research interests include the implementation of the Women, Peace and Security (WPS) agenda in the Mediterranean region, North Africa politics and sub-Saharan peace and security studies – with a particular focus on Central Africa. She also works as consultant for the Peace Programme of the Community of Sant'Egidio and she regularly contributes with *La Stampa* covering sub-Sahara security and political issues.

Silvia Colombo is Senior Fellow in the Mediterranean, Middle East and Africa Programme at IAI. She is an expert on Middle Eastern politics and, in this capacity, she is working on Euro-Mediterranean cooperation, transatlantic relations in the Mediterranean and domestic and regional politics in the Arab World. Among her research interests there are also the relations between the European Union and the countries of the Gulf Cooperation Council (GCC). She holds a Ph.D. in Comparative Politics from the Scuola Normale Superiore of Pisa (Florence Branch) and a Master's Degree in Near and Middle Eastern Studies from the School of Oriental and African Studies (SOAS) in London. She speaks Arabic fluently and has travelled extensively in the Middle Eastern region.

Andrea Dessì is Head of the Italian Foreign Policy Programme at IAI, Senior Fellow within IAI's Mediterranean, Middle East and Africa Programme and Editorial Director of IAI's English-language series *IAI Commentaries*. Andrea is also a Non-Resident Scholar at the Strategic Studies Implementation and Research Centre, Başkent University, Ankara. He has worked extensively on US and European foreign policy towards the Middle East with a particular focus on the diplomatic and military history of the Arab-Israeli conflict, US policy towards Israel and Washington's alliance frameworks in the Middle East. His research interests include security studies, the geopolitics of the Middle East and the intersection between global and regional trends and developments. Andrea holds a Ph.D. in International Relations from the London School of Economics and Political Science (LSE) with a thesis on the US-Israel relationship during the 1980s. He has worked with IAI since 2011 and has contributed to a number of EU-funded projects and research tasks (FP7 & H2020).

Carmen Geha is a Tenured Associate Professor of Public Administration and Leadership at the American University of Beirut (AUB). She is also a co-founder and Research Associate at the Center for Inclusive Business & Leadership (CIBL) for Women, which serves as a focal point for advancing inclusive employer practices, policies and national strategies for women's participation and representation in the MENA region. Geha's research examines the nexus of politics and public institutions with a focus on the politics and policies of inclusion/exclusion around: women's political and economic participation, refugee crisis, and civil society and protest movements. She is a non-resident fellow at the European Council on Foreign Relations (ECFR), a Research Associate at GRITIM Interdisciplinary Research Group on Immigration at Pompeu Fabra University, and has held visiting positions at Harvard University, Brown University and the Institute of Advanced Studies.

Mattia Giampaolo is a Research Fellow at the Centro Studi di Politica Internazionale (CeSPI) and former Pan-European Fellow at the European Council on Foreign Relations (ECFR). He conducts research on political movements and parties in Egypt and Tunisia at CeSPI and he focused, at ECFR, on Libya-Italy relations. He is now working on the Egyptian state-society relations in the aftermath of the 2011 Revolution.

Hafsa Halawa is an independent consultant working on political, social and economic affairs, and development goals across the Middle East and North Africa (MENA) and Horn of Africa regions. A former corporate lawyer, Halawa has held positions in government, the UN, INGOs/NGOs, corporate multinationals, private firms, and think tanks, now consulting for a similar set of clients. She is concurrently a non-resident Scholar at the Middle East Institute and a Visiting Fellow at the ECFR, based between the United Kingdom and the Middle East.

Daniela Huber is Head of the Mediterranean, Middle East and Africa Programme at IAI and Editor of *The International Spectator*. She is also adjunct professor at Roma Tre University where she teaches a M.A. course on International Politics. Between 2016 and 2019, she has co-coordinated the Horizon 2020 Project MEDRESET which critically examined Euro-Mediterranean relations.

Aurora Ianni is Research Fellow at the Centro Studi di Politica Internazionale (CeSPI). Her research areas cover the Middle East/North Africa region and

Turkey. Among the latest projects she focused on the role of women during Sudan and Algerian uprisings (2018/2019) and on the migration issue in Turkey–EU relations.

Lorena Stella Martini is Advocacy and Communication Assistant at the Rome office of the European Council on Foreign Relations (ECFR). Her research interests revolve around socio-political dynamics in the MENA region, with a focus on Morocco and Iraq. Martini holds a double Master's degree in Comparative analysis of Mediterranean societies and International studies from the Mohammed VI Polytechnic University (Morocco) and the University of Turin. She previously obtained a Master's degree in Middle Eastern studies from the Graduate School of Economics and International Relations (ASERI) at the Catholic University of Milan, and a Bachelor's degree in Languages for international relations (majors: English and Arabic) from the same university. Martini has prior professional experience with think tanks and NGOs, and she has done research on individual freedoms in Morocco.

Theodore Murphy is the director of the Africa programme at the European Council on Foreign Relations (ECFR). From 2007–2011, Murphy worked in conflict resolution/mediation with the United Nations and the non-governmental sector in the Horn of Africa and Middle East. He served as Expert Advisor to the AU/UN mediation team in Darfur in 2007–08. In 2011, Murphy was appointed by the UN Secretary General to the Panel of Experts for Libya where he served in the post of Regional Expert. From 2012 onwards, Murphy oversaw mediation initiatives throughout the Horn of Africa, where he negotiated an internationally recognised political agreement in Darfur and supported efforts towards creating a Red Sea Forum.

Arturo Varvelli is Head of the Rome office and a Senior Policy fellow at the European Council on Foreign Relations (ECFR). His research interests include geopolitics and international affairs; the Middle East and North Africa; EU and Italian relations with the region; and transnational terrorist movements. He focuses on Libya and Italian-Libyan relations in particular. Previously, Varvelli worked as the Co-head of the MENA centre and Head of the terrorism programme at the Italian Institute for International Political Studies, where he organised the 'Rome MED – Mediterranean Dialogues' alongside the Italian Ministry of Foreign Affairs. Varvelli holds a PhD in international history from the University of Milan, and a post-PhD degree from the CRT Foundation, based in Turin.

Abbreviations

20FM	20 February Movement
AAM	Adel Abdel Mahdi
AMDH	Association Marocaine des Droits Humains (Moroccan Association for Human Rights)
ANDCM	Association Nationale des Diplômés Chômeurs du Maroc (National Association of Unemployed Graduates in Morocco)
ARM	Anti-Racism Movement
AU	African Union
AWI	Al-adl wa'l-ihsane
BBA	Beirut Bar Association
COP	Conference of the Parties
CSO	Civil Society Organisation
DCFTA	Deep and Comprehensive Free Trade Agreement
DPKO	Department for Peacekeeping Operations
EEAS	European External Action Service
ENI	European Neighbourhood Instrument
ENP	European Neighbourhood Policy
EPCSPI	Egyptian Popular Committee in Solidarity with Palestinian Intifada
ETUF	Egyptian Trade Union Federation
EU	European Union
FDI	Foreign Direct Investment
FFC	Forces for Freedom and Change
FJP	Freedom and Justice Party (Egypt)
FLN	National Liberation Front (Front de Libération Nationale)
GCC	Gulf Cooperation Council
GDP	Gross Domestic Product
GoSS	Government of South Sudan
IMF	International Monetary Fund

INGO	International Non-Governmental Organisation
ISIS	Islamic State in Iraq and Syria
JCPOA	Joint Comprehensive Plan of Action
JEM	Justice and Equality Movement
KB	Khaddit Beirut
KRG	Kurdistan Regional Government
KSA	Kingdom of Saudi Arabia
LGBTQ	Lesbian, Gay, Bisexual, Transgender, Queer
MALI	Mouvement Alternatif pour les Libertés Individuelles (Alternative Movement for Individual Freedoms
MB	Muslim Brotherhood
MENA	Middle East and North Africa
MESA	Middle East Strategic Alliance
NATO	North Atlantic Treaty Organisation
NDP	National Democratic Party (Egypt)
NGO	Non-Governmental Organisation
NISS	National Intelligence and Security Service
PJD	Parti de la Justice et du Dévéloppement (Justice and Development Party)
PKK	Partîya Karkerên Kurdistanê (Kurdistan Workers' Party)
PM	Prime Minister
RND	Democratic National Rally (Rassemblement National Démocratique)
RNI	Rassemblement National des Indépendants (National Rally of Independents)
RSF	Rapid Support Forces
SCAF	Supreme Council of the Armed Forces
SAF	Sudanese Armed Forces
SLA/M	Sudan Liberation Army/Minni Minawi
SPA	Sudan Professional Association
SPLM-n	Sudan People's Liberation Movement-North
SPRING	Support for Partnership, Reform and Inclusive Growth

SRF	Sudan Revolutionary Front
SUPF	Socialist Union of Popular Forces
TMC	Transitional Military Council
UAE	United Arab Emirates
UfM	Union for the Mediterranean
UGTT	Union Générale Tunisienne du Travail (Tunisian General Labour Union)
UK	United Kingdom
UNAMI	United Nations Assistance Mission for Iraq
UNDP	United Nations Development Programme
UNEP	United Nations Environment Programme
UNFPA	United Nations Population Fund
UNHCR	United Nations High Commissioner for Refugees
UNICEF	United Nations Children's Emergency Fund
UNIFIL	United Nations Interim Force in Lebanon
UNSC	United Nations Security Council
US	United States

GLOBAL POLITICS AND SECURITY

Series Editor:
Prof. Lorenzo Kamel,
University of Turin's History Department,
and Istituto Affari Internazionali (IAI)

"Global Politics and Security" publishes high-quality books authored by leading academics, think-tankers and policymakers on topical questions in international relations and modern and contemporary history, ranging from diplomacy and security, to development, economy, migration, energy and climate. The series publishes works produced by the Istituto Affari Internazionali (IAI), Italy's leading foreign policy think-tank, as well as by authors affiliated to other international think tanks or universities. The aim is to promote deeper knowledge of emerging issues and trends through constant exchange between the worlds of academia and practice. Publications include original monographs and edited volumes which combine a grasp of the past, an understanding of present dynamics, and a vision about potential futures.

www.peterlang.com